DETENTE IN EUROPE

Real or Imaginary?

BY THE SAME AUTHOR

Tito's Communism. Denver: University of Denver Press, 1951.

Danger in Kashmir. Princeton: Princeton University Press, 1954 (revised paperback edition, 1966).

The Communist Subversion of Czechoslovakia: 1938-1948. Princeton: Princeton University Press, 1949 (paperback edition, 1963).

Poland Between East and West. Princeton: Princeton University Press, 1963 (paperback edition, 1965).

DETENTE IN EUROPE

Real or Imaginary?

JOSEF KORBEL

PRINCETON UNIVERSITY PRESS
PRINCETON, NEW JERSEY

In gratitude
to
Dr. Ben M. Cherrington
Dr. Elizabeth L. Fackt
Mrs. Harriet S. Lawton

Preface

IT IS a perilous undertaking to write a book about contemporary history; documents of confidential nature are not yet accessible and such sources of information as official statements, interviews, and newspaper reports are incomplete and may be misleading.

Nevertheless, studies of events that shape history cannot be postponed until the last document is declassified. The policy of détente in Europe is such an event: it has changed the configuration of political, economic, and cultural forces as we knew them in the period of the Cold War. The significance of this development for Europe, for the United States, and the rest of the world appears to justify the risk inherent in the nature of the study.

Without any responsibility on their part for the final product of the study, I owe profound gratitude to several institutions and individuals for their assistance or advice.

The European Institute, Columbia University, and its distinguished Director, the late Professor Philip E. Mosely, saw the beginning of my research when I was there as senior research fellow. The Graduate School of International Studies, University of Denver, aided my two research trips in Europe. The Rockefeller Foundation extended to me a unique hospitality at the Villa Serbelloni, Bellagio, Italy. Officials in the EEC Headquarters and the United Nations ECE, in the British, French, and West German Ministries, in the British Council, as well as those in Inter Nationes and Radio Free Europe gave me materials and generously granted interviews. The librarians of the Council on Foreign Relations and of the Royal Institute of International Affairs opened their invaluable press archives. Special thanks go to the research assistants, John West and Eduardo Feller.

Professors John Armstrong, Vice-Chancellor Alan Bullock, Oxford University, and Bernhard Abrahamsson read the full text of the manuscript or parts of it. The final copy was in the careful and sensitive hands of Miss Miriam Brokaw, Associate Director and Editor, Princeton University Press. Mrs. Cynthia Johnston typed and retyped the manuscript with her characteristic efficiency and patience.

To all these institutions and persons, I express my sincere thanks. Special gratitude goes to my colleague and friend, Professor R. Russell Porter, who edited the manuscript with his unusual flair for English.

J. K.

Denver, Colorado
February, 1972

Table of Contents

DETENTE IN EUROPE

Real or Imaginary?

Introduction

POLITICS has a tendency to produce handy terminologies, designed to characterize some condition in international affairs or to enunciate some new political concept. The world has been inundated with such expressions: peaceful coexistence, satellite or client countries, cold war, communist world domination, containment, imperialism, neo-colonialism, revanchism, liberation, liberalization, building bridges, convergence, Socialist Commonwealth, Truman Doctrine, Eisenhower Doctrine, Nixon Doctrine, Brezhnev Doctrine, etc.

These terms, coined mostly in the West, conveniently crystallize our thinking and reduce a complex problem to a comfortable and understandable size. Sometimes they reflect the reality of the moment, at another time they have no significance beyond propaganda, but in almost every case they have tended to lead to gross oversimplification and consequent serious errors in judgment. Often they have survived long after the policy that they described had proved inapplicable and, as clichés, have constrained our capacity for the consideration of alternative solutions.

For almost fifteen years, both Western and Eastern Europe have used one such term in regard to their relationships—détente. But this term (beyond its literal meaning) has not as yet been crystallized. It stands for no particular policy or concept that could serve as a framework for a new international system in Europe. Rather, the word is as yet only an abbreviated expression of a desire, perhaps even a determination, on the part of European governments to lessen the tensions between Western and Eastern Europe that have kept them divided for the quarter of a century since the close of World War II, to regain in one way or another and to some extent that mutual trust which is the most precious ingredient in relations between any two countries or groups of countries.

Between friendly states, when national interests prompt them to take different positions on individual questions, good

3

will and good faith continue to provide a necessary foundation for the reconciliation of different positions in a give-and-take fashion. But if a series of hostile political actions, unfounded or imagined accusations, and vituperative language damages that element of mutual trust, it takes a long time and acts rather than words to reestablish it.

This basic prerequisite for a constructive or even a livable relationship between the East and West was utterly destroyed by the Cold War. As long as it continued there was no chance of solving any major wartime problem and the only alleviation of those tensions which resulted from the division of Europe took place when both sides found it to their interest to reach an agreement, as, for instance, in the case of the Austrian State Treaty in 1955. On the contrary, deep-seated suspicions led to increased rigidity and to a hardening of positions of power, the latter serving as a barometer of the trust or mistrust of the other side's intentions.

Perplexingly enough, the causes of this division were not a result of the war. Rather, they are to be found in ideological conflicts between the East and West, and they persisted in spite of those strong bonds of common purpose which had been the necessity of common military goals during the war years. Once the imperatives of allied solidarity had ceased, however (and even before the end of this need), the processes of power politics based on fundamental ideological differences surged to the surface and there came into East-West relations an entirely new configuration of forces. These not only failed to solve the problems resulting from the war—in particular the question of divided Germany—but even promoted the development of new frictions and conflicts. Fundamental ideological, social, and economic changes in the countries of Central and Eastern Europe, the subservience of their governments to the Soviet Union, and the radical reorientation of their foreign policies triggered off a series of reactions in the West that in turn created a network of still more novel political and economic concepts in the East.

By 1946 the division of Europe was complete. The numerous conferences related to war problems tended only to obscure the paramount conflict between the Eastern and Western worlds. It is therefore small wonder that it has taken some fifteen years for an atmosphere to be generated that would permit a return of even minimal credibility of words and actions between nations on either side of the once impregnable Iron Curtain.

Today, in Europe, the word "détente" is on everyone's lips. For Western Europe, the Cold War belongs to the past. The numerous efforts of all West European countries to seek some rapprochement with the East are indicative of their sincerity. These efforts have not been limited to the less "risky" contacts at economic and cultural levels; they have been extended to the political sphere, even though the consequences of political attempts at European pacification are so sensitive that any effort to alleviate tensions may actually heighten them, indeed could lead to a serious crisis. Nevertheless, no responsible statesman can afford to ignore any opportunity to remove the causes of such tensions or fail to examine any prospect for bringing to his country and the whole of Europe a sense of security and stability.

The Soviet Union and its European allies appear to have offered several such opportunities. They have also on numerous occasions expressed a desire to remove the barriers dividing Europe; they have indeed submitted more concrete propositions than have the Western capitals for a solution of critical problems and they have initiated a number of moves that, if implemented, would seem to give Europe a sense of common identity.

However, general statements and individual proposals from either side are not enough. It is critically important to probe into their motives, whether apparent or ulterior; to weigh their real, not imaginary, value; to undertake the hazardous task of evaluating possible consequences. Last but not least, it is important for each side to test the other's words and actions not so much in terms of one's own values and standards but by what experience and judgment tell us of the values and standards of the other. And at that point one returns directly to the problem of credibility and trust.

Détente in Europe has lasting significance only as it may be an important step toward a new European system that might one day assure the old Continent of a sense of security, possibly a degree of integration that crosses national boundaries. This ultimately requires a mutuality of fundamental political interests, a complementarity of production and services, and a free exchange of intellectual and cultural accomplishments—and all this, presumably, with no expectations of major changes in present political and social systems. It is, indeed, a big order.

In the face of this, one must ask whether the word "détente" will in the end only enrich the long list of useless political clichés. Only a careful examination of mutuality of interests, based on the past record of various policies of détente in Europe, can lead us (and then with uncertainty) toward a correct evaluation of the real prospects for détente.

There is one way of minimizing the dangers inherent in an analysis of contemporary problems: to examine facts and publicly avowed policies against the background of accumulated evidence of the past and in the light of the obvious national interests of the principal actors on the scene of European politics. A mass of materials related to détente is available and, in contrast to the freezing immobilism of the Cold War period, this fact is itself significant.

The title "détente in Europe," which will focus on the policies of Western Europe toward the states of Central and Eastern Europe and vice versa, has been used advisedly. Several reasons justify the narrowing of the topic to this geographical area. First, policy-makers in the United States, while speaking about "building bridges" (President Lyndon Johnson's speech, October 7, 1966), have not demonstrated an active interest in American relations with Central and Eastern Europe since Western Europe began to develop a policy of détente. (Even the spectacular visit of President Nixon in Rumania, in August 1969, fell short of practical consequences.) United States engagement in Central and Eastern Europe is, indeed, far down on the list of priorities of her foreign policy, though the results of a détente in Europe will inescapably affect, one way or another, her international position. She will be its beneficiary if it develops satisfactorily, just as she will inevitably become involved in renewed tensions and crises should it fail.

Second, the states of Central and Eastern Europe have reciprocated America's lack of interest in their development. Their contacts, political, economic, and cultural, with the United States have limped far behind their contacts with Western Europe. This can be explained not only by the difference in geographical distance, by differences in cultural traditions, and by the degree of mutual dependence, but also and primarily by conflicting views on such critical international issues as the war in Vietnam and the crisis in the Middle East.

Third, the policy of détente in Europe appears to justify the limits of this study by the significant fact that West Europe treats Central and Eastern Europe not as a compact area or an appendix of the Soviet Union, but rather on the basis of the individuality of each country, as limited as that individuality may be due to ideological affinity with the USSR and political and economic dependence on Moscow.

In a sense, of course, the minor interest of the United States in this current European struggle toward détente plays an important, though principally a negative, role. For the absence of the West's most powerful ally and the continuing presence of the East's counterpart—the Soviet Union— creates an assymetry in relationships between East and West that cannot be ignored. Further, any designs for European détente must ultimately include a reduction of tensions between these two major powers.

By the same token, and in an even more significant way, U.S.-Soviet relations constitute an overall framework for the policy of détente in Europe. Although these relations (and indeed the whole concept and conduct of both U.S. and Soviet foreign policies) are of such magnitude and such complexity that they cannot be placed within this study of détente in Europe, nevertheless they must always be kept in mind, and the reverberations of these relationships between these two great powers are, when appropriate, apparent in this study. It is quite clear that in the past, these relations—whether they found expression in mutual confrontations or attempts at a bilateral solution of conflicts of interest—have influenced the thinking and the actions of the European protagonists of détente in both Moscow and the West European capitals. In the future, the solution (or the failure to solve them) of such continuing problems as the war in Vietnam, the conflict in the Middle East, the armament of the two super-powers and the presence of their armies in Europe will inescapably affect the relations between the West and East European countries. In the final analysis, a lasting détente in Europe is interlocked with developments in U.S.-Soviet relations and these, though sometimes encouraging, are as often foreboding. The same may be said for the prospects of détente in Europe.

CHAPTER 1

Ideology

THE WARTIME allied coalition did not limit itself to the defeat of nazism and fascism. It also enunciated a program of building a Europe of national governments that would be committed to the principles of democracy; a number of international agreements, signed by the Big Three, laid down foundations toward this end. The Declaration on Liberated Europe signed at Yalta provided a framework for this program for all countries of Europe, victorious and defeated, and obligated the signatories to see to its fulfillment. The agreement on Poland, also signed at Yalta, contained specific provisions for establishing democracy there. The Potsdam Agreement foresaw a slow and carefully calculated growth of democracy from the local to the national level in Germany. The Paris Peace Conference in the summer of 1946, obligated the other defeated countries—Italy, Hungary, Rumania, Bulgaria, and Finland—to "secure [for] all persons under [their] jurisdiction . . . the enjoyment of human rights and of the fundamental freedoms. . . ." The United Nations Chapter solemnly confirmed the principle of non-intervention in internal affairs as a sacred article of international law.

Thus, ideology was to be removed as a divisive factor from the scene of international politics. The fact that the big powers themselves adhered to virtually contradictory ideologies was of necessity ignored, even though the West could hardly see in Stalin's Russia a democratic regime and the Western world did not qualify as a democracy by Moscow's standards.

As a practical measure, to eliminate or minimize internal political strife within nations at the time of their urgent need for rehabilitation and reconstruction (and in some countries also as a result of profound social changes resulting from the war), coalition governments that generally included com-

9

munist parties came into existence. In Central and Eastern Europe communist parties assumed a dominant role in the government; in such countries of Western Europe as France and Italy they occupied important governmental positions, reflecting their popularity in the electorate. However, the parties all pledged themselves to respect the principles of political freedom and to follow an evolutionary process of economic and social reform. Indeed, the communist parties appeared to have rejected the Lenin-Stalin strategy that dictated the violent overthrow of bourgeois governments as an inevitable and necessary prerequisite to the establishment of a socialist society.

The actualities of that period and those agreements are now history. The commitments proved to be only a series of tactical moves, patterned after Lenin's prescription for pursuing an enemy who zigzags. Elections, after short or long delays, did take place in Central and Eastern Europe but none of them were free, with the exception of the first elections in Hungary (which resulted in the victory of the non-communist parties) and in Czechoslovakia, though even there, contrary to widely held beliefs, psychological pressure, making full use of mass media, influenced many voters in favor of the communist party. In all other countries of the area the elections were managed by communist machinery, with direct assistance in varied forms from Soviet sources. The overpowering presence of the Soviet armies did the rest, as was subsequently admitted by Stalin in his correspondence with Tito.

Even if, as in Poland, Hungary, Rumania, and Bulgaria the grave social injustices of the prewar period called for profound political and social change, the results of the "elections" did not reflect the wish of the populace as to how to break away from the oppressive past. Thus, in spite of repeated domestic pledges and international commitments, the ideological factor was injected in both national and international politics and played a decisive role in shaping the future of Europe.

10

It would be difficult to argue that the elections in Western Europe were subject to the same illegitimate or manipulated domestic pressures. Nor can the United States be accused of direct interference in the internal affairs of West European countries, though certainly financial help in the form of grants or loans was recognized as an instrument for the encouragement of democratic elements to give their vote to the non-communist parties. Thus, it cannot be doubted that the West, as it was watching the ominous development in the East, was also aware of the ideological dimension of the situation.

The Paris Peace Conference in the summer of 1946 turned into anything but a peaceful conference. Speeches by representatives of countries that only one year before had in the name of democracy been staunch allies in a bloody war, abounded with accusations, from one side of dollar diplomacy and capitalist imperialism, parried by the other with protests against communist subjugation and infiltration. Many matters on the agenda were discussed almost exclusively in the light of the ideological gains that were expected to result from their disposition.

The civil war in Greece, each faction supported by one side or the other of the ideological fence, gave birth in March 1947 to the Truman Doctrine, a policy with unconcealed ideological overtones. The ejection of the communist parties from the French and Italian governments in the spring of 1947 was certainly not free of ideological considerations. The Marshall Plan in the summer of 1947, though originally extended to all Europe, grew out of the idea of arresting the process of economic chaos and social misery, the familiar breeding ground of communist agitation. The conferences of the Big Four on Germany provided the Soviet Union with a platform to accuse the West of reviving nazism in the western zone of occupation while the United States, Great Britain, and France pointed to the communization of the eastern zone.

The establishment of the Cominform, in September 1947, which included two West European communist parties (those of France and Italy) was another critical step in the ideological division of Europe. Its proclamation, following ever harsher voices from Moscow, returned to the revolutionary vocabulary of the 1920's as the problems of Europe were once again analyzed in the light of class struggle.

As time went by, the ideological war became uglier, the alienation deeper, and, with the communist putsch in Czechoslovakia in February of 1948, an Iron Curtain descended across Europe, from north to south, making the ideological separation complete. From then on, for eight years, the policies of the communist governments were guided by outdated Marxist, Leninist, and Stalinist perceptions of the noncommunist world, based on a "scientific socialism" supposedly equipped with methodological instruments capable not only of an unarguable analysis of the past and present but also an equally unerring prediction of the future—an unavoidable collapse of the capitalist system. As late as October 1952, Stalin considered the war among capitalist countries inevitable, and the 19th Congress of the CPSU bristled with revolutionary phrases.

The West reacted to the East's ideological onslaughts with the policy of containment. Implicitly reconciled to the developments in Central and Eastern Europe, though they ran against the spirit and the letter of wartime agreements and of the peace treaties, the policy was intended to prevent the spread of communism farther West. However, with the change of administration in Washington in January 1953, from President Truman to President Eisenhower, the United States government injected its own ideological element into the struggle between the West and East. Critical as it was of the concept of containment, which it considered self-defeating and defeatist, it enunciated the policy of liberation. West Europe cautiously declined the American proposition, and such events as the revolt of workers in East Germany in June 1953, and the national revolution in Hungary in November 1956, suppressed as they were by Soviet intervention and accompanied as they were by mere diplomatic protests, demonstrated the futility of this new, seemingly dynamic approach.

By 1956, both sides had reached a stalemate.

Detente: A Problem of Convergence

Measured against such a yardstick as the Cold War, the policy of détente in Europe has made remarkable progress. Nevertheless, viewed as a potential for establishing a new and stable international system, its prospects continue to be related, among other factors, to the continuing reality of the ideological division of Europe. However, a number of interesting changes have taken place.

In the second part of the 1950's, nationalism began to reassert itself in the thinking of East European nations. Many observers saw in this development an erosion of communist ideology as a significant factor in the division of Europe. Communism as an ideology has undeniably lost much of the revolutionary fervor it had had in the early 1920's when the Third International was capable of directing the policies of communist parties the world over. The European parties of that era tailored their activities to Moscow's command, and the working masses were inspired by revolutionary zeal.

Certainly, communist ideology suffered a serious blow from the rigidity that Stalin imposed on the Soviet satellites. Revolutionary appeals were abandoned as Soviet state interests took priority over ideological considerations. Then Tito's defection in June 1948 marked still another chapter in the history of communism as it eroded one of the fundamental tenets of Marxism: the international solidarity of the working class. The change in party leadership in Poland and the national revolution in Hungary in the autumn of 1956 and the "Czechoslovak Spring" in 1968 were evidence of Moscow's failure to impose upon these countries its "official" version of communist thought, though all professed that they acted under the banner of Marxism. Polycentrism undermined the foundations of "scientific socialism," which, as a science, was supposed to guide all communist countries regardless of their national heritage, the degree of their political consciousness, or the stage of their economic development.

Nevertheless, communism as a state system still rests on a unified ideological foundation. In all such states there is still the one-party societal structure, an economy based on nationalized property, and, to all intents and purposes, a single world outlook. Communism still views the dynamics of international politics as a conflict between the forces of capitalism and socialism. It still believes in the inevitable collapse of capitalism and rejects the concept of the possible convergence of the two systems. Patently, therefore, Marxist ideology does play a role in the policy of détente.

The Twentieth Congress of CPSU, held in February 1956, was a landmark in the history of the communist movement. It was meant to divest the movement of the burden of the Stalinist past, and, in something of the same spirit, it enunciated the principle of the equality of all communist parties and countries and recognized their right to follow their own paths of socialism. In addition, Khrushchev presented the Congress with a new interpretation of the Leninist policy of peaceful coexistence. Both pronouncements had a material impact on East-West relations.

But the principle of equality was not implemented. In fact, it was first modified only one year after its announcement, when the communist parties assembled in Moscow in November 1957 and accepted the CPSU as *primus inter pares,* acknowledging its position of leadership. It was abrogated in September 1968, when the so-called Brezhnev Doctrine enunciated the policy of the limited sovereignty of the communist states. The doctrine represented not only a retreat from the principle of party equality but also an attempt to return to Stalin's understanding of the relationships between communist regimes and in turn their relationships to the noncommunist world.

The second principle—the right of the communist countries to follow their own path of socialism—also proved to be an important ideological factor in East-West relations, in this case a positive one. Deemphasizing Stalin's maxim that every communist party must learn from the experience of the October Revolution and follow the Soviet example, the resolution of the Twentieth Congress signaled a fundamental change in the process of building socialism. Whatever Khrushchev's motives were—whether ideological or pragmatic, whether they were a part of the struggle for leadership in the CPSU or a counter-product of Stalin's intolerable controls over the satellites, whether they were dictated by serious economic problems or by an urge for reaffirmation of their intellectual identity—the pronouncement triggered off many a search for a reformed economic system and for indigenous cultural values. The governments of Central and Eastern Europe freed themselves from some of the most oppressive aspects of the Soviet curbs; introduced with greater or lesser intensity some flexibility in industrial planning, production, and marketing policy; and halted the process of the complete collectivization of land. Communist scholars began to scrutinize some basic tenets of Marxism or to reinterpret them in the light of the experience of their respective countries. They pointed to the problem of alienation in the socialist society, which according to Marx was characteristic of the capitalist system only. Intellectuals in general stood in the forefront of this impressive struggle toward liberalization, asserting once again their traditional role of leadership in the centuries-old striving for freedom.

This period of liberalization contributed substantially to the development of a climate for détente. Not only did it offer a precious opportunity for developing contacts with the West, but West European governments, comprehending the significance of liberalization and fully grasping its potential for a relaxation of tensions, began to treat the East European countries as individual national entities rather than as Moscow's obedient satellites.

But none of this would have been feasible had not the Soviet government acquiesced in it. Whatever prompted the Twentieth Congress to promulgate the principles of the equality of the communist countries and parties and of individual roads toward socialism, this ideological innovation extended a degree of autonomy to the client states. One may define it as Moscow-made, prefabricated Titoism, as a strategy that was designed to give its allies a sense of identity without, however, endangering the Soviet government's command position.

Moscow's new attitude was closely related to Khrushchev's equally novel interpretation of peaceful coexistence. Although he declared that he acted in the spirit of Lenin's meaning of the term, he maintained that conditions in the world situation had changed and that war between the two social systems was not only no longer inevitable but that in a nuclear age it must be avoided.

In fact, Khrushchev's position clearly contradicted Lenin's (and Stalin's) views on peaceful coexistence. They had viewed it as a tactical, conditional, and temporary stance; Khrushchev considered it a necessity for an indefinite period of time. This is not to say that Khrushchev's understanding of peaceful coexistence was free of ideological bias. He stressed that the class conflict continued, that the Soviet Union continued to compete with the capitalist world in the sphere of economics to demonstrate the superiority of the socialist system, that the ideological struggle went on. His exclamation "We shall bury you!" is still remembered.

The proceedings of the Twenty-First, Twenty-Second and Twenty-Third Congresses did not deviate from these ideological overtones. Nor did the leaders of the Central and East European parties, particularly Walter Ulbricht, miss a single opportunity to regard East-West relations in the light of this ideology.

It is difficult if not impossible to separate Soviet foreign policy from ideology and thus be able to discern when and under what circumstances Soviet leaders are acting pragmatically in the interest of the state; when and under what circumstances they continue to foster the ideal of international proletarian solidarity; or when and under what circumstances their pronouncements of ideological tenets are meant only to cover the realities of international life. Lenin's writings abound in theoretical principles that can be handily extracted to explain any situation in ideological terms. If Moscow at any moment is compelled to act in the interests of the state at the risk of an apparent contradiction of its ideology, this certainly does not mean that it has abandoned its ideological base. Moscow's stubborn persistence in explaining every move within an ideological framework attests to the fact that it continues to regard Marxism as the final social theory, that it remains the prisoner of its doctrine. Whatever the apparent contradictions between policy and ideology, the communist frame of mind, the institutional, economic, and cultural structure of communist societies, and the profound conviction of the exclusive righteousness of Marxism remain.

In the midst of Moscow's acceptance of the policy of rapprochement with Western Europe the Central Committee of the CPSU stated that "the present stage of historical development is characterized by a sharp aggravation of the ideological struggle between capitalism and socialism." [1] Still more recently, at the meeting of seventy-five communist parties in Moscow in June 1969, the international situation was characterized as "a sharpening of the historic struggle between the forces of progress and reaction, between socialism

[1] *Pravda,* April 11, 1968, as quoted in John Sontag, "International Communism and Soviet Foreign Policy," *The Review of Politics,* Vol. 32, No. 1, January 1970, p. 84.

and imperialism." [2] Brezhnev, speaking at the Twenty-Fourth Congress of the CPSU, held in the spring of 1971, abstained from analyzing world developments in the light of class struggle, but he did state that in "confrontation with socialism, the ruling circles of the capitalist countries are afraid, as never before, that the class struggle will develop into a mass revolutionary movement. . . . The general crisis of capitalism continues to deepen." He also adhered to the old-time Leninist "truth" that contradictions between imperialist states persisted and "the complete triumph of the cause of socialism throughout the world [was] inevitable." [3]

Some Western scholars considered a gradual change in the economic system and in the political atmosphere in the East an encouraging component of the policy of détente. Their analysis led to what became known as the theory of convergence. But the East, sensing a danger in these expectations, denounced the theory. On August 7, 1969, Konstantin Katushev, the Soviet delegate at the Tenth Congress of the Communist Party of Rumania, rejected the bridge-building policy as "perfidious tactics" of the "imperialists" who were pursuing the goal of "undermining the unity of the socialist countries. . . ." The East German delegate, Kurt Tiedke, warned on the same occasion against the West's efforts to drive a "wedge" between socialist states and install a "Trojan horse" in the socialist camp: "The imperialists of the United States and West Germany regard ideological diversion in the socialist states to an increasing extent as their primary state policy." [4]

A Czech magazine attacked the West—which had allegedly in the past used the frontal attack in its anti-communist crusade—for now following a more subtle imperialist in-

[2] *Ibid.,* quoting *Pravda,* June 18, 1969.
[3] *The Current Digest of the Soviet Press,* Vol. xxiii, No. 12, April 20, 1971, pp. 8, 11.
[4] Radio Free Europe, Research, *Rumania/19,* August 14, 1969.

18

trigue by developing a theory of "so-called convergence." It identified Henry Kissinger, Zbigniew Brzezinski, and George Kennan as the fathers of a broadly designed plan of gradual and determined penetration called "gradualism." According to the article, all the disciplines of the social sciences and humanities were engaged in analyses of life in the socialist countries in order to find the most effective methods of exerting influence. The article summarily rejected the whole idea of convergence.[5]

A similar article in a Hungarian paper took a more patronizing attitude toward the theory of convergence, regarding it as an admission on the part of the West that socialism cannot be annihilated by an armed conflict. It recognized certain technical similarities between the two industrial systems—such as production methods, including computers and automatic assembly lines—but it pointed to the unbridgeable differences between the two as long as capitalism remains capitalism and its social classes continue to exist. Accordingly, the whole theory of convergence was invalid, although some theoretical and political circles in the West saw it as a weapon against the socialist countries.[6]

East Germany, which had reason to be most concerned about prospective applications of the theory of convergence since it was exposed to direct influence from West Germany, took the lead in its denunciatory attacks. Some articles, condemning wholeheartedly the prospect for economic convergence, asked instead for closer economic relations among communist states, particularly with the Soviet Union. Ulbricht stated that all important political, scientific, technological,

---

[5] *Život Strany*, No. 43, October 22, 1969; for full translation, see Radio Free Europe, Research, *East Europe*, November 20, 1969. For another article, "Anti-Communism and the Ideological Struggle," see the same source, *Czechoslovak Press*, July 17, 1970.

[6] *Magyarorszag*, May 4, 1970; for full translation, see Radio Free Europe, Research, *Hungarian Press*, June 22, 1970.

military, and economic problems had to be solved by the socialist commonwealth itself for the simple reason that economic collaboration with the West, and in particular acceptance of credits for capital investment, would result in political dependence. Another article criticized East German foreign trade organizations who dallied with the concept of convergence for "ideological carelessness"; another source warned that cooperation of different social orders would lead to abandoning socialism and national sovereignty. Still another article cautioned against ignoring class considerations and stated that so-called cultural and ideological convergence was nothing more than an attempt of the capitalist countries to alter or eliminate socialism.[7]

Sensing a threat to their political system from Brandt's *Ostpolitik,* speakers at a session of the Central Committee of the Communist Party of East Germany, in December 1970, warned against the "danger of imperialist subversion," against "ideological subversion," and the impossibility of any "ideological coexistence." They considered "social democratism" more dangerous than any other kind of imperialist propaganda and asked for a strict "economic delineation" from the West. Erich Honecker, the successor to Ulbricht, rejected the convergence theory at the Eight Congress of SED in May 1971.[8]

A book by Henry Florek and Stanislaw Szefler, *Subversion in the Economy,* launched a major attack against Polish revisionists. In its denunciation of the theory of convergence, it added to the list of "subversive" scholars such names as Jean-Jacques Servan-Schreiber, John Kenneth Galbraith, W. W. Rostow, Daniel W. Bell, and Raymond Aron; their

[7] Radio Free Europe, Research, *GDR: Foreign Affairs,* August 13, 1969.
[8] Radio Free Europe, Research, *GDR: Political Internal Affairs Party,* December 18, 1970; *GDR: Party,* June 16, 1971.

works are considered as the theoretical basis of economic subversion.[9]

In the Soviet Union, a group of sixteen scholars met under the auspices of the Academy of Sciences and unanimously condemned the theory of convergence. They labelled it as a desperate attempt on the part of apologists for capitalism to subvert the communist system, and they branded convergence as a particularly dangerous attack against socialism for its enormous success. They saw the theory as a product of capitalism's profound crisis which can be solved only by its replacement with socialism. It is the duty of Marxist scholars to unmask the theory since it is meant to provide imperialists with a framework for a class offensive against socialism. These Soviet scholars condemned various sociological, political, and economic analyses, published in the West, as unscientific and described their methodology as a mixture of idealism and vulgar materialism. Quoting, naturally, from Lenin, they pointed to the principal flaw of the theory of convergence, namely the unbridgeable difference between capitalism and socialism: the ownership of the means of production and distribution of products.[10]

In general, all East European newspapers condemned the theory of convergence and a closer development of contacts with the East on two grounds: cultural exchanges serve no purpose other than the corrosion of Marxism, and economic cooperation is clearly aimed at undermining the confidence of the populace in the superiority of the socialist system. They called for closing the ranks of the socialist countries in all fields—ideological, political, economic, and military.

These well-orchestrated attacks were motivated by fears of the effectiveness of gradualism and they clearly reflected ideo-

[9] For a review of the book, see Radio Free Europe, Research, *Poland/15,* September 15, 1970.

[10] Akademiia nauk SSSR, *Sovremennye burzhuaznye teorii o sliianii kapitalizma i sotsializma,* Moskva, Izdatel'stvo "Nauka," 1970.

logical concern over East-West relations. It must then be expected that, although not only economic and technological considerations but also a hunger on the part of the scientific, literary, and artistic élite in the East for further intellectual contacts with the West will be important in any concept of détente, they will always be colored by and must operate within the limits of ideological considerations. One can hardly imagine any lasting solution to the problems that divide Europe or any sturdy political relationship, based on mutual trust, as long as the communist countries view Western Europe as a hostile capitalist camp and suspect it of attempting to subvert the socialist system. The ruling circles of the communist bloc will see to it that a policy of détente does not exceed manageable bounds. False hopes in West Europe may lead to profound disappointments. Or, indeed, as Phillip Mosely put it, "A miscalculated détente, far from leading to mutual trust and possibly even to cooperation, would bring the world abruptly into new conflicts, panic, and catastrophe." [11]

Nationalism in Central and Eastern Europe has undoubtedly affected the rigidity of Marxist-Leninist dogmas. It has not, however, appreciably weakened the ideological foundations of the systems. The communist countries, in spite of national peculiarities, find in Marxist determinism a firm common denominator. No matter that such "truths" of the Marxist-Leninist theory as "capitalists digging their own grave," "inevitability of wars between capitalists for colonies," "the international chain of capitalism breaking at its weakest link," and "cyclical economic crises in capitalist economy" have proved to be pathetically incorrect or are a part of a now ancient history; communist countries will nevertheless persist in their belief in the sanctity of the science of Marxism, because without it they would lose their sense of

[11] "The United States and East-West Détente: The Range of Choice," *Journal of International Affairs,* Vol. XXII, No. 1, 1968, p. 6.

direction, their *raison d'être*. It is this myth that has created strong bonds among them and from which they are unable to free themselves. In addition to this ideological allegiance, pragmatic considerations bring the communist élites in East Europe close to the Soviet Union. In spite of, or indeed because of, the intensive nationalism of its peoples their political existence rests on Soviet support, as the events in Hungary in 1956 and Czechoslovakia in 1968 clearly demonstrated.[12]

In March 1948, when Milovan Djilas was still the second most influential man in Yugoslavia, in a conversation with the author, he mused about the future of relationships between communist countries: "Personally, I am of the opinion that a period is forthcoming, and it may last several decades, when the individual socialist states will develop independently but closely linked together. They will form a bouquet of socialist flowers bound by common ideals, but of different scents because of their different traditions, culture, and economic standards, and ways and means of solving their political and economic problems." It was a daring prophecy for that time, and in a sense a true one: the individual states do vary from each other but of more significance to the prospect for détente is the common ideology that has withstood the pressures and the conflicts of nearly a quarter of a century.

Ironically, years later, Djilas became skeptical of the common ideal of communism; in fact, it became repugnant to him.

---

[12] A public opinion poll, addressing itself admittedly to an unusual group of interviewees—those nationals of East European states who visited West Europe but were to return to their home countries—indicated that only a small minority (three to five percent in 1970) of the citizens would in case of free elections cast their vote for the communist party and that they would give preference to the social democratic party. Radio Free Europe, "Party Preference Trends in East Europe," July 1971.

"The world is satiated with dogma," he wrote, "but people are hungry for life. . . ." [13]

This groping toward national identity is a curious paradox of history. These are the same peoples who in the nineteenth century turned to nationalism for the recovery of their nationhood, who in 1940 succumbed to its destructive extremism—fascism and nazism—and who now seek refuge from imposed dogma through these same assertions of nationalism. The West welcomes this development, viewing it as an encouraging factor of détente and as a corrosion of communist ideology. However, these expectations may either turn out to be false hopes or, if not, could result in a balkanization of the area, thus offering the Soviet Union an opportunity for another intervention, even more brutal than the world has witnessed in the past. Thus, nationalism, seen today as détente's hope, could prove to be its death.

Be that as it may, the growth of nationalism made the first large dent in the theory of proletarian internationalism and shattered the Marxist myth that "the workingman has no country." It did produce polycentrism, autonomous tendencies, rivalries in the COMECON, Yugoslavia's defection, the Hungarian national revolution, the Czechoslovak Spring, cultural re-identification, and Rumanian national self-assertion. These developments were accompanied in some countries by economic reforms and structural decentralizations that resulted not only from practical considerations but also from a regard for national interest. Nationalism has certainly affected relations among the individual communist countries. The question remains, however, whether and to what extent nationalism has contributed to the prospects for détente and how much can détente—as a contradiction of communist ideology—expect to benefit from its potential.

[13] *The Unperfect Society,* New York, Harcourt, Brace & World, 1969, p. 57.

Pragmatic considerations of national interests have partly turned the economics of the East European states toward Western Europe, and a longing for intellectual companionship did open some windows to the West's literary and scholarly world. In this respect, economic nationalism and cultural indigenous surges have contributed to the policy of détente. However, in matters of paramount national interests one can point to a number of occasions when the East European countries took a stand that cannot be explained in terms of their national interests.

There is, of course, no objective way to identify national interests; it is a matter of value judgment. One could say, for example, that it would have been in the interest of the Central-East European countries to normalize their relations with their neighbor to the West, the Federal Republic of Germany (FRG), as soon as the passions of the last war had subsided. Their national security and chances for greater independence from the Soviet Union would have increased had they accepted Bonn's proposals to settle their mutual problems. One must assume that their membership in the Council of Europe and an association with the EEC would have broadened their political and economic vistas. One can hardly see national interest motivating their stand on the Soviet-Chinese dispute and the Arab-Israeli conflict. Nor can their accusations of United States imperialism serve their true national interests. In every such case, and many others, their attitude, far from serving their apparent national interests, has been identical (with the qualified exception of Rumania) with Moscow's policies.

Nor does it matter (insofar as the prospect for détente is concerned) whether these communists governments in East Europe act spontaneously on the basis of their own ideological convictions or whether they submit their national will to Soviet pressures. Their attitudes, restrained either by Soviet domination or by an indigenous ideological outlook, impose certain limits on the scope of détente. Moscow may permit them to cultivate contacts with Western Europe within the framework of certain ideological restrictions and under Soviet guidance but never to the detriment of Soviet interests or the ideological substance of their regimes.

But once again and nevertheless, one cannot write off the role that regular contacts on any basis with Western Europe must play in the policy of détente. An exposure to the fruits of freedom, the intensive search for cultural values, a growing economy—all these inescapably must open, if only ever so slightly, the ideological blinds of the East European leaders. But there are limits. For if close cooperation—not merely détente—with the West were to be achieved at the expense of ideological considerations, the ruling parties would, to paraphrase Stalin, stop being communist. Therein lies the crux of the policy of détente; these are the realistic limitations to its achievements.

CHAPTER 2

Politics

THE ideological struggle between the West and East was, naturally enough, accompanied by a power conflict and a new political alignment. As long as the necessities of war compelled the Big Three to work together, their attention was focused on Germany. Numerous statements made during the war, particularly at Teheran and Yalta, contained only general principles of their policy toward postwar Germany, such as denazification, democratization, reparations, punishment of war criminals, disarmament and occupation. A final solution of the German problem was to be decided at a peace conference, the date of which was postponed, according to the Potsdam Agreement, *sine die.*

Only two political agreements related to postwar cooperation between the major allies were signed during the war. In May 1942 Great Britain and the Soviet Union signed a twenty-year treaty of alliance against Germany. In December 1944 General De Gaulle signed a similar treaty with the Soviet government. Soviet suggestions, made in 1942 to the American government, to join forces in such a pact failed, for Washington did not wish to prejudice its position in regard to a peace conference. At a later period, between 1945 and 1947, the American government changed its position on alliances; first James Byrnes and then General George Marshall offered to sign a twenty-five or forty-year treaty with Stalin, against any threat of German aggression. This time Russia declined.

By that time, Stalin viewed Soviet power interests in an entirely different light. As early as December 1943 he had signed a treaty of alliance with Czechoslovakia and then, in quick succession, identical treaties with all other countries of Central and Eastern Europe. Subsequently, all these allies of the Soviet Union signed bilateral treaties of friendship and mutual assistance among themselves. The die was cast: Central and Eastern Europe were merged into a compact political and military bloc, the announced purpose of which was to defend the security of the East. In fact, these alliances were also aimed against the West and served the Soviet government as an instrument for tightening its political and military controls over its neighbors and for creating a sense of uncertainty in the West about further Soviet intentions.

The West could not ignore these arrangements of power. First, in March 1947, France and Great Britain solidified their close ties by the Treaty of Dunkirk and then, in March 1948, the Benelux countries joined in. The United States continued to prefer to stay out of any formal commitment to Western Europe. When, however, in February 1948, the communization of Czechoslovakia completed the circle of Soviet control of Central and Eastern Europe, and when Soviet policy in East Germany turned their zone of occupation into another satellite of Moscow, Washington could not remain oblivious to possible Soviet designs toward Western Europe. The Vandenberg resolution, in June 1948, provided a political basis for a formal alignment of the United States with the countries that felt threatened by the aggressive Soviet policy. On April 4, 1949, for the first time in the history of her relations with Europe, the United States put her signature on a multilateral pact, NATO. Permission of the Western powers for West Germany to establish the Federal Republic of Germany, with limited rights of sovereignty, in September 1949, and the Soviet reaction the following month, elevating East Germany to the status of the German Democratic Republic (GDR), led to an indefinite postponement of the most crucial European problem, the reunification of Germany. These two events also paved the way for the eventual incorporation of West Germany into the military system of NATO in February 1955; this was followed on the Soviet side by the establishment of the Warsaw Pact alliance and by a series of bilateral alliances of the Soviet bloc countries with East Germany. In addition, to sever the last ties between the wartime Allies, the Soviet government responded to the inclusion of the FRG in NATO by the renunciation of its treaties with Great Britain and France. The process of gradual crystallization of the two mutually hostile blocs was brought to peak and had seemingly reached a point of no return. On the wider scene of U.S.-Soviet relations, and in close connection with the progressing confrontation in Europe of the military strength of the Soviet and Western blocs, attempts to bring the armament race under control yielded no results.

The Baruch Plan, which might have served as a basis for submitting the production and use of atomic fuel to UN controls and the eventual destruction of the existing American nuclear arsenal, was rejected by Moscow. When the Soviet government exploded its own atomic and hydrogen bombs, all prospects for bringing the nuclear arms race to a halt vanished until the Soviet Union had reached a level of parity with the United States. Under this umbrella of the "balance of terror" the two blocks reached a stalemate in military power in Europe. Viewing each other as political enemies, with apparently mutually exclusive goals of subverting the other side to its own philosophical beliefs, each side braced itself with conventional and nuclear weapons and gave their armies one principal mission: to deter the other side from real or possible threats to their own security and social systems. All political contacts between the two parts of Europe were suspended, and since communists view intellectual contacts in the light of politics these were also brought to a complete standstill.

The Stalinization of Central and Eastern Europe brought particularly grievous results to the nations of the area in their cultural life. With the exception of Bulgaria and old Serbia, they had centuries-old cultural ties with Western Europe. Though the ethnic affinity with Russia triggered off the

29

slavophile movement in the nineteenth century, the scale of these feelings ranged from political hopes (as in the case of Bulgaria and Serbia) through rather intellectual ties (in Bohemia, Croatia, and Slovenia) to outright rejection of Slav solidarity (in Poland). The non-Slavic nations of the area (Rumania and Hungary), surrounded by the Slavic "sea," were understandably frightened by the political implications of pan-slavism.

As has been said before, Russia, with her orthodoxy, Byzantine pompousness, self-imposed isolation, political and economic backwardness, false pretenses of Chiliasm, was, though *in* Europe, not *of* Europe. Not even the monumental intellectual achievements of the "Westerners" would turn the tide as the outbreak of the war in 1914 dashed their hopes of progress toward political constitutionalism and intellectual freedom. The victory of Bolshevism and the continuing weight of Russian tradition only deepened the abyss between the sense of Russian and Western values of life. As "no nation can dissociate itself from its past" neither could the Soviet Union sever its umbilical cord from its Makropulos mother, Czarism. Or, as Thomas G. Masaryk put it succinctly, "The Bolsheviks destroyed the Czar but failed to destroy Czarism."

However, the main stream of cultural life in Central and Eastern Europe, in its broad sense, flowed from the West. The great forces of Western culture—Christianity, the philosophy of humanism, the renaissance, the Reformation, the Enlightenment, libertarian nationalism—as well as its arts and architecture found receptive soil in Central and Eastern Europe.

This homogenous culture was abruptly rejected by the Stalinist regimes, which compelled the creative mind to turn its back on the West. Intellectuals as well as other strata of society were forbidden to travel to Western centers of culture and learning; to continue contacts with them; to receive Western literature; to see a Western painting; to produce a Western play; to present a Western film; to read Western scholarly journals, magazines, newspapers; and to listen to Western broadcasts, which were made largely ineffective by an elaborate system of jamming.

On the contrary, the intellectual life of the people of Central and East European nations was subjected to a deliberate process of russification and sovietization. Learning Russian was made obligatory, and translations of Lenin and Stalin at cheap prices inundated the book market. The products of Soviet playwrights, movie-makers, painters, and men of literature and science assumed a dominant role over indigenous national works. In the name of socialist realism, creativity was all but choked out.

The separation of the East from the West took many forms. The most compelling, the ideological, was meant to provide a theoretical base for this alienation. The military served both as a protective shield and as a potential aggressive weapon. The economic was to revolutionize old social structures, prove superiority over the "bourgeois" systems of the West, and make the new economy responsive to Soviet economic needs. The most humiliating form of all, the cultural, was designed (as Marxist theoreticians alleged their system was able to do) to create a new, Soviet type of man.

The central point of all change was to be Moscow, and the West had no opportunity to make any contacts with the individual nations of Central and Eastern Europe. The only road leading to Warsaw, Prague, Budapest, Bucharest, and Sofia (and to Belgrade until 1948) led through Moscow, and Stalin barricaded it thoroughly. Then, some five years after his death, the change began to take place.

Detente: A Problem of Perceptions

It would be difficult to name any date to mark the origin of the policy of détente. It started modestly in the late 1950's when the West sensed an element of sincerity in Khrushchev's exuberant calls for peaceful coexistence, as Western Europe regained a feeling of self-confidence, and as the countries of Central and Eastern Europe began to grope for a new stance in European politics, less dependent on Moscow's authority. Even such dramatic and foreboding events as the building of the Berlin Wall in August 1961 and the Soviet-led occupation of Czechoslovakia in August 1968, which spoke eloquently of Moscow's understanding of détente, had no lasting effect on the West's quest for a relaxation of tensions. On the contrary, after a brief period of popular indignation and official protests, the West tacitly though reluctantly appeared to accept the Soviet position that both acts reduced the danger of serious conflicts between the East and the West.

In general, over the past ten years, all West European countries have developed steadily increasing contacts with the Central-East European countries. They followed a certain pattern, common to all contacts at the cultural, scientific and trade level. Agreements on cultural and scientific exchanges were signed and were followed by streams of mutual visits of theatrical groups, orchestras, individual writers, actors, film directors, and scientists. Cultural and scientific exhibits were exchanged and closer contacts established at international meetings, exhibitions, and sports events. Trade unions and parliamentary representatives exchanged delegation visits, children's summer trips were arranged, and sister-city relationships were entered into. West European tourists swamped the beaches of Rumania and Bulgaria, not to mention Yugoslavia. Many West European scholars, other intellectuals and even politicians, many of them communists, visited East Europe on a private basis.

With the exception of West Germany, these trade, cultural, and scientific contacts were accompanied by corresponding political developments. Official visits were exchanged between governmental representatives of practically all East and West European countries, starting at the inconspicuous level of Chambers of Commerce, directors of governmental departments, and leading to visits by Ministers of Foreign Trade, and culminating in trips by Foreign Ministers and in some cases by Prime Ministers. Official communiques and speeches were worded in warm terms, signaling the end of the Cold War and the beginning of a new era of détente and cooperation.

The Federal Republic of Germany, until 1970, was the sole exception to this trend of détente in Europe. Though relations with her neighbors to the East are at the heart of a policy of détente, her political contacts with them continued to be practically nil (except for Rumania). On the contrary, she was exposed to an incessant barrage of accusations of militarist, expansionist, and revanchist policies.

A close examination of the motives for these policies on the part of either the West and East, of their real achievements in the arena of politics, or of the goals of either side suggests the wisdom of a cautious attitude toward the outcome of the currently optimistic mood in European affairs.

The Soviet goals of détente can be divided into two categories: those which are clearly defined and those which are only implied. The Soviet Union has sought consistently for almost fifteen years to achieve, through détente, an international legal confirmation of the status quo in Central and Eastern Europe. It has repeatedly asked, despite the commitments of the Potsdam Agreement, for international recognition of East Germany as an independent state and of her boundaries with West Germany and Poland, and for turning West Berlin into an independent political entity. It has persistently defied attempts on the part of West Europe to reach a political accommodation with Soviet allies in East Europe, making it clear that their relations with West Europe are to be limited to Soviet interpretations of détente. Thus, the policy of détente, in Soviet eyes, was to serve the Soviet effort to reconfirm its dominant position among the countries of the Warsaw Pact.

In addition, the Soviet government has constantly tried to

eliminate the presence of the United States in Europe, first by way of dissolution of the military blocs, NATO and the Warsaw Pact, and more recently by proposing a European security conference.

The Soviet Union has pursued some other implicit goals that are related to its policy of détente. In the attempt to eliminate United States influence in Europe it has developed political contacts with individual countries of Western Europe, playing upon their sensitivity in matters of national independence and pride. In this respect, it found an eager partner in France. Its continuous attacks against West German militarism and revanchism had the dual intent of making Bonn's policies suspect among its European allies and of increasing their doubts about Washington, which was pictured as the instigator and supporter of Bonn's expansionist goals. When the Soviet government signed a treaty with the FRG in August 1970, the focus of détente switched from Paris to Bonn and produced—as Moscow had expected—a growing concern in France about the future of West German policy. The cardinal question, therefore, is whether Moscow sees in détente any basis for a constructive policy of cooperation, rooted in a new system of security, or whether détente is thought of only as a strategic device to weaken West Europe, by playing one country against the other and by awaiting a time when Moscow may apply massive political pressure against them.

The Soviet policy of détente also reflects its interests in Asia and the Middle East. By contributing to a relaxation of tensions in Europe it encourages the governments of West Europe to avoid entanglement in the Arab-Israeli conflict and to take a hands-off or even hostile attitude (as in the case of France) toward United States engagement in South-East Asia. Thus, the Soviet commitments in the two areas face a confrontation with an America, isolated from her allies, who do not wish to chill the glow of détente in Europe. In addition, since détente gives the Soviet Union a sense of political peace and military security in Europe, it can focus its political attention and strength on the conflict with China.

The countries of Central and Eastern Europe have stood solidly behind the Soviet concept of détente and have patterned their own to Moscow's methods in establishing and expanding their contacts with Western Europe. However, a careful analysis of East Europe's moves toward détente and its reactions to the West's friendly initiatives indicates that its various interests in closer contacts with Western Europe do differ from country to country and from case to case. Moreover, many countries seem to welcome the policy of détente as an opportunity to reduce Soviet influence in the area and gain some sense of independence. Nevertheless, a review of their efforts over the decade clearly indicates that Soviet policy remained the decisive factor in their attitude toward West Europe. Rumania has been the only exception.

West Europe's perceptions of détente differ considerably from the Soviet Union's. The latter follows certain indentifiable goals; the first engages more in elusive generalities. The two policies may complement each other in some respects but their final concepts may prove mutually exclusive. Both sides want to achieve a relaxation of tension; they both favor development of trade and scientific and technological cooperation; both express the wish to remove the seeds of political animosity. But it has been West Europe that acquiesced to one of the Soviet Union's principal demands, the de facto recognition of the status quo in East Europe; it has been West Europe that reconciled itself to both the political system and Soviet dominance in that area. It has been West Europe that has adjusted itself to the "realities of the situation," to use the Soviet term. Soviet contributions to détente are less evident, save that Moscow has for the time being relaxed its attacks on West German "militarism and revanchism."

There are a number of reasons for this inequality in give

and take. The Soviet Union and its allies view the policy of détente within a common framework, whereas Western Europe regards it with much less specificity, as a slow, undefined process of alleviation of tensions. This general concept is common to all West European countries, but a closer look at the substance of the policies of three of the major powers—West Germany, France, and Great Britain—suggests that their motivations and to some extent their goals in regard to détente differ and indeed in some respects are in conflict with each other.

West Germany sees in détente an avenue toward normalization of her relations with the East. From the inception of the FRG in September 1949 until Kiesinger's government in December 1966, reunification was considered in Bonn as a precondition to a general détente in Europe. Kiesinger reversed the order: he recognized that détente must precede successful efforts for reunification. He failed to make any progress in this direction, however, because he refused to abandon that basic principle of West German foreign policy (the Hallstein Doctrine and the claim to the exclusive representation of the whole of Germany). The Soviet Union under these circumstances refused to establish any relationship of détente with Bonn. Brandt's coalition government, however, went the whole way by renouncing these principles and meeting most of the Soviet demands.

France has been the most ardent promoter of the policy of détente. Since 1959 General De Gaulle had often repeated his grand but vague design of a "Europe from the Atlantic to the Urals" (a slogan which had been coined by Guy Mollet) as he had talked on frequent occasions about a policy of "détente to entente to cooperation." Assuming that the forces of nationalism would prevail over communist ideology, he expected that the Central and East European countries would reassert their national identity, free from the domination of the Soviet Union, and that they would cheerfully open the door to the political presence of France in the area. If the German understanding of détente was motivated by the need to remove tensions on her eastern borders, but within the context of ideological realities, France on the other hand was moved by considerations of prestige and power, ignoring ideological barriers. By the same token, West Germany, acting in the belief that normalization of relations with the East would serve as a substantial contribution to détente in Europe, continued to stress her ties with the rest of Western Europe, to work toward its political integration, and to emphasize the necessity of a United States presence in Europe. De Gaulle, on the other hand, sought in détente an opportunity to bolster France's independent policy and minimize America's influence in Europe. Bonn worked toward strengthening the attitude of NATO toward the Warsaw Pact alliance and would have preferred a common stance by the West in negotiations with the East. Paris reduced its military commitments to NATO and chose to approach the East on a bilateral basis. Bonn was careful to take a stand-off attitude toward the process of liberalization in Central and Eastern Europe. It was aware of the potential of unrest in East Germany, which might be triggered off by such events as the Hungarian revolution in the autumn of 1956 and the Czechoslovak Spring in 1968, and of the possibility that these events might bring intra-German relations to the brink of a conflict. Paris officially encouraged this process toward independence and in fact perceived it as an avenue of détente. West Germany was aware that her power was inferior to the Soviet Union's and of the latter's preponderant influence in East Europe; France pictured herself as a power equal to Russia in matters of European politics. In addition, France envisaged the policy of "détente to entente to cooperation" as a vehicle for exercising restraint on West Germany and for keeping a vigilant eye on her growing power. The language of détente of the two countries was similar, but the meaning was different and in some aspects contradictory.

Great Britain, in contrast to France, saw in the policy of

détente a way to an accommodation and reconciliation between the two parts of Europe. Détente was to her more a matter of style, of political atmosphere, of some mutual trust rather than of some momentous and overt policy. Unlike the FRG, but rather like France, Great Britain has no direct dispute with the Soviet Union and with the countries of East Europe over concrete problems, nor is she burdened by the heritage of past hostilities in pursuit of political ambitions in the East. As is the case with other West European countries, her democratic system separates her from the East, but similarly to West Germany and in contrast to France she does not expect, nor does she encourage, a disengagement of the nations of Central and Eastern Europe from their totalitarian ideology; nor does she assume diminution of Soviet influence in the area. She is reconciled to the political and ideological status quo. Her own economic need compels her to attend to her special interest of developing a prosperous trade with the East without ulterior political motives as is the case in Bonn. Great Britain regards American contributions to the defense of Western Europe as essential to the maintenance of the balance of power in Europe.

Thus, there are some slight, some marked, distinctions in the understanding and practice of détente by the three West European powers. This difference may not be of major concern as long as détente is in the initial stage of removing tensions between the East and West. However, if the suspicion is justified that the Soviet Union uses détente not only for the immediate purpose of international stabilization in Central and Eastern Europe but also as a long-term proposition to undermine the political cohesion of the West and thereby exert increased political pressure on West Europe (in particular on West Germany), then this difference in the understanding of détente on the part of the FRG, France, and Great Britain may have serious consequences. Past experience indicates that the Soviet Union might see détente as a tranquilizer for West

Europe, hoping to lull it into a precarious feeling of security. This is not to say that détente should be opposed, but it does suggest that when the Soviet "package" is offered the West should look carefully beneath the wrapping.

The story of negotiations with totalitarian powers is sadly familiar. How often during and after the war have the Soviets and the West used the same language but with what contradictory interpretations? The history of negotiations with totalitarian powers has direct bearing on any assessment of the value of détente, particularly in the light of the West's badly splintered attitudes. The East may differ in its internal councils on some tactical or perhaps even substantial issues of its détente policy but when facing the West in regard to any concrete question it presents a united, well-coordinated front. As has been shown, not so Western Europe. Should the Soviet Union intensify its efforts to weaken NATO in the name of a policy of détente, should it succeed in undermining the solidarity of the West European nations among themselves and with the United States, then indeed the vine might bear bitter grapes. It is conceivable, indeed probable, that West Europe had no other alternative than to meet the Soviet Union on the latter's terms once the Cold War confrontation had abated and the desire for détente has gained momentum. However, in the long run it is West Europe's security under Soviet political and military pressure, the problem of Germany, and the elimination of periodical threats to West Berlin that must be the standard by which West Europe must test the real meaning of détente.

The policy of détente is both a hope and a danger. It may lead to a real pacification of Europe or it may turn into disillusionment or even sudden threats and tensions. Its outcome depends not only on Soviet goals but also on the policies of France, Great Britain, and West Germany and on the extent to which they will be able to coordinate them.

39

French Policy

The interests of France and those of the Soviet Union and its allies in some instances appear to be complementary and in others conflicting. General de Gaulle, minimizing the latter, tried to blend their mutual interests in his vision of "l'Europe des patries," a vision of independent national entities that would resurrect the grand destiny of the old Continent, free from the hegemony of the two super-powers. Moscow welcomed his efforts to reduce United States presence in Europe but certainly not his calls for the independence of Soviet allies. It followed with satisfaction De Gaulle's persistent opposition to Britain's entry into the European Common Market, but viewed with misgivings his policy of close cooperation with West Germany. Though this policy (in that it was really designed to keep a wary eye on the growing of power of the FRG) was in consonance with Soviet interests, it also lent support to Bonn's quest for reunification which De Gaulle originally considered a prerequisite to peace in Europe. Nor could the Soviet government accept De Gaulle's consistently firm position on West Berlin. Russia wanted to establish it as an independent political unit, while France insisted on guarantees of the city's ties with West Germany. While Moscow appreciated De Gaulle's abrogation of military commitments to NATO and the consequent weakening of the West's military posture toward the forces of the Warsaw Pact countries, it viewed with no pleasure at all France's build-up of an independent nuclear capability. All nations of the East bloc were gratified by De Gaulle's recognition of the Oder-Neisse boundary, but they found him not so helpful in their long struggle for recognition of East Germany. In one significant aspect the attitude of the Soviet Union and its allies toward De Gaulle's policy differed: the countries of Central and Eastern Europe were heartened by his appeals for the reestablishment of their national sovereignty; Moscow neither approved nor responded.

40

As regards non-European affairs, the Soviet Union could observe only with a great deal of contentment De Gaulle's stand on the war in Vietnam, his support of the Arabs in their conflict with Israel, his spectacular trips (with anti-American overtones) to Canada and Latin America, and his recognition —though here perhaps with mixed feelings—of the People's Republic of China.

De Gaulle's approach to the policy of détente inevitably carried the imprint of his forceful personality. Enamored with grandiloquent rhetoric, he coined many flamboyant phrases designed to create a profound impression today and to be quoted by the historians tomorrow. His program of détente was undeniably consistent. His method, within the framework of his vision of a future Europe, was systematic and reminiscent of nineteenth-century diplomacy. Never losing sight of the "grandeur de France" and consistently projecting her as a leading power on the European continent, he advanced boldly, step by step, on all diplomatic fronts— cultural, economic, and political. France was to him an equal partner with the Soviet Union. As to the Central and East European nations, his attitude was the beneficent paternalism of a superior power, acting in their interest and in the tradition of historical ties with the countries of the area.

After De Gaulle had established the first cultural and trade contacts and authorized visits at lower levels, he moved onto the scene of politics. After the members of the cabinet of the East European countries in charge of foreign trade, industry, agriculture, education, and technological development had paid visits to Paris, he sent French counterparts to their respective capitals. After their Foreign Ministers, Prime Ministers, and some Heads of State paid their respect to France, he dispatched his Minister of Foreign Affairs, Couve de Murville, to their countries. He finally extended to Poland and Rumania the honor of a personal visit and accepted the invitation of other states as well. In his attempt to avoid the antagonism of the Soviet Union and inevitably concerned about this carefully designed plan for French cultural, economic, and political penetration into its own domain, he had carefully preceded these contacts with similar ones with Moscow. It was an impressive, old-fashioned strategy. Unfortunately, for France (as well as East Europe), the balance sheet of a decade of relentless efforts records no major results. Realities have proved stronger than rhetoric, even De Gaulle's.

In matters of cultural and scientific contacts, France proudly and justifiably claimed a rich heritage, and the reputation and prestige of her cultural achievements in the inter-war period were particularly high in Poland, Czechoslovakia, and Rumania. Under a policy of détente, abetted by the desire of East European nations to revive their cultural past and their contacts with the West, France's cultural resurgence was welcomed by their intellectual circles. The French government signed agreements on cultural and scientific cooperation with all East European countries. They provided for such arrangements as the exchange of scholars and students, information on scientific and technological developments, and radio and television programs; for conferences and for cooperation in the field of atomic energy; for the establishment of cultural institutes, lecture halls, and libraries; and for the exchange of artistic groups and exhibits of cultural and scientific works.

The fragmentary information about the implementation of these agreements does not permit an evaluation of their effectiveness. The French Ministry of Foreign Affairs saw them as "modern diplomacy," pursued "for the people, by the people," and it noted with satisfaction that "of all geographical areas East Europe and Latin America are most favored." Conversely, "the socialist republics, in the increasing number of their exchanges with West Europe, reserved a privileged place to France." [1]

[1] Ministère des Affaires Étrangères, *Relations culturelles, scientifiques et techniques 1968-1969,* p. 5; *1965,* pp. 59, 18.

According to official data, and in harmony with the increasing thrust of Paris' policy of détente, the number of students and teachers exchanged with the East European countries has steadily grown. While the total number of university stipends, accorded by the French Ministry of Foreign Affairs to foreign students, more than doubled between 1963 and 1968, that of stipends for students from East Europe increased nine times, reaching the figure of 912 in 1968. Of these, students from Czechoslovakia were in the greatest number, mainly due to the admission of applicants who had escaped to France after the Soviet occupation of Czechoslovakia. These were followed by students from Poland, Yugoslavia, Bulgaria, Hungary, Rumania, and the Soviet Union, in that order.[2]

Of 5,700 stipends offered by the Ministry of Foreign Affairs for study abroad, over 1,000 were allocated for studies in East Europe. In addition, the East European governments extended 187 stipends to French students.[3]

France put great emphasis on teaching French in East Europe, and the language now holds an important place in their secondary schools. In Bulgaria, 70 percent of students were learning the language in 1966; in Hungary 10 percent; in Rumania 60-65 percent; and in the Soviet Union about 25 percent. The number of French professors in East Europe as well as the number of adult people attending classes in French has grown.[4]

In the field of scientific and technological exchanges in 1965, the program with Poland increased 40 percent; with Bulgaria by about 500 percent; and with Czechoslovakia by 100 percent. In 1968, out of some 1,200 French scientists who were sent abroad, over 500 worked in the Soviet Union and close to 150 in East Europe.[5]

[2] See Table XVI and *ibid,* 1968-1969, p. 105.
[3] *Ibid.,* p. 89.
[4] *Ibid.,* 1966, pp. 15-17.
[5] *Ibid.,* 1965, p. 67; 1968-1969, p. 55.

This record is impressive and it speaks convincingly of French understanding of cultural détente. Nevertheless, it does not seem to fare well by comparison with the cultural contacts of other countries with Central and East Europe. Incomplete data lead to misleading conclusions, but one can state that the number of French students in East Europe represents only a small fraction of foreign students in that area. It would be unfair to compare two different years of study, but one can at least note with interest that some 26,000 foreign university students were in the area in 1967 and only 912 French students were there in 1968-1969. On the other hand, it must also be observed that over a period of twelve years, from 1955 to 1967, the number of foreign students in the area almost doubled (though it was still only about one fourth of the number of foreign students in the United States).[6]

It must also be observed, however, that despite French vigor in these affairs, in 1966 more Czechoslovaks and Hungarians studied in the United States and in West Germany than in France, and Poles chose America (though not West Germany) over France. Rumanian and Bulgarian students, however, gave preference to France over both the United States and West Germany. Indeed, students from all countries of the area *in toto* (including the Soviet Union and Yugoslavia) chose the United States over France. On the other hand, it is undoubtedly of political significance that over one hundred students went to France from East Germany, whereas none came to America or West Germany. To what extent this reflected their desires and to what extent visa problems, is not known.

Finally, it should be noted that the total number of East European students in the leading West European countries was small, altogether slightly under 2,500, with Yugoslavia

[6] See Table XVII.

44

and Poland in top place and Bulgaria and the Soviet Union at the bottom.[7]

Another indicator of France's *mission civilisatrice* in East Europe is the number of translations of books written in French as compared with literary works in other Western languages. In the four years between 1964 and 1967, translations from English and German led translations from the French in Bulgaria and Czechoslovakia for every year; in Hungary for three years; in Poland, English books took precedence over French books for four years. Only in Rumania were French books more popular for three years. Translations from the Russian, of course, took preference in almost every instance, but, interestingly enough, in decreasing amounts and particularly (and conspicuously) in Rumania.[8]

Nor could France claim a privileged place in instruction in the French language in East Europe. For instance, her Foreign Minister, Couve de Murville, during his last visit in Warsaw in 1966, noticed that the language was "in retreat" and behind Russian, German, and English. In Czechoslovakia only 15 percent of students were learning French, far less than those studying the other three languages; and in Hungary 23 percent, just about the same as English and German.[9]

On the other hand, if tourism can be considered an aspect of cultural contacts, it should be noted that French visitors to East Europe of all kinds (not only tourists) took second place only to Germany in 1968. They went to Bulgaria, Czechoslovakia, Poland, Hungary, and Rumania, in that order (not counting East Germany). Over a period of ten years, from 1958 to 1968, they visited East European countries in an almost steadily increasing number, a fact all the more significant in that the French are not considered to be avidly

[7] See Table XVIII.
[8] See Table XIX.
[9] *New York Herald Tribune,* July 27, 1966; *Le Monde,* July 28, 1966.

devoted to travel abroad.[10] In summary, it would seem that although both the French government and French intellectuals carried French culture into Central Europe with some vigor, they did so with modest results, and also that the states of that area, to the extent to which meager data justify a generalization, reciprocated with similar modesty.

French activities in détente in trade offer a picture similar to that in the cultural sphere: intensified efforts but with results less than those achieved by the FRG, or even Great Britain and Italy (this is largely covered in Chapter 3).

Whatever progress France achieved in cultural and economic détente, her political policy plays the determining role in her relations with East Europe. One rereads De Gaulle's speeches with profound awe. Whatever the occasion—a press conference (which as a rule turned into lectures) or his statements before the U.S. Congress or in Moscow or Warsaw, or Bucharest—they all testify to his erudition, his intellect, his rhapsodic spirit, his unbounded patriotism, and the steadfastness of his vision of the Europe and the world of the future. They testify as well to his sense of form and manner, to his majestic and even dynastic style.[11] But the feasibility of his ideas is an entirely different matter.

De Gaulle's policy toward East Europe must be viewed in the light of the domestic and international situation in France when he took office in 1958. His country was exhausted materially and morally by the war in Vietnam and Algiers, and he rallied her spirit. France's freedom of action in world affairs was imperilled by U.S. military and political preponderance. To meet this, he removed from her shoulders the burden of her colonial heritage, the while exalting her

[10] See Table xv.

[11] For the texts of De Gaulle's speeches, see *Major Addresses, Statements, and Press Conferences of General Charles De Gaulle,* New York, Ambassade de France, Service de Presse et d'Information. From here on, *MASPCG.*

greatness and focusing her ambitions on the task of building a new Europe—under French leadership, to be sure—but free from the hegemony of the two super-powers. "A European Europe," he called it, "our Europe." In the pursuit of this design he faced a threefold (and in ways self-contradictory) problem: how to reconcile the Soviet policy in East Europe with his concept of national independence; how to change the historical antagonism between Germany and France into a lasting and constructive partnership without arousing suspicion in the East; and how to contribute to a solution of Germany's division, but with due regard to the growth of her power. The working plan that was to lead to the solution of this multifaceted problem was summed up in his often repeated and appealing sentence, "from détente to entente to cooperation." It was a grandiose plan, thought through in neatly devised phases.

The first step, détente, was to be achieved by replacing the confrontation of the two hostile blocs (and their mutual use of invectives) with bilateral, not bloc to bloc, negotiations, and with mutual ideological tolerance. The second step, entente, would presumably lead to a negotiated settlement of the problems of the boundaries of Germany, of armaments, and of security. The third step, cooperation, would culminate in a new European system that would give to the old continent, so rich in wisdom and culture, its rightful place in shaping the destiny of mankind. De Gaulle profoundly believed, and said so on numerous occasions, that he was proceeding in the interests of the whole world.

His attention was first focused on Germany; having found in Adenauer a worthy partner he worked diligently for the close cooperation of France with the FRG. According to him, on French-West German "solidarity [depended] all hopes of uniting Europe on political and defense levels as well as on the economic level. On this solidarity depends, in consequence, the destiny of the whole of Europe, from the Atlantic to the Ural Mountains." He saw as early as 1960 that "Federal Germany [was] rendering the greatest possible service to coexistence by incorporating itself as it does into Western Europe," which will establish, through organization, some equilibrium with the Soviet bloc and "enable the old continent to bring a reconciliation between its two parts. . . ." [12]

De Gaulle's efforts were crowned by the French-West German treaty, signed in January 1963, which was to lay a firm foundation not only for cooperation between the two countries and the successful political organization of West Europe but also for his still distant goal of détente all over Europe. He was not deterred from pursuing this goal by the hostile reception the treaty received in the East. The Czechoslovak government in an official note pointed to its "dangerous consequences", and the Polish government protested, viewing the pact with "profound disquiet," as one that encouraged German revanchism and militarism. *Izvestiia* termed De Gaulle's idea of a Europe from the Atlantic to the Urals "pure adventurism," and said further that "one can only marvel at the vanity of the actor trying on the crown of the new Charlemagne." [13]

In an attempt to reconcile his policy on Germany with a desire for rapprochement with the Soviet bloc, De Gaulle faced a real dilemma. On the one hand, he considered the division of Germany an "absurdity" and spoke of the right of the Germans to self-determination and reunification. He also refused to recognize the GDR, which was to him an "artificial" creation. He was consistently firm on the question of West Berlin, stating that France was not ready "to give way

[12] *MASPCG, op.cit.*, Vol. May 19, 1958 to January 31, 1964, p. 179; Vol. April 7, 1960 to October 17, 1963, p. 12.

[13] *Le Monde*, February 17, 1963; *The Current Digest of the Soviet Press*, Vol. xv, No. 7, p. 15. The idea was not only adventurism; it was also a phantasy. André Malraux told C. L. Sulzberger that De Gaulle, speaking of a Europe from the Atlantic to the Urals, "implied partitioning the Soviet Union." *New York Times,* January 21, 1972.

before the threats of the totalitarian empire." [14] On the other hand, the Soviet Union and its allies insisted on the recognition of East Germany as an independent state and West Berlin as an independent political entity. The cleavage between the two claims again became apparent when De Gaulle, on the occasion of his celebrated trip to their capitals, attempted to persuade the Soviet and Polish governments to move closer to his position. The efforts ended in failure.

How determined De Gaulle was in regard to Germany is open to speculation. Publicly he was certainly advocating German reunification, without which, he asserted, there could be no lasting peace in Europe.[15] But he fully appreciated, being the incarnation of Gallic wit, and probably enjoyed the deliberate inversion of the famous words of Gambetta, applied now to German reunification—"Parlez-en toujours, n'y pensez jamais" ("Talk about it constantly but never think about it"). Moreover, on several occasions during Erhard's chancellorship, of which he was rather critical, he indicated that he was in the position, precious to any statesman, to choose an alternative course if Bonn was reluctant to follow his European and anti-American leadership. At the end of 1963, he made an oblique reference to the existence of the East German state when he included "Pankow" among other communist capitals and expressed the hope that their totalitarian regime "will gradually come to an evolution compatible with our own transformation." [16] In February 1965, at a press conference, he gave an elaborate lecture about the role of Germany in the history of Europe and then acknowledged that "fruitful relations between East and West [would] not be established so long as the German anomalies . . . continue." Whatever

[14] *MASPCG, op. cit.,* Vol. May 19, 1958 to January 31, 1964, p. 142.

[15] H. Siegler, *Wiedervereinigung und Sicherheit Deutschlands,* Vol. 11, 1964-1967, Bonn, Verlag für Zeitarchive, 1968, p. 56.

[16] *MASPCG, op.cit.,* Vol. May 19, 1958 to January 31, 1964, p. 244.

that term means, he failed to mention reunification, and the statement was subjected to criticism in the *Bundestag* while *Pravda* attached to "the press conference of the French President a highly important significance." [17] Gromyko, at a press conference in Paris two months later, remarked that the policy of "the French government [proceeded] from the fact of the existence of two German States" and that "formal recognition or no recognition of a government changes nothing of these facts." The French government, embarrassed as it was by Gromyko's statement (certainly indiscreet if not unfair) tried to correct the situation by commenting officially that it proceeded "from the fact Germany [remained] divided but this [meant] no recognition of the GDR." [18]

When De Gaulle was in Moscow in June 1966, he referred to East Germany, as "the zone of occupation." However, the French-Soviet declaration, issued at the end of the visit, mentioned only in general terms that the two parties exchanged views on the German question. On the other hand, they agreed that their prime objective was normalization and then "a gradual development of relations between all European countries. . . ." [19] Whatever possible ulterior thought was on De Gaulle's mind, the wording undoubtedly included East Germany in terms of the Soviet interpretation.

De Gaulle's publicly expressed displeasure over Erhard's policy, and in particular his close cooperation with the United States, cooled the relations between France and West Germany in the mid-1960's and the German press was increasingly critical of De Gaulle's policy toward East Europe. For instance, *Die Welt* asked, "Did the General get the impression that he can decide the fate of the Federal Republic over the head of Bonn?" Or, *Die Zeit* explained that France was afraid

[17] *Ibid.,* Vol. March 17, 1964 to May 16, 1967, p. 85; Siegler, *op.cit.,* Vol. 11, p. 61.

[18] *Ibid.,* Vol. 11, p. 73.

[19] *MASPCG, op.cit.,* Vol. March 17, 1964 to May 16, 1967, p. 108.

of another Rapallo but perhaps De Gaulle was seeking "a Rappallo on a European scale and under French leadership." [20]

After Kiesinger became Chancellor in December 1966 French-German relations improved. The new government in Bonn, in contrast to its predecesor, turned East in an attempt to seek a solution of the German problem in cooperation with Moscow. De Gaulle was supposed to help in the matter. He still spoke about reunification as "a historical necessity," but at the same time recognized that reunification might take many long years, perhaps decades. He still considered Germany's division to be an "abnormal situation" which, however, "must be settled by the Germans themselves within the framework of an agreement of Western, Central, and East Europe." [21] Nevertheless, he was moving closer to the Soviet position, which excluded the United States from the right, guaranteed by the Potsdam Agreement, to participate in the solution of the problem. He stated several times that it was a European question.

His statements in Poland in September 1967 enraged the German press and even Kiesinger was reported to have been "outraged" and said that "there [were] limits to what a country that wants to protect its dignity can take." [22] By February 1969, in an interview with C. L. Sulzberger, De Gaulle "took no trouble to disguise his growing feelings against West Germany and was clearly frightened by the increase in German power." [23]

It would appear that West Germany had good and serious reasons to question the sincerity of De Gaulle's publicly professed friendship and his insistence that he was working toward a solution of the German problem. Contacts that

[20] March 3, 1965; January 22, 1965.

[21] *Die Welt,* December 19, 1966.

[22] *Washington Post,* September 22, 1967, quoting *Der Spiegel.*

[23] *New York Times,* November 11, 1970.

France developed at the non-official level with the GDR only strengthened this suspicion. In addition to a growing trade (see Chapter 3), a lively exchange of visits developed, some of them sponsored by the French Committee for Exchanges with a New Germany, which had been founded in 1948 and others, after 1961, by Franco-German exchanges. In 1962, the German-French society was established in East Berlin, with the goal "to offer to French people a true picture of the peaceful intentions of the GDR and to permit the citizens of this Republic to know better the progressive democratic traditions of the French." [24] Two years later, it was noticed that "not a single week [passed] without East Berlin making a friendly gesture toward Paris" and still later that "thousands of French citizens visited the GDR in 1966 at the invitation of the German-French Society." [25] Little wonder that a responsible West German daily, describing the flow of these contacts, concluded, "One can only hope that it will not happen that this movement, cleverly nourished by the East, gains a decisive weight in French public opinion." [26]

This attitude toward the German problem, whether official or non-official, was an integral part of De Gaulle's concept of détente. In the early 1960's, he still recognized the division of Europe into two blocs and spoke of Russia's hegemony, its empire, and its control of satellites. Later, however, the terminology changed as he expressed warm regard for the great Russian people and France's traditional friendship for Russia. Sensing, in advance of other Western statesmen, a trend toward liberalization in the nations of East Europe, he addressed himself to their "national personality" and mentioned them by their individual names, rejecting the collective

[24] *Le Monde,* January 31, 1962.

[25] *Neue Zürcher Zeitung,* September 5, 1964; *Neues Deutschland,* December 16, 1966.

[26] *Frankfurter Allgemeine Zeitung,* February 25, 1961.

and derogatory designation, "the so-called East Europe." He condemned the Cold War as "silly."

The governments of the East European countries responded to De Gaulle's approaches as an opportunity for asserting at least some of the prerogatives of sovereignty. As was only fitting for a country that had begun to grope for an independent stance in international affairs, the Rumanian Prime Minister Gheorghe Maurer in July 1964 opened the pilgrimage of East European political representatives to Paris. He was followed by the Chairmen of the Council of Ministers and Foreign Ministers of all East European countries and in some cases even by the first secretaries of the communist party. In the spring and summer or 1966, Couve de Murville was the first Foreign Minister of France to visit the capitals of the area since World War Two. The policy of détente appeared to be moving toward singular success. Maurer called De Gaulle the "eminent personality of our epoch." One Czech daily considered his policy "reasonable," and a Czech weekly paid tribute to his "realistic views, intelligence, and energy." A Polish publicist characterized him as "a man of the 21st century with features of a man of the 19th century." A Polish paper thanked him for the understanding "that the Cold War [was] out-of-date." Todor Zhivkov, the Bulgarian party chief, valued "very highly the effort of France and particularly of General De Gaulle to strengthen peace in Europe and in the world." Jenö Fock, the Hungarian Prime Minister, spoke of the prospect of "institutionalizing the friendship" by signing a treaty with France. Even Willi Stoph, the head of government of the GDR, considered De Gaulle's policy "realistic." According to *The Economist,* "In East European eyes, General De Gaulle [was] the messiah of the détente and Couve his prophet." [27]

[27] Quotations are in sequence, from *Le Monde,* July 31, 1964; November 27, 1964; April 27, 1966. *Christian Science Monitor,* March 30, 1965. *The Guardian,* May 19, 1966, quoting *Trybuna*

All visits were carefully prepared and received increasing publicity in the press. Official communiques and statements spoke of traditional friendships with France, common interests, close views, even convergence of views, and détente.[28]

On one important question, the visiting parties continued to find themselves in disagreement: the status of East Germany. The East Europeans insisted on her recognition; De Gaulle, in spite of subtle references to her "existence," continued to refuse to accept their position.

In his drive for détente De Gaulle outwardly sought Moscow's acquiescence. When in Moscow he expressed the conviction "that there [was] reason to strengthen and multiply, in all fields, the relations between [the] two countries." Without, however, "ceasing . . . to be a country of freedom and a Western nation *par excellence*," France would like to see "the start of the implementation of new relations with the so-called Eastern European states toward détente, entente, and cooperation." To avoid Soviet suspicions that his policy in East Europe was designed to infringe on the Soviet role, De Gaulle recognized that "Russia [was], indeed and in all respects, the leading power in the part of the world where she [was] located." [29] Thus, while he ascribed to France an active role in East Europe, he excluded Soviet influence from West Europe. Neither of the two propositions could have been acceptable to Moscow, and it was in this conflict—again, two different perceptions of détente—that Paris was to face the hard realities of that term.

This became particularly evident on two occasions: De Gaulle's visit to Poland and to Rumania which he considered to be highlights of his ceaseless efforts toward détente.

Ludu, Times, November 11, 1966, *Le Monde,* March 31, 1968, June 6-7, 1965, *The Economist,* July 30, 1966.

[28] For the text of the communiques, see *La Politique Étrangère de la France,* Textes et Documents (from here on, PEF).

[29] *MASPCG, op.cit.,* March 17, 1964 to May 16, 1967, p. 128.

On his triumphant journey to Poland, as he was welcomed by enthusiastic crowds, placards greeted him not only with such slogans as "Hands Off Vietnam" but also with "Down with the Revanchist Policy of Germany," "Long Live the GDR." The latter were as unpleasant as the first was acceptable. Before the trip, De Gaulle had agreed with Kiesinger that he would try to ease the tensions between Warsaw and Bonn. Thus, on several occasions he alluded to the necessity of reconciliation, but the Polish leaders rebuffed him unmistakably as they continued to insist on recognition of the GDR. On the other hand, they were gratified by his repeated assurances that France had stood for a long time—in fact since 1944—for Poland's boundary on the Oder-Neisse rivers. They were particularly delighted with his unplanned visit to Zabrze, where he singled out the community formerly called Hindenburg, "the most Silesian town of all Silesian towns which means the most Polish of all Polish towns." [30] Needless to say, the German press reacted violently to the statement and governmental circles expressed astonishment. Willy Brandt commented that "it was the simplest thing to understand [De Gaulle's] interpretation of the future. It is more difficult to understand that of the present but his appreciation of the past is with the best will in the world incomprehensible." [31]

De Gaulle spoke audaciously about the greatness of Poland and her role in European affairs. As his visit proceeded, the cadence of his appeals for her independent policy increased. He saw Poland's "compact territory," in full possession of her "national personality," regaining her "own national soul," and expressed the hope and expectation that she would "see perhaps a little farther, a little greater than [she] has been obligated until now. If you do that, if you see far and great, you will undoubtedly overcome the obstacles that appear to

[30] *Le Monde,* September 12, 1967.
[31] *Ibid.,* September 17-18, 1967.

you today insurmountable. . . . You understand what I want to say." [32]

The Poles understood, but they made De Gaulle understand as well. Gomulka, after having heaped praise on De Gaulle, "who acquired a special place in the hearts of Polish people," first reminded the distinguished visitor that the old-time French-Polish alliance saved neither France nor Poland, and they had indeed drawn conclusions from past experience. "The fundamental conclusion," he stated, "is expressed in the adoption of the path of friendship and alliance with [her] great neighbor to the East, the Soviet Union. This alliance, jointly with the socialist states of Central, Eastern, and Southern Europe, including our Western neighbor—the German Democratic Republic—is the cornerstone of the Polish Peoples' Republic and the principal guarantee of her security." He expressed readiness to normalize Poland's relations with the FRG, "the second German state, when its official policy will accept as a starting point new and realistic principles." [33] Thus, although De Gaulle at no time had mentioned the Soviet Union, appealing rather to Polish national pride, and had sought an understanding on the part of his hosts for the problem of Germany, the first secretary of the Polish party made it perfectly clear to him where Poland's place, interests, and expectations were. And they were out of joint with De Gaulle's exhortation that "the French-Polish solidarity [was] not comparable to any other, particularly any other in Europe." [34] Indeed, even though according to the final communique, similar to the French-Soviet communique of June 1966, the two parties agreed that "they would pursue regular consultations on questions of interest to France and

[32] *Ibid.,* September 12, 1967.

[33] *Voyage en Pologne du Général De Gaulle,* Textes et Notes, No. 216, pp. 20, 22.

[34] *Le Monde,* September 12, 1967.

Poland," [35] there is no evidence that Poland (or for that matter, the Soviet Union) consulted at all with Paris when her troops took part in the invasion of Czechoslovakia. Presumably, the act was of no interest to France.

Thus it is apparent that the dramatic eloquence of De Gaulle's discourses could not bridge the gap between his views of Poland and those of her leaders. Characteristically enough, while he, the visitor, thundered for Polish independence, they themselves politely but realistically declined. A Polish newspaper pointed succinctly to the differences in French-Polish understandings of the sequence of happenings that should lead to a peaceful Europe. France thought in terms of achieving détente first, which would then lead to agreements on certain concrete problems. Poland and other socialist countries wanted, in an inverse fashion, "to consider the détente as a result of ententes." [36] An analysis by Alfred Grosser focused on the most sensitive aspect of De Gaulle's scheme when he wrote, "However, if it appears incontestable that nothing can be done without the USSR, nothing will be done either with the USSR if it does not want to do anything. Therein lies the veritable obstacle to the European policy of General de Gaulle and the new policy of Bonn. Warsaw can perhaps do a lot but it is in Moscow where the answer must be sought to the question, how to pass from détente to entente, if the first signifies for some the beginning of an evolution and for the others the perpetuation of the status quo." [37]

Moscow did eventually answer the question: it signed a treaty with Bonn that confirms the status quo in East Europe. Paris, no longer the leading power in the policy of détente, can perhaps console itself by stressing that it had long advised the FRG to seek a rapprochement with the Soviet Union.

The aftermath of De Gaulle's next, equally flamboyant

---

[35] *Voyage en Pologne. . . , op.cit.*, p. 26.

[36] *Sztandar Mlodych* as quoted in *Le Monde,* September 8, 1967.

[37] *Le Monde,* September 12, 1967.

journey to Rumania also proved to be disappointing. True, he found the situation in Bucharest different from that in Warsaw. In the courageous leader Nicolae Ceausescu he found a partner responsive to his patriotic challenges. In fact, Ceausescu used the occasion to address himself, indirectly, to the Soviet Union rather than to France, and to reassert Rumania's independence.

On May 14, 1968, passing through the streets of Bucharest in an open Cadillac (the identification of which had been removed)[38] De Gaulle received a tumultuous welcome, this time without placards aimed against West Germany. However, his allusions to the necessity of solving the German problem were met with the same plea as in Warsaw: recognition of the GDR. His rejection of the "artificial and sterile" division of Europe into blocs, his calls for unity of "our Europe," and his emphasis on France's ethnic affinity with the Latin Rumania, surrounded by Slavs and Magyars, Ceausescu politely countered by stressing his country's alliance with the Soviet Union and the Warsaw Pact. De Gaulle, in answer, recognized that Rumania was Russia's neighbor with whom she had special ties and whose power designated her as an essential pillar of the continent but the "artificial separation which resulted from Yalta [was] contrary to the nature of Europe, for which there [was] no more [either] ideology or hegemony which could have any value in comparison with the benefits of détente, entente, and cooperation. . . ." Ceausescu agreed that the "anachronistic division of Europe must be ended" but added Rumania would not alter her policy toward the Warsaw Pact and the Soviet Union and "the Rumanian nation [was] today free and master of its destiny." [39]

The communique, published at the end of De Gaulle's visit, indicated the rather meager political results of his conversations. It spoke about a newly established commission for

[38] *New York Times,* May 15, 1968.
[39] *Le Monde,* May 16, 1968.

economic cooperation, about a new consular convention, and about opening a French library in Bucharest and a Rumanian library in Paris.[40]

State visits and official statements may seem impressive, but they do not make history unless they confirm the results of agreements already achieved through painstaking negotiations. De Gaulle's visit in Bucharest was not an exception to the rule. Surrounded by pomp and with the Rumanian press heaping praise on his head, he nevertheless carried back to Paris little he had not known before—Rumania's enthusiasm for his views on independence but also her political attachment to the Soviet Union. Despite the pomp and circumstance of his visit, the Moscow press devoted few lines to the occasion and *Neues Deutschland* simply announced it in one paragraph. Czechoslovakia, which was experiencing the inspiring "Prague Spring," was busy hosting the ominous visit of Kosygin and Marshal Grechko; Hungary and Poland renewed their treaties of alliance; and, even as De Gaulle spoke in Rumania about "national dignity," France itself passed through *les événements* and a most critical general strike.

Thus, the results of De Gaulle's valiant efforts and magnificent oratory fell far short of his expectations. He failed to reach any agreements on a solution of the German problem; he failed to change the position of the East. As *Le Monde,* which was in general sympathetic to De Gaulle's foreign policy, stated, "Three years of flirting with the Kremlin did not make the Soviet policy deviate one inch in regard to the German problem, the key to a European settlement 'from the Atlantic to the Urals' of which Elysée continues to dream." [41]

De Gaulle had also accepted an invitation to visit Czechoslovakia, Hungary, and Bulgaria, but the trips were never made. In April 1969 he resigned the presidency. Though his

[40] *PEF, op.cit.,* 1er semestre, 1968, pp. 131-139.
[41] February 21, 1968.

successor, President Pompidou, continued in the path of détente, using the same language, and though he and the Foreign Minister, Maurice Schumann, visited Moscow, their policy lacked De Gaulle's *éclat,* the thrust of his arguments, the forcefulness of his personality. France, without De Gaulle, was confronted with the reality of her limited power and influence. In line with this evaluation of her international position, Pompidou materially softened his predecessor's attitude toward the United States, even became an advocate of England's entry into the EEC, and discontinued the illusion that France could act independently from other Western powers and as equal of the Soviet Union in European affairs. When Brezhnev visited France in October 1971, the French government accepted the Soviet position on holding a European security conference at an early date and agreed that French-Soviet cooperation was "a permanent factor of international life." It declined, however, Moscow's idea of signing a treaty of friendship. Instead, Brezhnev had to be satisfied with a document on "enunciation of principles" on the inviolability of Europe's frontiers, non-interference in internal affairs, independence, equality, and renunciation of force. These are generally accepted (though not always respected) rules of international behavior; they do not contribute in a specific way to Soviet-French relations, nor do they advance the cause of détente as once envisaged by De Gaulle.

British Policy

Great Britain's policy of détente requires no elaborate discussion. Just as the French mind is inclined to define concepts of foreign policy in precise terms, the British have traditionally believed that life is too complex to be confined by rigid conceptual definition. Relations among nations are open to changes and what is left unsaid may facilitate the process of international developments, as much or more so than what is spelled out in detail. The British government has, therefore, seen détente as a pragmatic proposition that should serve and be served through a variety of processes that seem to alleviate tensions and contribute to European peace. In contrast to France's concept of détente based on analytical assumptions, London has shunned away from grandiose schemes, spectacular state visits, and eloquent phrases. It has given preference to the ways of quiet diplomacy and practical steps of rapprochement.

Regrettably, however, Great Britain has neglected to capitalize on the enormous reservoir of admiration and respect that the nations of Central and Eastern Europe had held for her because of her heroic stand during the war. Whereas the French overestimated the determination (or the practicality) of these nations to assert their national independence, the British were overcautious in recognizing or encouraging any polycentric development in Eastern Europe, even by any display of active interest in their political ambitions.

Great Britain has always given to the FRG, without any apparent ulterior motives, full support in its *Ostpolitik*. She has firmly supported France and the United States on the question of Berlin. As to the reunification of Germany, she has taken the same attitude as all other members of NATO, i.e., openly in its favor but with the full knowledge that neither she nor the other allies can do anything about it. In the early 1960's, and of course before, she stressed that peace in Europe depended on such reunification and affirmed the position of the government in Bonn that it was the sole representative of the whole German nation. In December 1966, when the British Foreign Secretary, George Brown, assured the British public, which had since the war been suspicious of Germany, of the FRG's dedication to peace, he declared the division of Germany to be the greatest problem of the future stability of Europe.[42]

[42] *Parliamentary Debates* (Hansard), House of Commons, Vol. 737, No. 111, Col. 1,172.

However, two months later, on the occasion of Kosygin's visit in England, a communique spoke of "the respect for . . . sovereign equality and territorial integrity" of all European countries. Bonn was disturbed as to whether the phrase possibly extended to East Germany; when the intractable George Brown was asked whether the communique implied recognition of the Oder-Neisse boundary he gave the answer, "Yes, in a certain sense. What we have said means that we respect sovereign, territorial integrity of the countries of East and West Europe. . . ." Retracting later under pressure from Harold Wilson, he clarified the statement by saying that in British "opinion Germany is, according to our definition, of course, one country." [43]

At the unofficial level, however, East Germany was evidently very much on the English government's mind. As was the case with France, cultural and scholarly contacts with this area grew from year to year and, according to incomplete records, they appear to be even higher in numbers and warmer in feelings. Summer excursions of children and the exchange of representatives of "twin cities" were fashionable over a period of years. Members of the Parliament from all parties, particularly the Labour Party, traveled to East Germany almost regularly, disregarding an official warning that their trips might be misrepresented; some of them expressed themselves for the recognition of the GDR as early as 1960. For instance, Konni Zilliacus stated, "Thank God for the existence of the GDR in which fascism and militarism was definitely exterminated. It has not happened in West Germany." Lord Boothby said, "I agree with Mr. Ulbricht: There are two German states." Similar statements were made by the Labour MPs, Sir Leslie Plummer and Ian Mikardo. Later, in 1968, groups of parliamentarians signed statements in favor of recognition, questions were asked in the House of Commons, and

[43] Siegler, *op.cit.,* Vol. 11, p. 241.

fifty Labour MPs submitted a motion calling on Harold Wilson to improve British relations with the GDR.[44]

Reading various sources, mainly newspapers, one has the impression that British unofficial contacts with East Germany were more intensive than with other East European countries. These contacts, however, were cultivated on a lower scale and, somewhat later, were less frequent than those by France.

Political contacts developed within the context of détente, broadly conceived and modestly implemented. Foreign Secretary Brown, in a speech in November 1966, which is considered a comprehensive and authoritative statement of British policy toward Central and Eastern Europe, looked at détente from a worldwide perspective. He vigorously disputed De Gaulle's concept, denying that East-West relations were limited to the frontiers of Europe itself. He was suspicious "of the very words 'East-West relations.' They have become a formula both too convenient and potentially misleading." They must not become "some theoretical concept, a slogan" with some value in and of themselves. What they mean lies only in their practice. He declined to "define Europe as stretching from the Atlantic to the Urals" since European culture, ideas, history, and interests "make it unreal to stop short at the Atlantic on the one side or at the eastern frontiers of Poland on the other." Speaking about the role of Germany in Europe he asserted that a "settlement in Central Europe must come some time" and before this happens tensions would continue.[45]

The speech revealed a substantial disagreement with De Gaulle not only on the role of America in European affairs but also on the way to relieve tensions. In contrast to

[44] *Neues Deutschland,* October 6, 1960; March 9, 1961; July 6, 1968, *Deutschlandsender,* March 2, 1970.

[45] Speech delivered November 21, 1966, before *Daily Mirror* International Editors' Conference, a reprint.

De Gaulle, George Brown believed that détente would ensue only after a solution of the German problem. This attitude explains why the British government did not attach much importance to political contacts with the countries of East Europe. "It did recognize that they were evolving," that there was "a change of political climate in Europe," and at one time prepared a "declaration on a code of conduct to which all nations of East and West will be able to subscribe." [46] However, nothing came of the draft of a collective declaration, and Britain's individual activities in East Europe remained modest. By comparison with France, she remained far behind in exchanges of political state visits and, to the extent that they did occur, the reception of dignitaries was restrained and press reactions measured. Except for exchange trips made by Ministers of Trade, Technology, Housing, and Industry, political visits developed as late as 1965 when the Foreign Secretary, Michael Stewart, traveled to Poland and Czechoslovakia. Rumania was given special attention in the autumn of 1968, but this appeared to be because the British wished to demonstrate their appreciation for her courageous opposition to the Soviet-led invasion of Czechoslovakia. The official communiques, issued on the occasion of such visits, indicate that consideration of such very complex and delicate issues as the problem of Germany and of boundaries was either avoided or that there was no change in Britain's conservative position, much to the disappointment of the host country. When in Poland, Michael Stewart stressed the need for German reunification and, contrary to De Gaulle, too, the old line that the Polish-German boundary could be finally determined only at a peace conference.[47] In Prague, on the sensitive problem of the Munich Agreement, he condemned it as "detestable, unjust . . . and dead"; as to the Czechoslovak insistence that

[46] *Parliamentary Debates* (Hansard), House of Commons, Vol. 737, No. 111, Col. 1,172.

[47] *Daily Telegraph,* September 23, 1965.

it be declared nul and void *ab initio,* he argued that it *was* signed and to pretend otherwise would create a dangerous precedent for the sanctity of treaties.[48]

It is therefore hardly surprising that England made little political headway in East Europe. First, she was not overly anxious to do so; second, her position on some basic questions of détente were close to the West German and American attitude, a fact that did nothing to endear her in the heart of the East.

In matters of cultural contacts Great Britain was rather active, though absence of complete records prevents a comparison with other West European countries. Those that took place were, however, more informal than the cultural programs of some other nations. England has a formal state agreement on cultural and scientific programs only with the Soviet Union. With East Europe, she enters into yearly arrangements, negotiated as a rule by the British Council. The government gives financial support to the Council and to Royal Societies that engage in exchanges without governmental control. For the programs with East Europe (excluding Yugoslavia and Poland), the Council's total budget in 1967-1968 represented a modest sum of $350,000—considerably less than that of West Germany and France. Such contacts had been established with all countries of East Europe after the war, but shortly thereafter they became a casualty of the Cold War (except for Poland and Yugoslavia) and were resumed cautiously and slowly in the early 1960's, when liberalization and détente provided a proper climate. In October 1967 the British-East European Centre was opened in London; it arranges and facilitates visits of scholars and artists on a private basis and without the governments' participation in the process of selection. Visitors sponsored by the British Council must be approved by both countries. Its

[48] *Times,* April 24, 1965.

programs in educational and scientific exchanges with individual countries of East Europe in recent years provide for exchanges of a small number (two to twenty) of scholars, language teachers, and researchers, and make general provisions for the encouragement of exchanges in the arts, exhibitions, films, radio and television, books, and of translations of literary works.[49]

One must not attach too much importance to tourist travel as a factor in détente, but in this respect Britishers showed no particular keenness to visit the East European countries, their numbers trailing the French and remaining far behind the Germans.[50] However, they have developed a lively trade (see Chapter 3).

All in all, Great Britain has not, at least by deeds, demonstrated any intensive interest in détente. Her primary interests have remained focused on the United States, West Europe, and general world problems. It is perhaps characteristic of her involvement in Central and East European affairs that the then leader of Her Majesty's opposition and now Prime Minister, Edward Heath, in an article about British foreign policy published in 1969, did not devote a single line to East Europe.[51]

Security

A policy of détente is related to numerous variables. A settled relationship between East and West Europe can come about only when all these variables interact harmoniously. Such factors as trade, co-production arrangements, technological and scientific cooperation, and cultural exchanges are constructive elements in contributing to a relaxed atmosphere;

---

[49] The British Council, *Programme of Cultural, Educational, and Scientific Exchanges between Britain and Czechoslovakia* [etc.], 1970-1972.

[50] See Table xv.

[51] *Foreign Affairs,* Vol. 48, No. 1, October 1969, pp. 39-50.

but they are all subject to political considerations and in this overriding field they can play only a limited, auxiliary role.

One overriding factor, crucial to any prospect for real détente, is each nation's assurance of its security. No lasting, peaceful relationship between East and West Europe could be obtained without such assurances. Assuming that Europe will continue indefinitely to be divided ideologically, the governments concerned face the task of finding a political arrangement that can reduce the tensions inherent in their warring ideologies. This goal appears all the more imperative as Moscow and its allies continue to emphasize that peaceful coexistence between the two social systems excludes an ideological reconciliation.

This being the case, and communist ideology what it is, there is quite a difference between this notion of peaceful coexistence and Moscow's frequently repeated assurances of non-interference in the internal affairs of other countries. As long as West Europe is politically and economically stable, as long as its governments work for social justice—assumptions that cannot be taken for granted—the slogans of communist ideology will be stripped of their effectiveness. However, for the present and for the foreseeable future, and in the absence of an overt and convincing refutation of the policy of ideological struggle—a futile expectation—West Europe would be ill advised to ignore the limitations of détente.

A reassuring way to minimize the ideological stance taken by East Europe would be a new system of security that would give both parts of Europe a sense of confidence and international stability. The record of the past five years suggests that both sides appear to be moving slowly in that direction. Should they succeed in converging their separate concepts of European security, the cause of détente would advance from secondary considerations to those overriding political and military solutions which would assure Europe of the ultimate purpose of détente: peace.

Military security is, of course, inseparably related to political problems. In Europe these problems generally fall into two categories: those questions which divide Europe into two camps and those specific questions connected with the problem of Germany, which continues to be the core problem of Europe's partition.

Outside of the ideological postures of the two parts of Europe, it has seemed to be apparent that no political problems substantial enough to justify a perpetuation of Europe's division exist once steps can be taken to solve the problem of Germany: the acceptance of the FRG by the East as a peaceful power; the reunification of Germany or an agreement on a workable relationship between her two parts; agreement on the future of Berlin and on the question of Poland's western boundary. By now, much has already taken place. The Brandt government has succeeded in creating in Moscow the image of West Germany as a society of progressive (peaceful) forces. It has renounced the right to the possession of nuclear weapons, recognized the existence of two German states, entered into direct negotiations with the GDR government about future relationships, and recognized the Oder-Neisse boundary. In addition, the Big Four Powers reached an agreement on Berlin. All of these factors have led to a major political settlement. It would then seem that no serious obstacles remain on the road toward the cardinal object of détente in Europe: its security. But it is not that simple.

The search for Europe's collective security has shifted with the changing scene of power politics. As early as March 1952 the Soviet government had presented to the three Western powers a sweeping proposal for mutual withdrawal of foreign troops and bases from a unified and neutral Germany. The motive of the Soviet initiative appeared obvious: it was intended to disrupt the process of the military consolidation of

NATO and West Europe's plan for political and economic integration, with West Germany's participation being essential to both goals. The West had then reacted with a renewed request for free elections in Germany. When, in January 1954, Sir Anthony Eden at the Berlin Conference advanced another proposal that would lead to German reunification by way of free elections and would give Germany freedom to choose her future alignment, Molotov counteracted with a Soviet proposal of European security, based on a previous Soviet proposition of a united but neutral Germany free from foreign troops and bases. The West was, however, resolved to proceed with the military consolidation of NATO, and the Soviet Union responded with the establishment of the Warsaw Pact.

The Geneva Summit Conference in July 1955 found both sides diametrically opposed even though each of them advanced far-reaching proposals for a security pact, accompanied by mutually exclusive ideas of a demilitarized zone on the eastern border of a reunited Germany (Eden), a withdrawal of foreign troops from European states, and direct negotiations between West and East Germany (Bulganin). The Soviet delegation also proposed an agreement on mutual renunciation of force, an idea that has since turned into a recurring refrain presented on every occasion that seems to call for a solution of the problem of European security or of Germany. The subsequent conference of the Council of Foreign Ministers and many other meetings and proposals, including the Rapacki Plan, wrestled with the same problems, but they all proved to be fruitless.[52]

Out of these efforts grew the general idea, initiated by Moscow, of assuring Europe of peace by way of a European

---

[52] The foregoing brief review is based on Timothy W. Stanley and Darnell M. Whitt, *Detente Diplomacy: United States and European Security in the 1970's,* Cambridge, University Press of Cambridge, 1970, pp. 23-30.

security conference. In the latter part of the 1960's this idea became the chief thrust of Soviet policy in Europe. It passed through several variations, all of them rather vague. Basically, however, it was a fairly constant demand to confirm the status quo in Europe without at the same time facing the concrete problems of European security. As the policy of détente progressed rather impressively in the field of trade and cultural relations and as it found additional encouragement by way of an increasing number of official visits to West and East European capitals, the Warsaw Pact countries began a synchronized political offensive, appealing to all European nations to convene at a security conference.

The offensive opened with the "Declaration on Strengthening Peace and Security in Europe," issued at a meeting of the Warsaw Pact countries held in Bucharest at the beginning of July 1966. It was a wordy statement but its main ideas emerged clearly.[53] It proceeded from the assumption that international relations must be based on "the renunciation of the threat of force or the use of force" and on the principles of national independence and "non-interference in domestic affairs. . . ." The Declaration then proceeded to identify the United States and West Germany as the chief villains threatening peace in Europe and deepening its division. It further pleaded for peaceful coexistence between states with different social systems; for strengthening economic relations; and for an increase in scientific, technological, and cultural contacts. Most importantly, it condemned the existence of military blocs and reaffirmed the signatories' readiness "for the simultaneous abolition" of NATO and the Warsaw Pact, which would be replaced by a European security system. The statement advocated as a partial measure of détente "the abolition of foreign war bases; the withdrawal of all forces from foreign territories to within their national frontiers; the reduction, on

[53] For the text, see *ibid.,* pp. 124-136.

an agreed scale and at agreed deadlines, of the numerical strength of the armed forces of both German states; measures aimed at eliminating the danger of nuclear conflict. . . ."

The Declaration asked for recognition of existing boundaries and of the two Germanys whose "reunion" (implying much less than reunification) can be achieved only through a "gradual rapprochement between the two sovereign German states." For all these purposes, a general European conference should be convened, with the participation of the members of the Warsaw Pact and NATO and the neutral European countries.

The document revealed Soviet aims fairly clearly: stabilization of the status quo in East Europe, the elimination of United States troops from Europe, and an inducement to neutrals to support the Soviet plans. Though a dissolution of the two military blocs would have meant the end of both NATO and the Warsaw Pact, the consequences would be rather one-sided: United States power would be eliminated from West Europe, while the Soviet Union would maintain its bilateral alliances with its client states in East Europe. However, the Declaration did not include any precondition to convening the conference and, regrettably, the West largely ignored the appeal.

The Bucharest Declaration proved to be only an opening phase of a systematic campaign for a European security conference. In April 1967 another meeting, this time of sixteen European communist parties (with the conspicuous absence of Rumania and Yugoslavia), met at Karlovy Vary and issued another call for a European conference. As the occasion of a party gathering warranted, the statement issued by this conference was rife with ideological overtones, but the purpose was essentially the same as that of the Bucharest statement.[54] The United States and West Germany were again the main

---

[54] For the text, see *ibid.*, pp. 137-144.

targets of the Karlovy Vary Declaration; and the uncertainties about the future of NATO, caused chiefly by France's repudiation of her military obligations, provided a rich opportunity to exploit NATO's "open crisis." The Declaration turned to "the democratic and progressive forces existing in West Germany," expressing its wish to lend support to "new and positive trends towards an international détente . . . appearing in the socialist and social-democratic movements in some West European countries." Since the NATO Pact was subject to renewal in 1969, twenty years after its establishment, the statement focused on this anniversary and asked again for the abolition of both military blocs, addressing its mass appeal along ideological lines to workers and to all other social strata of the West European populace. The statement differed distinctly from the Bucharest Declaration on one point: while the latter advocated "the withdrawal of all forces [including Soviet] from foreign territories to within their national frontiers," [55] the Karlovy Vary proclamation spoke only of "the withdrawal of foreign troops from the territory of European States," with the apparent implication of the elimination of United States, but not Soviet, troops from Europe.

Once again, the statement passed without official reaction from the West, although this time the Western silence could be justified by the explanation that governments do not respond to propositions originating from a political party rally. However, when the Foreign Ministers of NATO met in Brussels in December 1967, they indirectly acknowledged one point of the Soviet-led appeals: they were "studying disarmament and practical arms control measures, including the possibility of balanced force reductions." [56] When they met half a year later at Reykjavik in June 1968, they agreed on some general principles about a mutual reduction of

[55] *Ibid.*, p. 134.
[56] *Ibid.*, p. 117.

forces: this "should be reciprocal and balanced in scope and timing"; it should "maintain the present degree of security at reduced cost" and without the risk of "de-stabilizing the situation in Europe." The East European calls for a European security conference were answered with vaguely formulated expression of the NATO governments' readiness "to explore with other interested states specific and practical steps in the arms control fields" and with the decision "to make all necessary preparations for discussions" with the Soviet Union and its allies on the subject of mutual force reductions.[57] NATO headquarters studies in depth of the problems were begun, but its governments did not consider the political situation opportune for accepting the Warsaw Pact invitation to a European conference.

The Soviet occupation of Czechoslovakia halted, at least for a time, any prospect for narrowing the gap between the Warsaw Pact's and NATO's views about convening a European security conference. It also generated a substantial change in the former's position about the purpose of such a meeting.

The Ministerial Council of NATO, convened in the wake of the invasion in November 1968, called for "great vigilance on the part of the allies." After reaffirming its collective political obligations and spelling out the military measures to be taken in order to strengthen its defensive system, the Council recognized that "prospects for mutual balanced force reductions have suffered a severe setback."[58] If the NATO alliance had previously felt compelled to reevaluate its usefulness, the Czechoslovak experience reinforced its political and military ties and dispelled any doubts about its duration. It was not only that the invasion solidified the ranks of the

[57] For the text of the Brussels and Reykjavik communiques, see *ibid.*, pp. 115-120.

[58] For the text of the communique, see *NATO Letter,* December 1968, pp. 18-19.

alliance and subsequently brought even France closer to the military thinking of NATO, but that even some East Europeans who were shocked by the Soviet aggression were heard to stress the need for continuous existence of the NATO alliance as important to their own interests. These observers expressed the view that the continued existence of NATO served as a deterrent to increased Soviet controls over their own countries.

The Soviet Union after the Czechoslovak events also markedly shifted its attitude toward European security. The press campaign that tried to justify the occupation now emphasized the necessity of strengthening the Warsaw Pact alliance in order to provide a shield to the socialist unity of its members. Rumania was the only country that continued to plead for the dissolution of military blocs. As a result of a reassessment of the situation, the next round of appeals for a European conference differed materially in tone and emphasis from the earlier statements. When the Warsaw Pact countries met in March 1969 in Budapest, they addressed a "Message from the Warsaw Pact States to All European Countries." This message referred only obliquely to "forces in the world" (meaning mainly United States) that sought "to maintain the division of our continent"; it stopped short of proposing the discontinuation of the two military blocs; and it called for a meeting "of representatives of all interested European states," this time implicitly excluding the United States and Canada. It repeated the old-time demand for recognition of the status quo, but it seemed this time to insist on accepting it as a precondition of the conference.[59]

The next two occasions on which the Warsaw Pact countries resumed their persistent attempts to convene a European conference were at their meetings in Prague and Moscow in October and December 1969, respectively. Taking into ac-

[59] For the text, see Stanley and Whitt, *op.cit.*, pp. 149-152.

74

count the reactions of the West to their previous appeals, they conceded the need for preparing the conference in advance; since the NATO countries resolutely rejected the Soviet design of limiting the attendance to Europeans, they were now also willing to discuss the "range of participants" and made it clear through a Soviet spokesman that they would not object to U.S. and Canadian participation. Nor, it seems, did they insist on the recognition of the status quo as a precondition to the conference; they "only" demanded establishment of "equal relations with the GDR on the basis of international law" and recognition of "the existing European borders." The previous proposition for dissolving the two blocs was again ignored and in its place was the demand to place on the conference agenda "the ensuring of European security and renunciation of the use of force or threat of its use in the mutual relations among states in Europe." The Moscow meeting advanced the idea of "general and complete disarmament" that it must have realized was, under prevailing circumstances, a *fata morgana.* However, it had no inhibitions—fourteen months after the invasion of Czechoslovakia—about coming out again for "the principles of equality, non-interference in internal affairs, respect of sovereignty. . . ." [60]

The NATO countries failed to react to this Soviet-led drive for a European conference with a counter-initiative of their own. Rather, the West followed the Warsaw Pact declarations with misgivings, viewing them as propaganda moves and as an effort to legitimize the status quo in East Europe and, in particular, to gain international recognition of East Germany

---

[60] For the texts of the two communiques, see *ibid.,* pp. 153-156. For a detailed analysis of the Warsaw Pact campaign for a European security conference, see, by Charles Andras, " 'European Security' and the Security of Europe," Radio Free Europe, Research, *East-West Relations/1,* March 1970; "Die Warschauer-Pakt-Staaten und ihr Konzept der europäischen Sicherheit," *Ost-europäische Rundschau,* Vol. xvi, No. 6, 1970, pp. 8-16; "Through Berlin—To Europe," Radio Free Europe, Research, *East-West Relations/1,* February 11, 1971.

—and perhaps with reason. For it is highly probable that the Soviet Union did pursue this goal through the device of a European conference, giving no serious thought to the prospect of a new system of European security that would include such momentous but unrealistic ideas as the dissolution of the two military alliances or general disarmament. However, it would perhaps have been wise for NATO to have pursued its Brussels resolution and to make preparations for the discussion of a mutual reduction of forces in Europe and to have submitted to Moscow a concrete proposal as a basis for a conference. The Soviet Union had not reacted to the Brussels propositions; such a plan, if proposed and not accepted, would have at least called the bluff of the Soviet's declared concern for security. However, since the West remained largely passive, Moscow did accomplish one of the professed goals of a European conference—the legitimization of the East European borders—through direct negotiations with West Germany. Thus the West missed the opportunity to place this Russian goal within the context of Soviet intentions on matters of European security.

While giving the appearance of having a common policy, individual members of NATO indicated their interest in this Soviet lure of a European conference. France, true to the De Gaulle image that she was again a big power and to his fetish of independence, expressed aversion to a collective approach, preferring bilateral contacts. Britain and Italy limited themselves to conciliatory pursuits of general détente; West Germany was not averse to a security conference; and some smaller European members of NATO indicated approval. President Nixon, addressing a NATO meeting on the occasion of its twentieth anniversary, realistically stated that it was "not enough to talk about European security in the abstract. . . ," that conferences were "useful if they [dealt] with concrete issues, which [meant] that they must be carefully prepared. It was not enough to talk of détente unless at the same time we anticipate the need for giving it a genuine political content that would prevent détente from becoming delusion." [61] In a similar spirit, but with great caution, the NATO communique, issued on the same occasion, insisted that "any negotiations must be well prepared in advance. . . ." [62]

However, as pressures from the outside openly increased and subtle activities from within intensified, NATO moved cautiously somewhat closer to the Soviet position. At its meeting in Brussels in December 1969 it issued a declaration. It identified itself with the Soviet stand on the principles of sovereign equality, independence, non-intervention in the internal affairs of any state, and the renunciation of force against any state. However, with the Czechoslovak example in mind, it recognized that "past experience [had] shown that there [was], as yet, no common interpretation of these principles" and that "any real and lasting improvement of East-West relations presupposes respect for them without any conditions or reservations." The Declaration indicated in some concrete terms the areas in which "mutual and balanced force reduction" could be negotiated. As to a security conference, however, without rejecting the idea, the document stated "that a careful advance preparation and prospects of concrete results would in any case be essential" and that "any such meeting should not serve to ratify the present division of Europe. . . ." [63]

However, following the Brussels session, various comments revealed discrepancies among individual members of the NATO alliance in regard to preparatory procedures and the timing of a conference. The U.S. Secretary of State, William Rogers, considered the Soviet proposal to be "nebulous and

[61] *New York Times,* April 11, 1969.
[62] *NATO Letter,* May 1969, p. 11.
[63] For the text, see T. W. Stanley and D. M. Whitt, *op.cit.,* pp. 123-126.

imprecise" and stated flatly that Washington would oppose any conference that would be an "unrealistic and premature exercise." Not forgetting the case of Czechoslovakia, he said that the United States would "not participate in a conference which has the effect of ratifying the Brezhnev Doctrine." [64] Nor would she "be lulled into a false sense of détente." Some smaller countries—Norway, Denmark, and Iceland—appeared anxious to open the negotiations with the Warsaw Pact at an early date; others—Belgium, the Netherlands, and Luxemburg—took a middle position; and the rest of them shared the United States position, though they expressed it less openly. [65]

The differences of opinion about a European conference were not limited to the NATO members; some countries of the Warsaw Pact also began to have second thoughts about it. As the chances of reaching an agreement between Moscow and Bonn increased, the intensity of the former's interest in a European conference appeared to decrease. In the first part of 1970, for example, the Soviet government indicated that the cause of peace would be served by both bilateral and multilateral negotiations and agreements. This shift in emphasis created some problems within the Warsaw Pact alliance. Rumania, while welcoming the prospects of the normalization of relations between West Germany and her associates in the socialist camp, continued to see in a European conference another opportunity for asserting her independence and even to advocate the dissolution of the two military blocs. East Germany, at the other end of the spectrum, underwent some jittery mutations. As long as Soviet-West German relations were tense, until the end of 1969, she took the position that direct negotiations were the primary channel to recognition of the two German states. This strategy offered her a chance to exercise some influence over her allies

[64] *New York Times,* December 7, 1969.
[65] *Ibid.,* January 15, 1970.

in their contacts with West Germany and in extracting from them full and open support in her quest for recognition as a precondition to the solution of their own relations with Bonn. However, when the Soviet Union and Poland entered into serious negotiations with the FRG at the opening of 1970, without insisting on fulfillment of the precondition, East Berlin began to give preference to a European conference that would fall short of international recognition but would add to its international prestige and eliminate the danger of Ulbricht's isolation.[66]

At its next session, in Rome in May 1970, the NATO Council made much more specific its attitude toward a European conference. It formulated its own conditions for a conference, stating in its communique that "insofar as progress is recorded as a result of [exploratory conversations] and the on-going talks—in particular on Germany and Berlin—the Allied Governments state that they would be ready to enter into multilateral contacts with all interested governments." One purpose of such contacts "would be to explore when it will be possible to convene a conference, or a series of conferences on European security and cooperation." A special declaration addressed itself to the problem of reduction of forces in Europe. This statement invited "interested states" to exploratory talks on the subject, to be based on matters of vital security interests as well as of their concern not to operate "to the military disadvantages of either side having regard for the differences arising from geographical and other considerations. Reductions [in military forces] should be on the basis of reciprocity, and phased and balanced as to their scope and timing"; they "should include stationed and indigenous forces"; and "there must be adequate verification and con-

---

[66] For a detailed analysis, see Charles Andras, " 'European Security' and the Security of Europe," *op.cit.,* pp. 43-55.

trols. . . ." [67] The Foreign Minister of Italy was requested to transmit the declaration to all interested parties.

Thus, for the first time, NATO opened an official contact with the Warsaw Pact about the question of a future European conference. France declined to sign the declaration, her Foreign Minister, Maurice Schumann, explaining that the idea of reduction of forces was "absolutely unacceptable to the socialist countries." [68] He did express himself, in contrast to De Gaulle's previous attitude, in favor of a conference that, however, should be "a confirmation and not the first manifestation of the process of détente." [69]

The Soviet reaction to the NATO invitation was as inscrutable as it was confusing. For once, the Soviet press did not directly attack the NATO meeting; TASS even admitted that "certain interesting ideas and propositions were expressed at the session." [70] However, *Pravda* accused the United States of torpedoing the chances for a conference when she silenced the more constructive elements of NATO, and it condemned the proposition dealing with a reduction of forces since America could not be trusted because of her engagement in South-East Asia. [71]

When the Warsaw Pact countries met toward the end of June 1970 in Budapest, they prepared a memorandum that was sent to all "interested states." This document repeated the old goal of the conference to reach a guarantee on renunciation of force and to discuss an increase in economic, trade, scientific, technical, and cultural relations, for the purpose of developing political cooperation (a seemingly attractive amplification of the old demand). It advanced closer to

[67] For the text, see *NATO Letter,* Vol. XVIII, No. 6, June 1970, pp. 21-25.
[68] *Le Monde,* May 30, 1970.
[69] *Ibid.,* July 17, 1970.
[70] *Ibid.,* May 30, 1970.
[71] *International Herald Tribune,* May 29, 1970.

the Western position by proposing the establishment of an organ to study the questions of European security and co-operation, including reduction of "foreign armed forces on the territory of European States." It also officially and finally confirmed the previous informal assurances that Canada and the United States could send delegates to the conference.[72]

The Warsaw Pact statement got a rather favorable reception in the West, but even as the two sides appeared to be drawing closer in a broad sense, so also their attitude toward concrete issues demonstrated anew how deep were their fundamental differences. For instance, Pierre Harmel, Foreign Minister of Belgium, who became an ardent advocate of the conference among the NATO allies, envisaged a meeting of ambassadors before the end of 1970 that would formulate the objectives of a future conference.[73] However, hopes that the Warsaw Pact would be willing to consider reduction of forces (to NATO the principal point of the conference) were soon dissipated, at least temporarily. Harmel, after a visit to Poland, declared that the Warsaw Pact was not prepared to discuss reduction of armed forces at the conference.[74]

At their meeting in East Berlin at the beginning of December 1970, the Warsaw Pact countries merely repeated the old demands for recognition of the status quo, without, however, mentioning the question of reduction of forces but urging an early date for the conference because "sufficient preconditions for holding such a conference have now been created." [75] This was presumably a reference to the NATO meeting in Rome with Moscow's assumption that the Soviet-West Germany treaty and progress in the negotiations on Berlin had fulfilled the West's conditions for a conference.

Since the NATO meeting was taking place in Brussels at

---

[72] *The Current Digest of the Soviet Press,* Vol. xxii, No. 26, p. 27.
[73] *Le Monde,* July 15, 1970.
[74] Radio Free Europe, Research, *Poland/42,* July 31, 1970.
[75] *The Current Digest of the Soviet Press,* Vol. xii, No. 49, pp. 1-3.

the same time, it did not react directly to the East Berlin session of the Warsaw Pact. But its deliberations were dominated by two issues that were, to the West, mutually dependent: détente and defense. As to a European conference, NATO reiterated the stand it had taken in Rome.[76]

At another meeting, in Bucharest in February 1971, the Warsaw Pact's Foreign Ministers were as vague as ever in discussing concrete questions of a European conference. However, the communique, issued at the end of the meeting, conceded the West's point about holding preparatory meetings in order, as they put it, to remove serious obstacles that NATO was allegedly creating by setting various preliminary conditions to convening the conference. Once again, the question of a reduction of forces was not mentioned.[77] Nor did it appear in the communique about the Warsaw Pact's meeting that took place at the beginning of December 1971.

This tedious review of the Warsaw Pact's position demonstrates clearly Moscow's intractable attitude toward a matter of crucial importance to détente—Europe's security. It is not easy to read the Soviet mind.

To compound the difficulty even further, the Soviet leaders in the spring of 1971 opened an intensified campaign for a series of negotiations on a subject that had been ignored in the two previous Warsaw Pact communiques—the reduction of armaments. Brezhnev renewed at the Twenty-Fourth Congress of the CPSU, after four years of silence on the matter, the idea of a simultaneous abrogation of the Warsaw Pact and NATO and proposed again the dismantling of foreign military bases and reduction of armed forces, above all in Central Europe.[78] The statement failed to evoke any public reaction in the West, but Brezhnev pressed the point on reduction of

---

[76] *NATO Press Service,* Communique, December 4, 1970; Andras, "Through Berlin—To Europe," *op.cit.,* pp. 25-28.

[77] *The Current Digest of the Soviet Press,* Vol. XXIII, No. 8, p. 19.

[78] *Ibid.,* Vol. XXIII, No. 12, p. 13.

forces in Central Europe further in his speech at Tiflis two weeks later and answered NATO doubts about Soviet aims by inviting it to "start negotiations." At the beginning of June Kosygin and the Chairman of the Presidium of the Supreme Soviet, Nikolai V. Podgorny, paraphrased Brezhnev's offer. Then, on June 11, Brezhnev brought the campaign to its culmination when he spoke about prospects of SALT negotiations on the basis of "equal security"; proposed a conference of five nuclear powers, including China; and expressed readiness to strike an "equal bargain" with the United States on the problem of Soviet and American fleets cruising oceans "away from their native coasts." As to a reduction of forces in Europe, he considered this a "big and independent question . . . of great importance for a détente and lasting peace on the European continent" and made it clear that the Soviet government was prepared to discuss the reduction of both foreign and national armed forces.[79]

Brezhnev's speech at Tiflis came at the moment when Congress was ready to vote on Senator Mike Mansfield's amendment to a bill extending the military draft, an amendment that would commit the administration to cut by one half the number of United States troops in Europe by the end of 1971. The timing of the speech is a matter of puzzlement. If it was intended to lull the Congress into a belief that European détente was imminent and that troop reduction was therefore safe, it backfired. Actually, it helped administration forces in Congress to defeat the amendment, the administration forces arguing that to now reduce unilaterally U.S. forces in Europe would be sure to make the Soviet Union suddenly disinterested in any such mutual withdrawal as it had itself suggested. However, now that Moscow had advanced the idea of such a reduction, which in fact NATO has repeatedly presented since 1968, and with Mansfield's unwise proposal at least tempo-

[79] *Ibid.,* Vol. xxiii, No. 20, p. 5; Vol. xxiii, No. 24, pp. 3, 4-5, 19-20.

rarily shelved, the ground did seem to be ready for a serious exploration of the possibility of troop reduction.

The Foreign Ministers of NATO, meeting at Lisbon at the beginning of June, welcomed the new Soviet position on reduction of forces in Central Europe and proposed steps that would speed up further exploration of the idea.[80] Then, in October, Manlio Brosio, by now NATO's retired Secretary-General, received the mandate to visit Moscow in order to explore the problem with the Soviet authorities. However, as the year 1971 was drawing to a close, Brosio still waited for an invitation from the Soviet government, and the NATO Foreign Ministers, assembled at the meeting in Brussels in December, wondered again about the real nature of Soviet intentions.

Nevertheless, the idea of negotiating a reduction of forces in Europe appears to have gained momentum. Moscow, after having taken in turn attitudes of ambivalence or negation toward all such proposals, has now adopted it as its own proposition. NATO, on the other hand, has relaxed its position, no longer making such negotiations dependent on progress in solving the problems of Germany and Berlin. Both sides seem to have separated the question from the prospects of a European conference.

However, one must ask whether the problem is really negotiable and whether both sides really approach it with any actual sincerity. Experts consider as extremely complicated such questions as quantitative and qualitative comparisons of weapons and divisions in Europe, their inseparable relationship to SALT, on-the-spot inspection and verification that would have to serve as a basis for an agreement on mutual and balanced reduction of forces.[81] Both sides con-

---

[80] For the text of the communique, see *NATO Review,* Vol. XIX, no. 7-8; pp. 25-26.

[81] See for instance, The Institute for Strategic Studies, *The Military*

sider the present balance of power in Europe as relatively stabilized and a partial withdrawal of forces to carry with it the danger of disturbing that balance. If this should be the result of negotiations on the reduction of forces, Europe would be exposed to increased uncertainties and such attempts at détente could be counter-productive.

One situation is encouraging to the prospect of reaching an agreement, namely, past experience in regard to the ban on atomic testing and the non-proliferation of atomic weapons. Patient negotiations lasting several years were required before the treaties on the two problems were signed. Thus, while an open discussion at a formal, high-level conference could not possibly lead to an agreement on reduction of forces, nevertheless an expert conference, with both sides thoroughly prepared, could conceivably pave the way to a series of meetings that would establish whether there is a common will to reduce military power without disturbing the present balance.

As to a European conference, one may safely assume that a conference on the other issues advocated for so long by the Warsaw Pact will become again a matter of public diplomacy, with all of its flamboyant trappings: official communiques, strategic speeches, and managed headlines in the press. Nevertheless, each side has expressed itself clearly enough over the years that not only points of major friction but also similarities of views are sufficiently evident that the holding of a European conference might be justified.

As to the procedural matters, which have serious substantive consequences, both NATO and the Warsaw Pact countries appear to agree on arranging a series of limited

---

Balance, 1970-1971, London, 1970; Frederick S. Wyle, "Is European Security Negotiable?" *Survival,* Vol. xii, No. 6, January 1970, pp. 189-193; Admiral Sir Nigel Henderson, "NATO Facing the Warsaw Pact Forces," *NATO Letter,* Vol. xix, No. 3-4, pp. 4-8.

conferences. This is, indeed, the only reasonable approach because a spectacular European conference, held before basic agreement had been reached, almost inevitably would become more a platform for propaganda rather than a sound forum for negotiating complicated problems, and is calculated to produce mutual disappointment and disillusion rather than détente.

As to the substantive matters, the two sides have mutually expressed the desire to discuss technological, cultural, scientific, and economic cooperation. In addition, the West wishes to discuss the free flow of ideas and travel. Technological and scientific cooperation has so far been based on bilateral agreements and there have been ten years of useful experience and growth. Though its further development is of primary interest to the East, a multilateral conference at an expert level could examine areas of common concern, and scientists of both sides could undoubtedly prepare a number of concrete proposals. Positive results from such a conference would contribute to the general atmosphere of détente.

Cultural cooperation presents a different problem. Though cultural contacts have also been regulated by bilateral agreements, the experience has demonstrated (and this is particularly evident in the writing of the communist press) that the Warsaw Pact countries regard such contacts in the light of ideological considerations. However, there is no reason why the West's cultural experts could not submit to a European conference a number of ideas that would foster cultural cooperation, or would at least test the seriousness of the East in its often expressed desires for cultural contacts. It is doubtful that such cooperation could be extended to any truly free flow of ideas and travel, but the West has nothing to lose by discussing such proposals, demonstrating thereby the openness of its society.

Economic cooperation between East and West, though on a limited scale and on a bilateral basis, is now an established

fact. A number of questions—such as tariffs, quotas, con-
vertibility of currencies, standardization of products, and
balance of payments—could be discussed at a European
conference. The UN Economic Commission for Europe,
which has for several years recommended a multilateral
approach to the problem of intra-European trade, has a
wealth of materials that lend themselves to a study of practical measures that could be considered as avenues of economic cooperation. By the end of 1972 the EEC expects to
establish a unified policy toward third countries in matters
of imports of industrial products, in addition to such common
policies on imports of agricultural products as are already in
existence. The COMECON complains of the EEC's discriminatory practices and, although it is not prepared to recognize
the EEC officially, a conference could be the right place to
discuss these conflicting claims. Repeated criticism that the
differences between the two social systems set definitive limitations to trade could be examined and either confirmed or
put aside. However, such complex problems as trade, which
cannot be solved by any general declaration of intentions,
require the best thinking of experts who, at a conference
devoted specifically to economic cooperation, would at least
establish just how realistic the idea of a multilateral agreement
might be.

The Soviet proposal for discussing a pact that would commit all European signatories to a renunciation of force or
threat of force should not present serious difficulties, although
the lasting value of such a pact is, to say the least, questionable. The same obligation is already embodied in the United
Nations Charter and an additional stipulation certainly appears redundant. In addition, many states were committed
in the past to similar restraints in the form of nonaggression
pacts, which were frequently violated; the Soviet Union is not
guiltless of such violations. A general treaty on the renunciation of force would of course not assure Europe of security

and it could be viewed only as an expression of intent at the moment of signature and for the immediate future. But it would contribute to the atmosphere of détente and specifically might blunt the edge of the Brezhnev Doctrine, which laid down the ideological and juridical foundations for armed intervention on the part of the Soviet Union against its own allies.

In this connection, both NATO and the Warsaw Pact countries agreed that a European conference should confirm their adherence to the principles of sovereign equality, political independence, and non-interference in internal affairs. The NATO countries amplified their understanding of these principles by the stipulation that they apply to all states regardless of their social and political system. This was obviously an attempt to make the Soviet Union renounce its self-proclaimed right to intervene, according to the Brezhnev Doctrine, in the affairs of other communist states. It is a futile expectation. The Soviet Union, which initiated the idea of discussing these principles at a European conference, would have no reservations at all about including them in a European pact. However, as always, the interpretation of any such agreement would be left to Moscow and there has been more than one occasion in the past in which contracting parties have agreed on the language, but not at all on what the language means.

When all is said, however, the West cannot afford to postpone indefinitely some kind of meeting with the Warsaw Pact countries. Individual issues have been clarified by both sides in a general way, and the time has come to test the real intentions of the parties at conferences, prepared and conducted in an orderly, professional, non-propagandistic fashion. As crucial as is a limited détente between West Germany and East Europe to a general détente in the whole of Europe, one cannot be separated from the other; nor can NATO rest satisfied with Brandt's partial results vis-à-vis Moscow, Poland, and East Germany. On the contrary, a German-based and constricted détente could lead to a disruption of the present distribution of forces; this in turn could create an intensification rather than a relaxation of tensions. Nor can détente in Europe be achieved without the active participation of the United States. West Europe, splintered by individual national interests, cannot evidence the strength or influence of the Moscow-controlled Warsaw Pact. The situation was aptly condensed by one analyst: ". . . the West gains more from the reality of détente, whereas the East gains more from its mere appearances . . . so the tactical problem for the West is how to insure that the realities accompany appearances— or that appearances do not outrun realities." [82]

Brezhnev Doctrine

The Soviet-led invasion of Czechoslovakia on August 21, 1968, struck like lightning. Prior to this tragic event, the political skies across Europe had appeared to be clearing. West Germany had been engaged in confidential negotiations with the Soviet Union about a treaty on renunciation of force. She had been ready to accommodate the Czechoslovak government in its persistent demand for nullification of the Munich Agreement *ab initio,* and her Foreign Minister, Willy Brandt, had been unofficially invited to visit Prague. Kiesinger's policy of "practical steps" seemed to be paving the road toward a meaningful dialogue with the government of the GDR.

France was reaping the benefits of her friendly relations with all the countries of Central and Eastern Europe as her advocacy of a policy of national independence had found a receptive echo in their newspapers, and a continuous stream of official visitors converged on Paris. General De Gaulle had returned from a triumphant journey to Rumania and had accepted an invitation to visit Czechoslovakia. The French

---

[82] Stanley and Whitt, *op.cit.,* pp. 96-97.

concept of détente appeared to be on its way toward productive implementation.

Czechoslovakia was inhaling the exhilerating air of the "Spring." Dubček's "socialism with a human face," according to the leaders of the movement, was to introduce the ultimate chapter in the history of Marxism-Leninism, and economic reforms heralded a new era of socialist prosperity. Without any thought of abandoning the Warsaw Pact, Prague planned to open her windows to the West. After twenty years of restrictions, scholars, writers, and artists were free to travel and engage in conversations in the West European capitals. The Western press followed the Czechoslovak experiment with feelings of admiration, wonder, and here and there some apprehension.

The expectations, the hopes, the dreams were shattered overnight as the world woke to the reality of the occupation of Czechoslovakia by the armed forces of the Soviet Union and its four allies. The first reaction was one of consternation and condemnation. The Soviet ambassadors accredited to the NATO capitals advised all governments on the day of the invasion that the Soviet troops had entered Czechoslovakia at the request of her government (a cynical lie) and that the move was not directed against any other country. All governments, though with careful nuances, condemned the Soviet action, but before long détente prevailed over indignation.

Chancellor Kiesinger went before a microphone on the day of the invasion and, acknowledging the world's condemnation of Soviet aggression, declared that the FRG would "continue to pursue a consistent *Ostpolitik*," that "there [was] not, there cannot be any fundamental change" in the policy of détente.[83] Foreign Minister Willy Brandt acknowledged that the efforts at détente had suffered a "setback that will be felt for long"

---

[83] *Die deutsche Ostpolitik 1961-1970*, Kontinuität und Wandel, edited by Boris Meissner, Köln, Verlag Wissenschaft und Politik, 1970, p. 275.

but that the policy of "relaxation of tensions must continue." [84] The Bonn Cabinet, on the same day, privately condemned the occupation as an open violation of Czechoslovakia's sovereignty, but this action was made public only five weeks later when Kiesinger presented the government's declaration to the *Bundestag*. One week later, on August 28, the government advanced a bolder proposition when it stated that the serious international crisis could be brought to an end only after "the sovereignty of the Czechoslovak people would have been fully reestablished and the invasion called off." [85]

A few days later, September 2, the Soviet Ambassador to Bonn presented to Kiesinger a diplomatic note, the meaning of which became known in three weeks as the Brezhnev Doctrine. "The entry into Czechoslovakia was founded on the obligation which the countries of the socialist camp had mutually undertaken for the protection of their unity," read the note, and it further expressed satisfaction that "the hopes which the outside world had put in the counter-revolutionary forces have now been destroyed." To make the warning clear, the Ambassador accused the federal government of a hostile policy and made it responsible for the consequences. [86] Thus, an act of aggression was accompanied by a diplomatic offensive. Applying his statement to the problem of reunification, the Chancellor rejected the notion that the peaceful pursuit of this goal represented any hostility toward the Soviet Union and assured the Ambassador of Bonn's determination to pursue a friendly policy toward all of its eastern neighbors. Then, in his statement before the *Bundestag*, perhaps resigned to the imposing reality of the situation, he restated the position he had taken before the Cabinet on the day of the invasion, that "there [was] no alternative to the policy of building a

[84] *Ibid.*, p. 277.

[85] *Texte zur Deutschlandpolitik,* Vol. III, Bonn, Federal Ministry for Intra-German Relations, 1970, pp. 84-85.

[86] *Ibid.*, pp. 86-87.

European peaceful order. There is neither a possibility, nor a reason to change our policy." [87]

It would be unreasonable to argue that West Germany should or could have taken a different attitude toward the invasion of Czechoslovakia; her position prevented her from even considering anything more than its condemnation. However, it is open to question whether the cruel experience of Czechoslovakia did not demand a reexamination by Bonn of the Soviet understanding of détente.

France's policy of détente appeared to have been compromised by the Soviet invasion since that policy was based on the assumption that the countries of East Europe had regained a sense of national identity and that they were in command of their internal affairs. The French government was shocked by the Soviet action, but it also renewed its accusations against the United States and Great Britain, along with the Soviet Union, for their joint responsibility for the division of Europe that made Soviet control over East Europe possible. On August 21 the office of President De Gaulle issued a brief statement according to which the Soviet intervention demonstrated that "the Moscow government did not disengage itself from the policy of blocs which had been imposed on Europe by the Yalta agreements" and at which "France had not participated." It concluded that "the events of Prague . . . are of such a nature as to work against European détente. . . ." [88] The French representative at the United Nations went a step further when he expressed the hope before the Security Council that the invaders would "immediately withdraw their troops from Czechoslovakia." [89]

However, détente was the principal preoccupation of the French government and such an event as the occupation of a country with which France had developed friendly relations

[87] *Ibid.,* p. 85.
[88] *PEF, op.cit.,* 2ᵉ semestre 1968, p. 54.
[89] *Ibid.,* p. 55.

could not disrupt its pursuit of this political concept. Michel Debré, the Foreign Minister, explaining the official policy before the Foreign Affairs Commission of the National Assembly on August 29, declared, with a dose of cynicism, "One doesn't ban traffic just because there has been an accident on the road." [90]

General De Gaulle, on September 9, spoke with his usual moving eloquence about the events in Czechoslovakia. He reminded the audience of reporters of France's refusal to subscribe to the Soviet domination of East Europe or to adopt the Washington-Moscow decisions at Yalta about the fate of Europe, made without Europe's participation. He stated proudly that France had not ceased since 1958 (the year he came to power) its work toward a political détente, expecting from Russia much more than "to chain her satellites behind the bars by a fence of a crushing totalitarianism." Thus, the occupation was to be condemned, "particularly as [it was] absurd in the light of the perspectives of European détente." However, the moral cohesion of the Czechoslovak people, facing the invaders, as well as the resentment of Western Europe, was to him proof that the French "policy, as much as it appears at the moment counteracted, is in conformity with the profound European realities and, therefore, correct." Hence, France "will continue to work for the independence of nations and the liberty of men and for détente, entente, and cooperation. . . ." [91] The statement represents an admirable combination of a sublime ideal and statesmanship, but one cannot ignore the possibility that overeager cooperation may turn into appeasement to the ultimate detriment of détente.

Minister Debré made a number of speeches before the press, the United Nations, and the National Assembly that

---

[90] *Le Monde,* August 30, 1968. (The statement was not published in *PEF.*)

[91] *PEF, op.cit.,* pp. 60-61.

reflected De Gaulle's attitude. He condemned the invasion in severe terms, asked for the withdrawal of the troops, and pleaded at the same time for the continuation of the policy of détente.[92] When the Czechoslovak government succumbed to Soviet pressure and reached an agreement on the presence of Soviet troops on its territory on a reduced basis, the demand for their withdrawal subsided and the outside calls for national independence and freedom gave way to a reconciliation with the situation, again in the name of détente.

The reaction in Great Britain was similar: a restraint coupled with utter bewilderment. The government branded the invasion as an act in "flagrant violation of the United Nations Charter and of all accepted standards of international behaviour." When the Soviet Ambassador had the temerity to present the occupation as an act dictated by a concern to "strengthen peace," the Foreign Secretary, Michael Stewart, pointing to the crux of Soviet policy and to the real meaning of détente, asked him "what confidence any state that was not allied to the Soviet Union could be expected to have in the policies of a State which treated its allies in this way." [93]

Prime Minister Harold Wilson's address before a special session of the House of Commons on August 26 was a masterful balance between unconcealed scorn for the Soviet action and an ardent desire to alleviate the tensions. It was a product of a conflict between his conscience and his awareness of his country's powerlessness to change the course of events. With one finger he pointed to Soviet ruthlessness, while offering his other hand as a gesture of continuing good will. In his words, British people were "squally . . . chilled by the feeling" that they had experienced a similar tragedy thirty years before when Germany had occupied Czechoslovakia. He reminded his audience of the position that the British representative at

[92] *Ibid.,* pp. 62, 108, 158-159.
[93] *Parliamentary Debates* (Hansard), House of Commons, Vol. 769, August 26, 1968, Col. 1,275.

the United Nations was taking before the Security Council. However, he felt the lessons to be learned from the events were that it was necessary not only to maintain the NATO defensive alliance but also to continue its determination to create "the conditions of détente," to be ready to "respond to the opportunities for détente," and "to move more positively in the direction of European unity." For "whatever the tragic disappointments of the last few days . . . we all know that the only future for the world rests upon continuing to work for détente between East and West. . . ." He recognized that "détente means trust," which was now undermined, but he rejected a "relapse into the frozen *immobilisme* of the Cold War." [94]

In general, the official West German, French, and British reaction to the occupation of Czechoslovakia was one of painful and righteous anger, as well as an awareness of their impotence to remedy the situation. The appeals for the withdrawal of the invading armies were intertwined with somewhat pathetic expressions of a desire, even a necessity, for the continuation of the policy of détente. To the Soviet government these pleas could be only reassuring, an indication that the West would soon reconcile itself with Moscow's action. It must be added, however, that the Czechoslovak government's capitulation to Soviet blackmail facilitated the West's adjustment to the events.

West European statesmen condemned the invasion collectively when they met as the Committee of Ministers of the Council of Europe, but at the same time they pleaded for a continuation of the policy of détente while, in the words of Michel Debré, "keeping their eyes open." [95]

The NATO Council, however, when it met in Brussels in October 1968, concluded, on the basis of a detailed analysis of the consequences of the occupation, that "the military and

[94] *Ibid.,* Cols. 1,274-1,284.
[95] *Le Monde,* December 15, 1968.

security balance in Europe has been importantly affected" by the Soviet invasion and it recommended that "all Western political and military policies be based on the unpredictability of Soviet behavior." [96]

The NATO Ministerial Council advanced its regular session by one month. Its communique called for increased vigilance and for strengthening of NATO defenses; it confirmed NATO's stand on Germany and Berlin and warned against the expansion of Soviet activities in the Mediterranean. Although the intervention in Czechoslovakia set back hopes of settling the problems that divided Europe and threatened "certain of the results already achieved in the field of détente," the communique stated that "the alliance should work to promote a policy of détente." [97] Just how they intended "to promote a policy of détente" that must "be based on the unpredictability of Soviet behavior" was not elaborated in the communique.

Some practical measures did demonstrate in a most impressive fashion the depth and breadth of indignation in West Europe over Soviet-led aggression. Before the invasion, both parts of Europe had been engaged at an increasing pace in exchange visits at all levels.[98] In protest to the invasion, many planned trips were cancelled, except in the case of Rumania, which had refused to take part in the occupation, and of Czechoslovakia, which for the first four months of the occupation avoided, in spite of the presence of the Soviet armies, repressive measures against the populace and whose writers and artists received a demonstrative welcome in West European cities.

At the official level, UN Secretary General U Thant's visit to Prague was cancelled. This was a serious mistake, for he

---

[96] *New York Times,* October 17, 1968.

[97] *NATO Letter,* December 1968, pp. 18-19.

[98] For details, see Radio Free Europe, Research, *East-West Contacts,* Monthly Surveys.

should have proceeded according to his plans in spite of or indeed because of the Soviet invasion. Denmark and Norway called off the visit of Todor Zhivkov, the Bulgarian communist leader. Denmark also cancelled the trip of Hungary's Foreign Minister, Janos Peter, and France postponed the visit of Wladyslaw Gomulka. Austria declined the visit of the Soviet Foreign Trade Minister, the Hungarian Premier, Jenoe Fock, and Zhivkov. Michael Stewart, the British Foreign Secretary, called off his visits to Bulgaria and Hungary. West Germany postponed the meeting of her Minister of Economic Affairs, Karl Schiller, with his East German opposite member, Horst Soelle. Negotiations between Belgium and Poland on a cultural agreement were postponed. A Danish-Polish conference at the ministerial level on problems of disarmament was called off and the Danish Foreign Minister cancelled his visit to the Soviet Union. NATO's Council of Ministers at its November 16 meeting issued a communique that stated that "in view of the action of the five members of the Warsaw Pact, the scope and level of allied contacts with them had to be reduced."

At the unofficial level as well, a great number of visits were cancelled: for example, the trips to Russia of the Danish Federal Youth Council, the Italian Christian Workers Association, the Oslo Municipal Philharmonic Orchestra, the Swedish Confederation of Trade Unions; the performances of the Bologna Community Theatre in Budapest and East Berlin; the visit of a Dutch Parliamentary delegation to Poland; and of the Greater London Council and the Swiss Chamber of Commerce to the Soviet Union. Great Britain cancelled the tour of the Red Army Choir and the Anglo-Soviet historical exhibition in Moscow. The Council of the International Film Festival at Cork, Ireland, did not permit Soviet participation. The performances of the Russian ballet in La Scala were postponed. At some international conferences, the representatives of the five members of the Warsaw

Pact were not admitted; at others, they walked out after the invasion had been condemned.[99]

The list of cancellations offers eloquent testimony to the sincerity and intensity of the indignation in Western Europe over the occupation of Czechoslovakia. Less than six months later, however, by January 1969, East-West contacts had again reached the pre-invasion level, with the exception of Czechoslovakia itself, which was by then in the process of adjusting herself to her new position of subservience and whose representatives were forbidden to visit the West. No cancellations of trips for December 1968 and January 1969 were recorded.[100] Things were getting back to "normal."

One year after the invasion, the atmosphere of détente in Western Europe appeared to be fully reestablished, erasing the sad memories of the recent past. As a French official put it, the policy of détente was now pursued without illusions and with the awareness that Moscow would not make any concessions and wished to achieve a détente on its own terms. A U.S. State Department official pointedly commented on the aftermath of the invasion: "We don't harp on it and the Russians would like everyone to forget about it but it's still there . . . like a ghost at a banquet." [101]

Another year passed and by the middle of 1970 even the ghost had disappeared. Chancellor Brandt signed a treaty with the Soviet Union and Poland and resumed negotiations with the East German government after having met with Willi Stoph at Erfurt and Kassel. The division of Europe appeared to have been accepted as an unalterable fact and détente was conceived as a concept existing within the framework of Europe's partition.

The Soviet Union and its allies, on the other hand, drew

---

[99] For details, see *ibid.,* A Monthly Survey, September-December 1968.

[100] *Ibid.,* January 1969. For a six-month survey, see Table XIV.

[101] *New York Times,* August 22, 1969.

some telling lessons from the "Czechoslovak Spring" and the invasion. They made it abundantly clear that they would prevent any East-West relations from exercising influence upon internal developments in the East European countries and upon their relations with the Soviet Union. As early as April 1968, when it became obvious that the Soviet Union was following the happenings in Prague with apprehension, the Central Committee of the CPSU appealed to Party members to increase their ideological activities and to "wage an offensive struggle against bourgeois ideology and to oppose actively any attempt to sneak views alien to Soviet socialist ideology into individual works of literature, art or other works."

Events in Czechoslovakia served as "proof" to the Soviet bloc that the West was trying to infiltrate it by giving support to counter-revolutionary forces by way of economic, cultural, and scientific contacts. Thus, for instance, showing Czechoslovak films in West Germany was viewed as a measure "used by the reactionary forces to prepare the ground for imperialist ideology." Western organizers of the dialogues between Marxists and Christians that had attracted much attention were accused of attempts to convert even communists to their anti-communist faith. West German tourists and economists who had visited Czechoslovakia were labeled as "specially chosen anti-communists who had undergone training in subversive activity, ideological, cultural, and economic sabotage, etc." Technical contacts and co-production plans were branded as imperialist efforts to encourage revisionism and demonstrate the superiority of capitalist methods of production over the socialist system. The West's alleged ideological offensive led to the acceleration of national idiosyncrasies, to questioning of the validity of Leninism, and to spreading the false theory of convergence when, in the Marxist view, the socialist and capitalist system could never converge. The West was accused of trying to change the foreign policies of East European countries, particularly toward the FRG.

The Soviet Union and its allies decided to draw a lesson from these devastating experiences which surfaced in connection with the Czechoslovak events. They called for an absolute unity to make socialism "incorruptible" and resistant to Western advances. Ideological purity must be reestablished, ideological preparedness sharpened, and the cultural struggle, which knows no peaceful coexistence, must be intensified. Intra-bloc cooperation in economic and cultural fields must be strengthened and a dynamic socialist foreign policy pursued. The COMECON must reach a higher stage of development and achieve "the least possible dependence on capitalist countries and without any kind of danger from imperialism." [102]

Thus, the intensive campaign to isolate East Europe from the possible impact of détente upon its internal developments was only another expression of the old-time interpretation of peaceful coexistence: East Europe was to remain an exclusive domain of Soviet influence and pressure. The theoretical undergirding to this policy enunciated by the Soviet Union was dubbed by the American press the "Brezhnev Doctrine."

After failing completely to substantiate the original claim that the Soviet-led invasion of Czechoslovakia was in response to a request from Prague to arrest a counter-revolution, *Pravda* published an article, September 26, which interpreted the intervention as an act of socialist legal right and duty. This article, the essence of which was resubmitted, October 3, by Gromyko to the international forum of the United Nations, the General Assembly, is of enormous significance to future

---

[102] Radio Free Europe, Research, *East-West Relations,* "The Invaders' Approach to Europe," February 4, 1969, quoting *Izvestiia,* April 11, 1968; *Neues Deutschland,* August 30, 1968; *Trud,* October 16, 1968, September 5, 1968; *Red Star,* September 20, 1968; *Izvestiia,* September 22, 1968; *Red Star,* September 12, 1968, respectively.

developments in all communist countries and to the prospects for détente. Its significance is not that it would bring an innovative element into the body of communist theory; Lenin, Stalin, and Khrushchev had spoken before Brezhnev did about the duty of the Soviet Union to defend socialism everywhere, by arms if necessary. What does make it important is the fact that it purports to reestablish the legal and ideological basis for military interventions in situations that, if the Soviet government so interprets them, threaten socialism from within or without, and that this position is taken after fifteen years— ever since the Twentieth Congress of the CPSU—of repeated affirmations that every country has the right to follow its own path of socialism and that all communist parties and countries are equal. Moreover, it violates the equally frequently repeated principle of non-intervention and national independence and demonstratively excludes from the Soviet policy of détente Moscow's own allies.

The article rejected as untenable and as a "non-class approach," the arguments that the occupation "violated the principle of sovereignty and self-determination since every communist party is responsible not only to its own people but also to all socialist countries and to the entire communist movement." Accordingly, and in contrast to the international law embodied in the UN Charter that the invaders' governments had signed, "in the Marxist conception the norms of law, including the norms governing relations among socialist countries, cannot be interpreted in a narrowly formal way, outside the general context of the class struggle in the present-day world. Socialist countries resolutely oppose the export and import of counter-revolution." This means that no communist party can "fail to take into account . . . the struggle between two antithetical social systems—capitalism and socialism." Thus, "the weakening of any link in the world socialist system has a direct effect on all the socialist countries . . ." and the Soviet-led aggressors were fulfilling only "their

internationalist duty." They "had to act and did act in reso-
lute opposition to the antisocialist forces in Czechoslovakia."
What happened in Czechoslovakia was a "formal observance
of freedom of self-determination" as her "antisocialist path"
would have led the country "straight into the jaws of the West
German revanchists and . . . to the loss of its national independence." Since "world imperialism . . . was trying to export counter-revolution to Czechoslovakia" Soviet "assistance" was, in fact, "a struggle for the Czechoslovak Socialist
Republic's sovereignty" and "for the principles of self-determination. . . ." As to the "illegality" of the intervention, it
must not be forgotten that "there is and can be no such thing
as non-class law." Laws and the norms of law are subordi-
nated to the laws of class struggle "and the class approach to
the matter cannot be discarded in the name of legalistic considerations." Disregard for such an approach "to the question
of sovereignty means, for example, that the world's progressive forces could not oppose the revival of neo-Nazism in the
FRG. . . ." [103]

Pravda's pronouncement (a better than usual acrobatic
display) is not only in flagrant opposition to the fundamental
rules of international law; nor does it only spell a warning
to all communist countries should they attempt to follow a
path of internal development that might be interpreted in
Moscow as acts against the interests of the socialist commonwealth. Its meaning also reaches beyond the boundaries of the
communist bloc and materially affects the policy of détente.
Any change, whether in matters of internal or external affairs
of East Europe, which might weaken the Soviet position in
the world could be viewed as breaking the ranks of class
solidarity and class struggle. Any serious initiative toward
improving the East European countries' relations with the
West outside the framework of the collective interest of the

[103] *The Current Digest of the Soviet Press,* Vol. xx, No. 39, pp.
10-12.

bloc, as understood in Moscow, would justify an intervention (according to this class interpretation of international law) as an act of internationalist duty. Close cultural relations of the West with East Europe and extensive trips might be condemned as attempts to subvert the Soviet bloc's ideological foundations. Major intensification of technological and industrial cooperation might be seen in Moscow as an undermining of the socialist economy by way of capitalist incursions. Moreover, any internal development in West Germany of which the Soviet government might be critical could be interpreted as a preparation for exporting counter-revolution.

Past experiences suggest that communist theorems frequently provide a cover for sheer power politics, and one should not overanalyze the real meaning of *Pravda's* article. One may assume that in any concrete situation, Moscow will continue to direct its international activities primarily according to power, not ideological, considerations. However, the article sets a marked limit to prospects of détente; it makes it clear that the Soviet government will not tolerate another "Czechoslovak Spring" that might result, among other developments, in uninhibited cultural, scientific, and economic contacts with West Europe and friendly political relations. It also suggests that the nature and scope of détente will be determined to a large extent by Moscow's policy and not by the individuality and the intentions of its allies (the latter being one of the focal assumptions for West Europe's policy of détente).

The treaty the Soviet Union and Czechoslovakia signed on May 6, 1970, embodies the principles of the Brezhnev Doctrine. It is an expression, in the form of a legal document, of limited sovereignty with significant international implications and ideological consequences. Its preamble confirms that "support, strengthening, and protection of socialist achievements are an international duty, common to socialist countries." While it does reaffirm the policy of peaceful coexistence and of international détente, at the same time it promises "support to the countries which have freed themselves of the yoke of imperialism." [104] This promise, in and of itself, has the sound of a lofty commitment, but it opens the door to interventions that run counter to peaceful coexistence and détente, just as "protection of socialist achievements" may serve as a barrier to détente should it begin to affect the communist system. The Czechoslovak communist leader, Gustav Husák, made this clear when he stated on the occasion of the signing of the treaty that it was a guarantee for socialist development of the country, and Brezhnev saw in the pact an expression of the will "to take all measures necessary for the protection of the socialist achievements of the Czechoslovak and Soviet people." [105] Gromyko gave to the meaning of the treaty an international legal connotation when he declared that it constituted "a step forward in the elaboration of the norms of international law, of a new type of relations between the socialist states." Štrougal, another Czech communist, known for his subservience to Moscow, dutifully followed by stating that it was "a type of entirely new relationship between socialist countries conditioned by the character of the international [working] class and surpassing the framework of the general democratic law." [106]

Both the East and West have confirmed on numerous occasions that they adhere to the generally agreed upon principles of national sovereignty, political independence, and of non-interference in the internal affairs of other countries. But it is obvious that, despite the verbal gymnastics, the Brezhnev Doctrine and its specific product, the Soviet-Czechoslovak treaty, are in conflict with the commonly accepted meanings of these principles.

How, in a world of such political dichotomy, can hope for

[104] For the text, see *New Times,* May 19, 1970, pp. 30-31.
[105] *Le Monde,* May 8, 1970.
[106] *Ibid.,* May 29, 30, 1970.

a lasting détente survive? One alternative would be for Moscow to renounce this new interpretation of law and return to the traditional meanings of the commonly enunciated principles. Though this is possible (for such reversals are not unknown in Soviet interpretations of ideology) it is highly unlikely. The other alternative is more probable: that the West, eager for détente, will understand that the language was a mask for an exercise in power politics, and, hopefully aware of continuing Soviet unpredictability, will simply not press its abhorrence of such a position.

CHAPTER 3

Economics

SETTING THE SCENE: A STATE OF RIGIDITY

BEFORE World War II, the countries of Central and Eastern Europe had only marginal trade with the Soviet Union. The obstacles for developing this trade were both political and economic in nature. These countries did not even have diplomatic relations with Moscow until shortly before the outbreak of the war. The exception was Poland, whose political relations with Moscow were even more tense than those of some of the other nations of the area. The economic structures of the Central and Eastern European countries were not complementary to that of the Soviet Union. Russia's agricultural production was in continuing crisis and its growing industry was in need of imports of machinery rather than in a position to export industrial goods.

On the other hand, the exports of the nations of this area to the Soviet Union were hampered by the predominantly agricultural nature of their economy, the products of which Moscow could not afford to buy. The raw materials found eager purchasers in other markets and the possible sale of industrial products (mainly from Czechoslovakia) to Russia would have had to be financed by credits that the prospective exporters were ill-equipped to provide. Thus, the trade of the Central-East European countries with the Soviet Union in 1937 amounted to only seven percent of their total trade.

The political changes that took place after the war led to a radical reorientation in trade. First, in the process of communization, the economic structure of Central and Eastern Europe underwent a fundamental change. Agriculture was almost completely collectivized (with the exception of Poland) and the countries that before the war had produced an export surplus of agricultural products now needed to import them.

Second, these countries were forced by the Soviet Union and their own communist governments to embark upon a policy of frantic industrialization, particularly in the production of capital goods, in order to free themselves from dependence on trade with the West, to extend support to the Soviet economy, and to be able to pay in kind for the Soviet export of raw materials and wheat. Thus, by 1953, trade of the Central-East European countries with Soviet Union had jumped from a pre-war 7 percent to 80 percent. The establishment of the Council for Mutual Economic Assistance (COMECON) in January 1949, as Stalin's reaction to the Marshall Plan, was meant to coordinate the economies of the communist countries. But its program, in fact, remained largely a paper declaration because Moscow preferred to influence the economic development of each country separately and to negotiate trade agreements on a bilateral basis.

During the Stalin era and for another five years after his death, economic contacts between East and West Europe had been largely a matter of chance. Political separation created a profound uneasiness that extended to matters of commerce. The old established channels of contacts and commercial routes were severed and new avenues had to be cautiously opened. The systems of both the East and West were oriented inward: one toward autarchy, with an overpowering economic dependence on the Soviet Union; the other toward establishing its own markets, relying on assistance from the United States. The remarkable economic and technological progress of Western Europe and the slow advancement of East Europe led to a growing gap. Each bloc went its own way, not only politically but economically as well. Military alignment was accompanied by economic alignment and the Iron Curtain was impregnable both politically and economically; nor, in fact, was the West interested in piercing the economic curtain.

One international body, the UN Economic Commission for Europe (ECE), tried to alleviate the grievous consequences of Europe's economic division. Established in May 1947, its function was to "initiate and participate in measures for facilitating concerted action for the economic reconstruction of Europe, for raising the level of European economic activity, and for maintaining and strengthening the economic relations of the European countries. . . ." [1] In 1960, ECE membership had risen from the original eighteen to thirty countries, and it has become the only European economic organization bridging the gulf between the two political, social, and economic systems. Its enormous though largely unpublicized activities, even in the dark period of the Cold War, covered such vast and complex fields as agriculture, energy, steel, engineering, housing, transportation, timber, trade, statistics, technical assistance, water problems, automation, and productivity of labor. It achieved a number of agreements on technical matters of European economic cooperation. However, because it is limited to recommendatory powers, it has not been able to overcome the political abyss between the two blocs.

Toward the end of the 1950's, Khrushchev infused new life into COMECON in an attempt to reestablish Soviet controls over Central and East Europe through trade—an attempt that failed, to some extent, because of the simultaneous trend toward polycentrism. This development was paralleled in Western Europe by the establishment of the European Economic Community (EEC), which proved to be a remarkable success. In contrast, COMECON has passed through periods of revisions in planning and internal tensions, and plans for a socialist division of labor have largely failed. This disparate development of the EEC and COMECON and the imperative of Eastern Europe's needs for economic growth were precisely what opened the door to an economic détente.

[1] *Fifteen Years of Activity of the Economic Commission for Europe, 1947-1962,* New York, United Nations, 1964, p. 22.

Detente: A Problem of Pragmatism

This is not the place to examine whether trade follows politics or vice versa. One could cite many examples, with variations, of each. In some cases, development of economic contacts was a precursor to the settlement of political problems; in others, the solution of political disputes preceded expansion of trade. In still others, political and economic questions were viewed as inseparable and their solution handled simultaneously. However, whatever the cause-effect sequence, it is in foreign trade that détente in Europe produced the first tangible results.

As both West and East Europe began to search for political accommodation by the late 1950's, trade offered a welcome area for the relaxation of tensions. The number of East-West trips by trade delegations had grown; such exchanges offered opportunities for mutual acquaintance, for getting familiar with methods of production and marketing, and for a better understanding of each other's problems. These experiences could not but influence the political climate favorably, to some degree.[2]

One should not, however, overestimate the significance of East-West trade as a factor of political détente. Even though communist leaders have repeatedly distinguished between ideological conflicts and trade, even though they are eager for reasons of their own to increase trade with highly developed industrialized countries, they are not ignorant of the political impact of trade contacts on their political and economic systems and they keep a vigilant eye on this aspect of trade.

World trade has grown remarkably since World War II, due to the expanding economy of industrial societies, rapid

[2] For an analysis of the relationship between politics and trade, see J. Bognar, "The Role of East-West Economic Relations in Promoting European Cooperation," Radio Free Europe, Research, *Hungarian Press Survey,* February 24, 1971.

110

technological development, and vigorous trade policies. Such regional European groupings as OECD, EEC, EFTA, and COMECON have served as vehicles for the encouragement of intra-group trade, but they have at the same time created protective barriers to inter-group exchanges; while efforts have been made to overcome the problem of economic isolation, the members of the regional groupings continue to be inward-oriented in promoting their economic growth. Trade between Western and Eastern Europe remains modest, in spite of its acceleration, by comparison with the increase in the total trade of the West European nations or with total trade within the COMECON. The extent to which East-West trade is limited becomes evident when one examines it at four different levels: (a) between the NATO countries and the communist world; (b) between all European non-communist countries and communist countries; (c) between the EEC and COMECON; and (d) between the COMECON countries and the four most important trading partners—West Germany, France, Italy, and Great Britain. Such an examination reveals a certain pattern that permits us to assess not only the limitations on East-West trade but also its significance for détente.

NATO's Trade with the Communist World

Trade between the NATO countries and the communist world has been negligible by comparison with their respective total trade. In general, the former's exports have consisted mainly of industrial products (machinery, chemicals, plates) and the latter's primary products (petroleum, wood, and agricultural goods). In the period between 1962 and 1969, the total trade of all NATO countries with the communist world averaged 3.2 percent of their total imports and 3.5 percent of their total exports. For the European NATO members during the same time period, imports from communist countries averaged 4.3 percent and exports 4.5 percent of their total import-export volume. Canada's imports averaged 0.6 percent and exports 4.2 percent; U.S. imports averaged 0.6 percent and exports 0.7 percent. Trade between NATO countries and the communist world reached a peak in the years 1966 and 1967 and then decelerated. But for every sub-grouping of NATO countries, exports exceeded imports during the last four years of the period.[3]

When we compare the rate of growth of trade between the two blocs, we get a different picture. In the period between 1964 and 1969, the rate of growth of imports of European NATO countries from Eastern Europe first accelerated rapidly from 1964 through 1966, then dropped markedly in 1967 and 1968, and increased again in 1969; the rate of exports grew at a steady pace for the first four years, declined markedly in 1968, and resumed growth in 1969. The rate of growth of Canadian and American imports and exports was rather uneven, showing sudden peaks and valleys of growth, but it must be remembered that their trade with the communist countries had started from a very low base.[4] The figures of just the trade of European NATO countries shows a more significant increase though its acceleration has also decreased. The difference is due to several circumstances: on the one hand, the U.S. embargo on exports of strategic materials to the East, introduced in 1947; on the other, the step-by-step release by European NATO countries of many such export items from the embargo list. In addition, the United States regards her trade with the communist countries in the light of political considerations, while her allies view it essentially in economic terms and in some cases as an instrument of political détente.

West Germany, Great Britain, Italy and France have been, in that order, the highest NATO traders. Imports and exports with some exceptions show a steady increase though as a

[3] See Table XI.
[4] See Table XII.

percentage of the total trade of these countries the figures represent only a fraction of their world trade volume.[5] The figures lead to the conclusion that West Germany maintains a steady lead over its allies in trade with the communist countries, increasing in value, but still negligible in relation to its increasing total trade. Italy's trade shows a rapid increase, while France lags behind. The Soviet Union, of all communist countries, is the chief trade partner of NATO; imports of NATO countries from the Soviet Union account for one-third of the imports from all communist countries and exports to the Soviet Union make up more than one-fifth of all exports to the communist world.

Intra-European Trade

Trade between the West European groupings (the EEC and EFTA) and the COMECON countries has developed along patterns similar to those of the trade between NATO and the communist world, except for the fact that there has been extensive exchange. The ECE secretariat undertakes in-depth studies of East-West European trade and of its prospects for the future. It is not unaware of the political barriers to trade and it aspires to the role of catalyst that may serve to overcome political obstacles by further development of trade. As one of its reports states, "Indeed, it is much easier to disrupt trade by political measures than to revive and further promote mutually beneficial trade once the damage has been done." [6]

Studies undertaken by the ECE secretariat do not warrant an optimistic outlook about East-West European trade. The rate of growth of this trade shows a decelerating trend in the light of an increasing world trade in general and of the growth

[5] See Table IX.

[6] UN Economic and Social Council, Economic Commission for Europe, "Supplement to the Analytical Report on the State of Intra-European Trade," E/ECE/761/Add. 1, February 12, 1970, p. 1.

of the trade of the European groupings in particular. World trade has grown on an average at about 7 percent per year; within the EEC, imports in the period between 1957 and 1967 increased at an annual rate of 13.2 percent; within the EFTA at 9 percent; and within the COMECON at 8.7 percent. The share of COMECON in total intra-European imports of EEC and EFTA countries declined, but, more importantly, while in the same period the volume of trade between West and East European grew steadily, the rate of growth declined as well.[7]

As to projections of trade, the ECE secretariat expects, in spite of "indications of a possible tendency toward long-term deceleration in the growth of East-West trade," that West Europe by 1980 will increase its imports from East Europe, as compared with 1965-1967, five-fold in manufactures and only two-fold in primary products.[8] The growth will depend on many as yet elusive factors: the adaptability of East European production to the needs of West European markets, the increase of industrial production and marketability of East European goods, the replacement of the current practice of bilateral commercial arrangements with a multilateral approach, the removal of West Europe's discriminatory measures against imports, and the substitution of free trade for the quota system.

In view of the uncertainties of a political détente, these expectations may be overly optimistic. Even an improvement in political conditions will not in itself provide a sufficient basis for promotion of trade; in the long run, this depends fundamentally on mutuality of economic interests. But it is equally true that economic incentives can help to bring a divided Europe together.[9] On the other hand, given the politi-

[7] UN Economic and Social Council, Economic Commission for Europe, "Analytical Report on the State of Intra-European Trade," E/ECE/761, January 14, 1970, pp. 4-5.

[8] *Ibid.*, p. 12.

[9] *Ibid.*, p. 28.

cal separation between East and West Europe, and given the limited prospects of East Europe to be able to pay for its imports, it is doubtful that economic détente can develop fully to the point of a basically unrestricted trade.

EEC and COMECON

For several years, the COMECON countries viewed the EEC with unconcealed hostility. They branded it as a capitalist trick that was to serve as an instrument of American economic imperialism, as a plot against peace that was to serve as the right arm of NATO's expansionist designs; they predicted its downfall, the inevitable result of its internal, capitalist contradictions. All the communist East had to do was sit and wait for the economic disintegration of the West, the inexorable fate of its cyclical production and market crises.

Unimpressed by these dire predictions, the EEC grew into a solid and permanent regional organization, providing its members with a framework for economic prosperity. Beginning in the spring of 1962, the Soviet Union and its allies, cautiously and with varied emphases, changed their attitude toward the Common Market. While they still regarded it as an imperialist bloc, committed to the exploitation of economically underdeveloped Third World countries, and as a means of protecting its members' monopolistic economies (which they viewed as capitalist trusts, designed to strengthen their military policy), they also reluctantly recognized the achievements of the Common Market and took cognizance of its continued existence.[10] Attacking its commercial policy

---

[10] See for instance, N. S. Khrushchev, "Problems actuels du système socialiste mondial," *La Nouvelle Revue Internationale,* September 1962; and Institute of World Economy and International Relations of the Academy of Sciences of the USSR, "L'integration imperialiste en Europe Occidentale, Le Marché Commun," republished in *Notes et Etudes Documentaires,* "L'USSR et le Marché Commun," No. 3, 041, November 26, 1963, Paris, La Documentation française.

as discriminatory and as a closed shop, nevertheless by 1964 individual members of COMECON established informal contacts with officials and offices of the EEC in Brussels, and their newspapers and scholars, as time went by, examined prospects for developing trade with the EEC countries within the framework of EEC regulations. Rumania and Poland were in the lead, followed by Hungary and Czechoslovakia.[11] Only Bulgaria and the Soviet Union refused to recognize the existence of the EEC as an international organ, until the Secretary of the Soviet Embassy in Brussels visited its headquarters in December 1968, ten years after it had been founded.[12]

As the interests of the COMECON countries in the EEC grew, most of their embassies in Brussels included one official whose special assignment was to follow EEC policies and maintain what EEC headquarters called contacts "offi-

[11] Poland established first contacts in November 1964 and Rumania in the spring of 1964. *Zycie Warszawy,* for instance, published on March 30, 1967, an article titled "Ten Years of EEC: Condemned to Success." A Czechoslovak scholar advocated development of trade with the EEC, recognizing that it had become an economic and political fact and one of the decisive factors in the world economy (Arnošt Tauber, "The European Economic Community and Czechoslovakia," *Series of Studies, 1968,* Vol. 10, Prague, Institute of International Politics and Economics). The Deputy Foreign Trade Minister of Czechoslovakia stated in January 1968 that his country had "natural interests" in trading with the Common Market countries. The President of the Council of Ministers, Ion G. Maurer, discussed Rumania's trade with the EEC members when on an official visit to Rome. The Polish Foreign Minister, Adam Rapacki, answering on the occasion of his visit to Belgium in 1967 the question whether Poland would recognize the EEC, stated, "Whether you recognize it or not, the Common Market exists" (Radio Free Europe, Research Department, "The Communists and the Common Market, 1957-1967," August 11, 1967, Radio Free Europe, Special, *Brussels,* February 7, 1968). The Hungarian Prime Minister, Jenö Fock, stated in February 1968 that the Common Market was a reality, the existence of which must be recognized (Radio Free Europe, Research, *Hungary/ 55,* November 6, 1969, p. 5).

[12] *New York Times,* January 28, 1969.

cieux" or technical contacts. Nevertheless, the intensity of this interest fluctuated according to Moscow's political mood.

For example, after the occupation of Czechoslovakia, the communist press criticized attempts at close economic cooperation with the West, which it accused of trying to demonstrate the superiority of the capitalist over the socialist economic system. At the Tenth Congress of the Communist Party of Rumania in August 1969, the Soviet delegate, Katushev, attacked the "economic penetration policies of the West" and Radio Moscow warned against "broadening of trade with the capitalist states [for] this would sooner or later lead to the inclusion of one socialist country or another in the sphere of influence of the capitalist market." [13] At the meetings of the Warsaw Pact countries, the member states were urged to develop closer economic ties among themselves and to rely on their own resources.

However, the need for Western technology and the opportunity offered by the West European markets did not permit ideological considerations to prevail completely over economic exigencies; thus varied national interests clashed with the common ideological stand. In an attempt to reconcile the conflict and at the same time to maintain its control, the Soviet government at present appears to entertain the idea of a common policy among COMECON nations toward the outside trade world, including the EEC. A high official of the COMECON stated toward the end of 1969 that ". . . as a united body, [it] would not be averse, for instance, to a declaration of readiness for cooperation made by the organs of the European Economic Community." [14] This trend, however, should not encourage the thought that the East is willing to consider official negotiations at the level of the COMECON

---

[13] Radio Free Europe, Research, *East Europe, Economics/1,* "What Role for COMECON?" April 1970, p. 101.

[14] Angel Todorov, Deputy Secretary of the COMECON, as quoted in *ibid.,* pp. 107-108.

and the EEC in their capacities as regional economic organizations. Rather, Moscow is eager to utilize West Europe's technological achievements and concedes the same opportunity to its allies for reasons of its own interest. Further, a coordinated stand toward the EEC facilitates Moscow's desire to maintain control over its allies. But the Soviet Union continues to face difficulties in integrating the economies of the COMECON countries; it follows with great apprehension the process of integration within the EEC, in which it sees a hindrance to Moscow's understanding of détente.[15] As late as the fall of 1969 Radio Moscow still accused "the advocates of integration" of the aim of "the political and military unification of Western European States in some sort of alliance directed against the Soviet Union and other socialist countries relying on force, including nuclear weapons." [16]

In its continuing attempts to weaken the cohesion of the EEC and its economic position toward East Europe, the repeated appeals of the Warsaw Pact for a European conference since 1966 have included proposals for discussions of economic and technological cooperation. Thus, a regional economic organization embracing all European countries, including neutrals, would hopefully halt the process of EEC's own further integration; discourage neutrals (Austria) and Britain and other EFTA countries from joining the EEC; combat American political and economic influence in West Europe; and, last but not least, strengthen East Europe's economic position toward the EEC.[17]

On the other side of the economic border, EEC officials welcome their "technical" contacts with the East European

---

[15] Moscow Radio, October 18, 1969, as quoted in the EEC *Background Paper,* January 1970, p. 4.

[16] *Ibid.,* p. 3.

[17] For detailed analysis, see Henry Schaeffer, "Communist 'Westpolitik' and the EEC," Radio Free Europe, Research, *East-West Relations/2,* December 21, 1970, pp. 16-53.

representatives, although they are also aware of the limited possibilities of EEC as a vehicle for the promotion of trade with the COMECON countries. But it is not their first priority, either. Not only the EEC itself, but also its individual members, are too engrossed with the spectacular success of the EEC and too fascinated by the prospects for further development to give much time or attention to COMECON.

The chances of a major breakthrough in West-East trade are not very promising, whether through the mechanism of the EEC or on a bilateral basis, because efforts to encourage commerce continually run into serious obstacles. The two systems—one a free market economy, the other a command economy—have developed different practices in price policies, in marketing, in negotiation of trade agreements, and in individual contracts. The currencies of the East European countries are not convertible and the exchange of goods is basically carried as barter trade. The EEC countries try to overcome the problem by extending short- and long-term credits to the East European governments, but this policy only aggravates the question of balance of payments because the recipient countries, as a rule, lag far behind in fulfilling their own export commitments and they import more than they can repay in export.

Another of the chief barriers to trade is the quality of the East's industrial products. Officials of the EEC and of its member nations in charge of trade all complain about the low quality of products exported by East European countries. They point out that individual ministries may negotiate a satisfactory trade agreement, but then find it difficult to persuade importers to sign a contract because they know that they can buy the same goods in West Europe not only with greater confidence in high quality but also without being involved in the cumbersome procedure of discussing specifications with some central office in charge of a whole industry. Although some countries in the East have recently liberalized direct contacts between importing and exporting firms, the Western importer still has to overcome the frustrating impediment of a centrally planned and controlled economy. Western exporters face similar problems as the ministries of foreign trade and industry in East Europe prevent them from discussing—or at best make it difficult for them to discuss—with the managers of the importing concerns the technical, frequently complex, aspects of business. Little wonder that the Western trader, accustomed to conducting his affairs efficiently, tends to be unenthusiastic at governmental encouragement of East-West trade. Some of the restraining aspects of the East's trade with West Europe were recently alleviated when some East European state monopolies established sales companies in West European capitals that are owned and jointly operated by Eastern state agencies and Western private firms.[18] But the basic problem of cumbersome business relationships between a state monopoly and a free enterprise continues to plague prospects for the future.

Moreover, the EEC itself puts serious obstacles in the path of the import of agricultural products. To protect the agriculture of its members, imports are subjected to a system of price regulations according to which the total price of imported agricultural goods must correspond to the price fixed by the EEC. Should any member of the EEC negotiate with a prospective importer from the third world (not only from East Europe) agricultural deliveries at a lower price, the exporting country must pay into an EEC fund a levy to bring the total price up to the level of the fixed price. The exporting countries enter into "technical" agreements with the EEC on agricultural goods and in particular on the question of price, and the agreements must be approved by the Commission of Fourteen of the Common Market countries. It is a complicated procedure involving representatives of the ex-

[18] UN, ECE, "Supplement to the Analytical Report. . .," *op.cit.,* p. 105.

porting and importing governments, the EEC headquarters, and its commission. The East European governments are justified in their constant complaints that the EEC pursues a discriminatory trade policy.

The EEC exercises no authority over trade in industrial products. This is a matter of bilateral negotiations in which the exchange of goods is determined not only by need but also by protective pressures of domestic industries. The quantities of imports are limited by quotas negotiated from year to year on the basis of long-term trade agreements. In recent years all West European governments have liberalized their imports of industrial products by removing a considerable number of goods from the quota list. Since every West European government follows its own policy on industrial imports and extends different privileges to East European exporters, the EEC members keep a careful watch to insure that an industrial product exposed to import restrictions in one country does not find a market in another country, which may then try to reexport it to the restricted market. The member states are obligated to advise the EEC headquarters about the opening, the progress, and the result of trade negotiations. But in the field of industrial goods the office has no control except to investigate whether or not a trade agreement is consonant with the EEC regulations.

According to the Treaty of Rome, the EEC countries were supposed to establish a common foreign trade policy by December 31, 1969. However, due to the complexities of intra-Common Market trade, as well as to mutual differences in interest in external trade, the Council of Ministers of the Six prolonged the transitional period until the end of 1972, when the Commission of Fourteen is supposed to become the negotiating partner on behalf of the EEC. Should the East European countries even then continue to deny formal recognition to the EEC, its members would still have to comply with the EEC position.

Some experts believe that political and economic developments in East European countries encourage the trend toward a common EEC policy as those countries endeavor to establish some measure of political independence and are in need of Western products and technology. These observers also believe that the entry of Great Britain into the Common Market will give additional support to this trend. They express the hope that the Soviet Union may acquiesce in this development if it is no longer worried about the German problem and if it can overcome the suspicion that the West is trying to bring socialism to an end. Others are less optimistic, pointing to the fact that trade with Western Europe is of great importance to the East but of limited usefulness to the EEC.[19]

It is when one begins to analyze the statistics of trade between the EEC and the COMECON countries that a revealing picture emerges, reflecting the real scope of economic détente. Non-communist Europe accounts for about sixty percent of total East-West trade, of which the EEC member states supply about one-half, and of this trade, one-half is carried by West Germany.

Growth in trade between the EEC and COMECON countries in the past twelve years has been remarkable. In the period between 1958 and 1966, exports from the EEC to the COMECON increased by 168 percent while total EEC exports to all third countries advanced by only 85 percent. Yet, even with the continuously growing participation of the EEC in world trade the COMECON market did not attract more than 5.6 percent of the total EEC foreign trade in 1966.[20] The year 1967 registered further growth, but the rate of growth

---

[19] See for example Jerzy Lukaszewski, "Western Integration and the People's Democracies," *Foreign Affairs,* Vol. 46, No. 2, pp. 377-387; R. Sannwald, "Die Handelsbeziehungen zwischen der EWG und dem Ostblock," *Osteuropa Wirtschaft,* Vol. 12, No. 2, pp. 97-114.

[20] CEE, Direction générale des relations extérieures, "Structure et evolution des exportations de la CEE vers les pays de l'Est de 1958 à 1966," 1/773/68-F, p. 1.

declined in 1968. In 1968 total trade between the EEC and the COMECON grew only by 9 percent as against 18 percent in 1967. The slowdown was reflected in an increase in imports of only 5 percent in 1968 against 12 percent in 1967 and of only 13 percent against 25 percent, respectively, in exports. But the year 1969 again saw an upward trend as imports increased by 16 percent over 1968 and exports by 14 percent.[21]

These figures, however, tend to distort the real value of the EEC-COMECON trade; it can be accurately judged only in relationship to the foreign trade within these groupings and to their trade with other countries or areas. As one would assume, some three-fourths to two-thirds of total COMECON trade is conducted within the communist countries themselves. A review of the decade 1958-1968, however, points to a decelerating trend in the past five years, with the exception of Poland, East Germany, and Czechoslovakia, whose trade with the rest of the communist bloc, in fact, shows an increase in 1968 over 1958. On the other hand, of all other COMECON countries, only Rumania experienced a substantial change in orienting her trade toward non-communist countries. In 1958 she imported from other communist countries 79.2 percent of her total imports and exported to them 76.2 percent of her total exports; in 1968, the corresponding percentages were 51.4 and 59.5.[22]

While the trade of the communist bloc is oriented inward, its trade with the non-communist world, though modest, is not without significance. Over a period of ten years, from 1958 to 1968, some one-fourth to one-third of the imports of the communist countries came from the non-communist countries.

---

[21] *Ibid.,* "Échanges CEE—Pays de l'Est en 1968," XI/7,316/69-F, April 8, 1969, p. 1; XI/116,243/70-F, September 23, 1970, p. 5.

[22] See Table I. A note on terminology: communist world = all communist countries = socialist bloc; East Europe = COMECON, including Outer Mongolia and Albania, though the latter is not a member of the COMECON.

All COMECON countries registered an increase in this trade, except for Poland and Czechoslovakia; Rumania's imports from the non-communist countries jumped from 20.8 percent in 1958 to 48.6 percent in 1968 and her exports grew from 23.8 percent to 40.5 percent over the same span of time. The EEC share in the COMECON trade with the non-communist world shows a modest increase, with the exception of East Germany's slight decrease and of Rumania's considerable increase.[23]

The communist countries play only a modest role in EEC trade with third countries. In one decade, from 1958 to 1968, the communist countries imported an average of only 8.2 percent of the EEC total exports and exported 9.3 percent of the EEC total imports. However, there has been on the whole a more or less consistent (with the exception of some member countries) increase in their participation in EEC foreign trade, although the growth has been unspectacular.[24]

When analyzing COMECON's foreign trade with the EEC in terms of its trade with all non-communist countries, one reaches the conclusion that the EEC has had a lion's share, reaching 40.8 percent in imports and 36.7 in exports in 1968. This was partly due to the high level of foreign trade with Rumania and to the trade between West and East Germany. EEC's role in Polish, Czechoslovak, and East German trade and in Soviet and Rumanian imports has been steadily growing while trade with Hungary has changed but little and with Bulgaria it has declined.[25]

When we come to a breakdown of the extent of EEC's participation in COMECON's trade with non-communist countries as compared to individual countries over the period 1958 to 1968, some interesting facts surface. For instance, in trade with the Soviet Union, West Germany and

[23] See Table II and III.
[24] See Table IV.
[25] See Table V.

France took a consistent lead in their share of Soviet trade with non-communist countries, with West Germany taking the front seat in most cases. However, in foreign trade with all other East European countries, West Germany's share was conspicuously ahead of not only France but also all other EEC countries. Italy's share of this trade has increased rapidly over the past few years, surpassing France in all cases except for trade with the Soviet Union and East Germany. It should be also noted that the Benelux's share was by no means negligible.[26]

The picture is much the same when one looks at the distribution of exports to the COMECON countries from individual members of the EEC. In the period from 1958 to 1969 (taking into account the years 1958, 1966, and 1969), West Germany's share in exports averaged 40.6 percent, France's 21.4 percent, Italy's 22.9 percent, and Benelux's 15.1 percent. While the shares of West Germany, France, and Benelux in EEC exports to the COMECON declined, Italy's share substantially increased.[27] The exports were, understandably, unevenly distributed, due to enormous differences in the size of markets between the Soviet Union and the rest of the COMECON and in ability to pay to exporting countries. Thus, at one extreme, Albania's share in exports from EEC averaged 0.5 percent in the period from 1958 to 1969 and Russia's share, at the other extreme, averaged 33.2 percent.[28]

East-West Industrial Cooperation

In the face of the continuing difficulties of East-West European trade, inventive minds advanced a novel plan for broadening commercial contacts designed to scale down the barriers created by the differences between the two economic systems: industrial co-production. All countries on both sides of the

[26] See Table VI.
[27] See Table VII.
[28] See Table VIII.

economic boundaries have worked with increasing intensity on this development in industrial and technological cooperation. Such efforts are not considered as a substitute to normal trade but rather as a vehicle for the modernization of trade relations. It is estimated that the number of industrial co-production arrangements has grown three-fold in the past five years, reaching a total of some 350-400 by the end of 1969.[29]

This industrial cooperation includes exchanges of technological and scientific information, granting of licenses, management services, West Europe's exports of machinery or whole plants equipment, credit arrangements, and even common marketing in third countries. The East European partner supplies raw materials, low-cost labor, and some equipment, and pays, instead of cash, by exporting to the Western partner finished or semi-finished products.[30]

As examples of this type of trade cooperation, France delivered to Poland complete equipment for a nitrogenous artificial fertilizer factory worth 60 million dollars; Italy constructed in the Soviet Union a huge plant for production of Fiat cars; France delivered to Rumania and Bulgaria equipment for Renault automobiles; a Dutch firm signed an agreement with the GDR for cooperation in technical development of coal production and its marketing in their own and third countries; Rumania and France jointly built a refinery in India; Hungary and West Germany co-produce some machine tools; Czechoslovakia and Italy established a joint stock company to sell pumps and similar equipment on the world market.[31]

The East European partners first had to swallow a bitter

[29] UN Economic and Social Council, ECE, "Supplement to the Analytical Report. . .," *op.cit.,* pp. 132, 133.

[30] Emil Benoit, "East-West Business Cooperation: A New Approach to Communist Europe," *New Republic,* Vol. 156, No. 7, February 18, 1967, pp. 21-23.

[31] Radio Free Europe, Research, *Hungarian Press Survey,* No. 1,885, January 15, 1967.

ideological pill before they embarked on these and other similar enterprises. Such actions are hardly consistent with their fundamental hostility to capitalist countries now investing in their socialist economies and taking out production profits. However, under the pressure of the benefits of the West's technological and industrial achievements, they managed to ease their socialist consciences, explaining that such technological and industrial cooperation was really an effort on the part of the West European countries to counteract the U.S. invasion of their economies, to avoid technological colonization, and to eliminate American hegemony, and as evidence of the West's desire for new markets.[32] The arguments have some justification. The attractiveness of the idea of co-production stems chiefly from the benefits the West can derive from the labor situation, largely free from the costly consequences of strikes, and from improvement in the balance of payment that facilitates further exports to the East. However, even with the technological and advisory services provided by West Europe, the quality of Eastern products suffers from the apparently inescapable problems of the socialist economy. It is said, for instance, that considerable quantities of the component parts of Fiat, shipped from the Soviet Union to Italy, were unusable because of defects. Nevertheless, West European officials, manufacturers, and observers see in the industrial and technological cooperation a promising aspect of economic détente.

Trade of the Four Powers with the COMECON

The trade of Great Britain, France, West Germany, and Italy with the COMECON countries requires special attention. First, these are the four principal partners in trade with

---

[32] *Ibid.;* see also Dr. Karel Černý, "The Trade Policies of the West Towards the East after 1963 with an Attempt at Political Interpretation," *Series of Studies, 1968,* Vol. 20, Prague, Institute of International Politics and Economics.

the area. Second, Great Britain, in contrast to the other three countries, is not constrained by EEC regulations on imports of agricultural products and it is significant to notice the differences in and the results of their trade; third, they are all engaged, to a greater or lesser degree, in pursuing a policy of détente, and their trade achievements throw a rather revealing light on the relationship between trade and political détente.

Analyzing this trade, one must keep in mind that these countries continue to trade very little with the communist world. In the period from 1961 to 1969, West Germany's exports to the COMECON countries averaged 5.9 percent and imports averaged 5.2 percent of her total trade. The United Kingdom's exports averaged 3.9 percent and imports 4.4 percent; Italy's 5.4 percent and 6.5 percent, respectively; France's 5 percent and 3.1 percent, respectively.[33] Still, all of these countries have demonstrated a lively interest in developing trade with COMECON.

The Soviet Union is a special case in trade among the four powers and the COMECON countries because of the attractiveness of its vast market. Great Britain has put particular emphasis on fostering trade with Russia. Nevertheless, although Great Britain took a consistent lead in the value of imports in the ten years from 1960 through 1969, her exports to Russia surpassed the West German exports only twice, in 1963 and 1966. France took last place in the value of exports in six of those years.[34]

British-Polish trade placed England ahead of West Germany nine times (from 1960 to 1969) in the value of imports and only four times (in 1962, 1963, 1966, and 1967) in exports. France, who has been greatly interested in developing closer political ties with Poland, took last place in imports

[33] See Table IX.
[34] See Table X.

in every year of the time period and placed last seven times in exports.[35]

Discounting Albania, whose trade with the West is entirely insignificant, in nearly all other cases—whether with Bulgaria, Czechoslovakia, East Germany, Hungary, or Rumania—the FRG (with Italy an occasional exception) consistently led the big four in both imports and exports. France usually ran last. Eleven times (out of 140 variables over the period of ten years) she was in second place but on no occasion was she in first place in her trade with these countries.[36]

The trade of the four powers with the COMECON countries grew in the decade 1960-1969 almost uninterruptedly. To continue to investigate the linkage between political détente and trade, however, one must note with interest that West Germany's imports from Bulgaria in 1969 were about three times higher than were France's; from Czechoslovakia five times higher; from East Germany (a special case) eight times higher; from Hungary three times higher; from Poland and Rumania twice as high; and from the Soviet Union one-and-one-half times higher. West Germany's exports were about twice as high as those of France in the case of Bulgaria, Hungary, Poland, and Rumania; five times higher in the case of Czechoslovakia; twenty times higher in the case of East Germany; one-and-one-half times in the case of the Soviet Union.

Some aspects of the trade of the four powers with Eastern Europe show common features. After the opening years, until about 1965, when informal trade arrangements had extended over a period of twelve months, they signed regular agreements, first for two and now for five years. Mixed commissions or other similar joint bodies were established to implement the trade agreements. In conjunction with trade

[35] *Ibid.*
[36] *Ibid.*

agreements, accords on scientific and technological cooperation were signed. Step by step, industrial imports were liberalized and up to 85 percent of all items were removed from restricted lists. In some cases, importing countries were granted credits up to eight years in order to strengthen their buying power. These moves, however, tend only to intensify the perennial problem of payments that almost universally show a balance in favor of the Western powers as they accumulate from year to year. To alleviate this problem, the four powers have been reluctant recently to expand exports and have encouraged imports through a policy of liberalization. This imbalance in trade has been caused chiefly by its own structure. Since the Eastern European countries need to import industrial products but are able to export mainly raw materials and agricultural products, on which the EEC imposes restrictions, one cannot expect a marked change in the balance of payment until Eastern Europe can place a larger quantity of industrial products on the Western market and until the quality of those products is competitive with Western industrial goods.

In the absence of a common approach to East-West trade and in the effort to expand their trade, the four West European powers are engaged in a lively competition. British exporters particularly are aggressive (and sensitive) in this respect. They recognize that British prices are usually higher than those of other competitors, product designs are not always up to date, and credit charges relatively high.[37]

As early as 1961, two prominent visitors to Poland, Czechoslovakia, and Hungary—Lord Boothby and Sir Leslie Plummer—were impressed (and probably shocked) by West German penetration of the markets of these countries.[38] A few

---

[37] G. F. Ray, "Export Competitiveness: British Experience in Eastern Europe," *National Institute Economic Review*, No. 36, May 1966, pp. 43-60. See also *Financial Times*, Special Supplement, August 21, 1968.

[38] *Sunday Times*, July 30, 1961.

years later, Lord Limerick, leader of a commercial mission to Rumania, remarked, "You can't get into any Ministry office without tripping over half a dozen West Germans who have probably been camped there since your last visit." [39] Poland is one of England's largest customers in East Europe, second only to the Soviet Union. Yet even here the competition is keen. Japan, which is far down the list in trade with Poland, has five permanent representatives in Warsaw and German is most often heard in the capital's hotels.[40]

Two spokesmen for East European countries have described their experiences in trade with England. Ivan Bashev, Bulgarian Foreign Minister, complained on one occasion that he wished British businessmen "could grasp the single fact that selling to Bulgaria is completely different from doing business in a commonwealth country." [41] A Warsaw official remarked, "The British are very conservative. You can't do business quickly with them on the telephone as you can with the Germans." [42] He failed to acknowledge that no East European representative would be permitted to negotiate a deal over the telephone. By singling out the West Germans, however (as is frequently the case with other West European exporters), he played upon England's feelings of jealousy and her competitive spirit. Nevertheless, in spite of the difficulties and complaints, British exporters have taken the lead in some sectors of industry, such as selling computers and aircraft to some East European countries.

British trade with East Europe will suffer when Great Britain joins the European Common Market, since it will then be subject to the same restrictions in imports of agricultural products as other member states of the EEC. This will inescapably affect her exports. However, official sources are

---

[39] *Financial Times,* November 18, 1969.
[40] *Times,* December 18, 1969.
[41] *Financial Times,* June 7, 1967.
[42] *Ibid.,* July 11, 1969.

131

of the opinion that the gains stemming from her membership in the EEC will far outweigh the losses.

One can point to some instances when political détente and economic reforms in East Europe have encouraged expansion of trade. For example, exports from Britain to Rumania in 1967 had nearly quadrupled from 1959, though it was still "only a nibble at a very large carrot," according to Lord Brown, Minister of State, Board of Trade, considering that Rumania's industrial production has grown 13 percent annually in the last fifteen years.[43] British exporters drew high hopes from the events in Czechoslovakia in the spring of 1968, expecting that the new political climate in Prague and economic reforms would turn Czechoslovak commercial interests toward the West. And, indeed, even after the Soviet invasion of Czechoslovakia, her representatives in September 1968 hastily signed a number of contracts with British firms. Similarly, high hopes for British trade with Hungary have been cherished since Hungary introduced economic reforms in 1968. Hungarians enjoy an impressive reputation as businessmen in London, where they were once characterized as persons "who go into a revolving door behind you and come out in front." [44]

In contrast with the Rumanian-British situation, rigid policies and subservience to the Soviet Union account for Bulgaria's small volume of trade with Great Britain. Under the 1970 National Plan, the Bulgarian government allocated only 13 percent of its total resources, earmarked for overseas trade, to business with the West, as against 25 percent in 1969, a move that led to increased competition for a diminished volume of trade. Bulgaria also discontinued the policy of grouping various industrial concerns into trade missions that had the right to deal directly with foreign companies and passed a law

[43] *Ibid.,* February 28, 1967.
[44] *Ibid.,* October 19, 1970.

132

giving the Ministry of Foreign Trade "full, definitive and strict monopoly" over foreign trade.[45]

As to France, her political leaders have demonstrated an intense interest in furthering trade with East Europe.[46] As one official source puts it, trade with East Europe is to France a matter of "faith." However, faith does not seem to overcome the reality of disinterest among both French importers and exporters.[47] As noted before, France remains behind other West European countries in trade with East Europe in spite of a favorable political climate. One can expect a change in the picture only if and when the East European countries are able to export larger quantities of high caliber industrial products.

The French press appears to be less concerned than the British press with their country's lagging trade with East Europe. French media publish strictly factual information about new trade agreements, whenever such agreements are signed, and they publicize statistical data about trade developments. Nevertheless, some reports are indicative of uneasiness about the small volume of French trade with East Europe in comparison with that of West Germany.[48]

The trade of West European powers with East Germany deserves special mention. Although none of the Western countries recognize this government, they are still eager to develop trade with it. This eagerness is prompted in part by the knowledge that East German industrial products are of acceptable quality, in contrast to those of the other COMECON

[45] *New York Times,* November 23, 1969.

[46] As an example see Radio Free Europe, Research Department, "Selected Data on Polish-U.S., Polish-French and Polish-West German Relations, 1963-1966," September 12, 1967, pp. 4-6.

[47] Ministère de l'Economie et des Finances, Service d'Information, *Les Échanges Commerciaux entre la France et les Pays de l'Est* (n.d.).

[48] See for instance the chart "L'Allemagne augmente son avance," *Le Monde,* August 18, 1970.

countries. On the other hand, lack of permanent mutual trade missions and the difficulties East Germans face in obtaining visas for travel to the West hamper further development of trade. Nevertheless, in spite of political obstacles, trade now takes place within a more stable framework. Until 1969, British-GDR trade was governed by annual informal agreements and negotiated by the Confederation of British Industries and the East German Chamber of Foreign Trade. In November 1969 a three-year agreement was signed, renewable for twelve-month periods. Since January 1970 England has extended to the GDR the same policy of liberalization of imports as she applies to the other East European countries. The British held great hopes for an expansion of trade on the basis of a visit to East Germany by the largest mission yet to travel there, in May 1970. They expected trade, both ways, to double by 1971. The London Chamber of Commerce was to establish a GDR Department and the East Berlin Chamber of Foreign Trade was to install a branch in Great Britain.[49]

France has proceeded along similar lines in her trade with East Germany. Since November 1962 French Commercial Services in Bonn have signed an annual "arrangement commercial officieux" with the East Berlin Chamber of Foreign Trade. In February 1968 the arrangement was extended for a period of three years, and France lifted all restrictions on imports except for those which apply to imports from the other East European countries. In January 1970 a new arrangement was made to cover a period of five years and in the spring of 1970 French industries established an economic office in East Berlin and the GDR a foreign trade office in Paris.[50]

Trade between the FRG and the GDR has by far exceeded

[49] *Times,* May, 1970; *Frankfurter Allgemeine Zeitung,* May 16, 1970.

[50] *Neue Zürcher Zeitung,* April 27, 1968; *Le Monde,* January 30, 1970; *Frankfurter Allgemeine Zeitung,* June 8, 1970.

that between the latter and the other West European countries; Bonn considers it an integral part of its *Ostpolitik* and it is, therefore, analyzed in the chapter on West Germany's political relations with East Germany. But even though the British, French, and Italian trade with the GDR is negligible in comparison with the intra-German exchanges, it has grown considerably. Imports from East Germany to the United Kingdom and Italy doubled between 1960 and 1969 and France's imports tripled; the United Kingdom's exports to East Germany increased slightly in the same period, while those of France doubled and those of Italy quadrupled, although England remained the leading exporter.[51]

The trade of the Western powers with East Germany is motivated by economic considerations. The Bonn government, which sees the GDR's market as its own domain, is sensitive to these commercial contacts, attaching to them political connotations. Bonn's concern stems from the fact that these contacts are exploited by East Berlin officials for political purposes. The British government, for instance, has for years been greatly interested in the traditional Leipzig trade fairs and British firms have consistently taken a leading position among Western exhibitors. (The French have shown less interest because they see the fairs only as an opportunity for signing short-term contracts.) In 1968 the BEA for the first time flew directly to Leipzig and a two-seat sport airplane was presented to Willi Stoph.[52]

At such events as the Leipzig Fairs, the East German newspapers give an enormous amount of publicity to Western visitors, trying to convey the impression that the GDR is an attractive trade partner and that it has achieved political respectability. Some members of the Parliament who have business stakes in British industry travel regularly to Leipzig, extend press interviews (at times highly sympathetic to the

[51] See Table x.
[52] *Morning Star,* March 11, 1968.

regime), and are received by members of the government. Needless to say, such political use of economic contacts is displeasing to the FRG.

A certain Rudi Sternberg represents "the biggest of these merchant adventurers" accounting for two-thirds of the total British imports from East Germany in 1961. "The whole thing is done with panache. Sternberg sails through the Democratic Republic in the only Rolls Royce ever seen there, with a Union Jack floating from its aristocratic bonnet." [53] He started with imports of potash and today is recognized as one of the leading agents for exports as well.

East Germany has propagandized for trade with England through various societies, organizations, and exhibitions, even the BBC and British newspapers.[54] When the *Times* and *Le Monde* published an advertisement about developments in East Germany, *Neues Deutschland* reported the "great event" as if regular articles had been published in those two respectable dailies.[55]

However one analyzes the statistical data, the results present one conclusive picture: trade between West and East Europe is growing appreciably in amounts but not in proportion to world trade or, more important, in proportion to its potential. In addition, the rate of growth seems to be decelerating—this despite the fact that the two economies complement each other and both sides have demonstrated a desire for an expansion of trade. However, this desire is not equally intense. The East needs the West's technology and highly sophisticated industrial goods; the West welcomes trade as any free enterprise system would, but the progress of its economy does not depend on imports from the communist countries. The East, on the other hand, has few options in choosing partners other than West Europe countries. Among

[53] *Observer,* March 12, 1961.
[54] *Sunday Times,* May 14, 1961.
[55] *Frankfurter Allgemeine Zeitung,* December 12, 1968.

other developed economies, the United States continues to apply an embargo on strategic goods and shows no active interest in an expansion of trade with the East. Japan's trade contacts are burdened by the problem of transport costs, at least to the distant area of Central and Eastern Europe.

How, then, does economic détente affect political détente or vice versa? There is no doubt that West Europe does not hamper trade with the COMECON for political reasons; nor does it any longer wage economic war with East Europe as it did in Stalin's time and until the late 1950's, when it adhered to the enunciated U.S. policy of embargo on many of the West's industrial exports. The COMECON countries, on the other hand, although not ignoring the political aspects of trade contacts with the West, are inclined to subsume them to the reality of their economic needs. One may say, therefore, that Europe has experienced for whatever reason an economic détente and if trade between its two parts has not progressed accordingly, this is due to fundamental differences between the two economic systems and what those differences imply in terms of production, trade practices, currency exchange, and marketing. The diluvial method of barter trade, which remains essentially the form of East-West European trade, is not conducive to further development,[56] nor is West Europe's discriminatory policy against East Europe's agricultural products.

When one examines the mutual influence of economic and political détente, the results suggest rather interesting conclusions. As shown above, West Germany leads all other West European countries in trade with the COMECON countries. Yet, she has had no diplomatic relations with them

---

[56] For instance, the widely publicized Soviet-West German deal in the spring of 1970, according to which Manesmann pipes are to be exported to the Soviet Union in exchange for Soviet oil, took months of Manesmann's search to find in West Germany an importer interested in Soviet oil.

(with the exception of the Soviet Union, since 1955, and Rumania, since 1967). Until August 1970, when a West German-Soviet Union treaty was signed, all East European countries, in fact, constantly exposed West Germany to vicious accusations of militarism and revanchism. In spite of this political attitude their trade with West Germany was eagerly cultivated and is still growing. Moreover, there was a widespread impression—and its correctness or error will come to the surface before long—that the Soviet Union's treaty with the FRG, which supposedly ushered in an era of political détente between the two countries, was partly motivated by the USSR's desire for a substantial increase in trade with West Germany. This would be at least one case when economic advantages facilitated a political détente. Similarly the Polish-West German treaty of December 1970 was expected to lead to an expansion of trade. West Germany's trade with East Europe is generally recognized as an instrument of her *Ostpolitik* and its growth as a result of her vigorous use of this instrument.

Rumania's remarkable growth in trade with West Europe exemplifies a situation in which a political détente encourages an economic détente; her independent foreign policy found a positive response in West Europe's trade with her.

The experience of France, by contrast, points to an inverse relationship between political détente and trade. De Gaulle was the principal protagonist of the policy of détente, and the Soviet Union and its allies reciprocated. Yet French trade with the COMECON countries shows a decline in growth and lags far behind that of West Germany.

Italy and Great Britain have not played a particularly active role, and their trade with East Europe, as a factor in détente, is inconclusive. The latter's trade has developed slowly due mainly to the lack of enthusiasm on the part of British exporters; the former's trade has progressed considerably, chiefly because of the dynamic approach of her industrial concerns.

All in all, détente in economics has proved to be valuable as a general proposition for fostering foreign trade, but it has had little influence on political détente, which is principally determined by political considerations. The market place is clearly one thing; politics is another.

CHAPTER 4

The Problem of Germany

THE problem of Germany lies at the heart of détente in Europe. Today, no constructive relationship between the East and West is possible without German participation.

During and for a short period after the war, and under the assumption of cooperation among themselves, the Allies had planned a quite different alternative: Germany was to be subjected to occupation by allied forces for an indefinite period of time; she was to remain disarmed, her industry stripped of armament production; her political development was to be kept under the watchful scrutiny of the Allies. Germany was never again to be permitted to endanger the national security of her neighbors, either to the West or East.

That assumption was an early casualty of the Cold War as the Allies began to compete for the industrial and military potential of the two parts of Germany. Today, except for the Soviet Union, the FRG is the most advanced economic power in Europe and, except for the United States, the most important military factor in the structure of NATO. The GDR, on the other hand, is the seventh largest industrial country in Europe, tenth in the world, and an indispensable element of the Soviet political and military strategy. Today West Germany occupies a central position in West Europe's development of a polity of détente, while the Soviet government, in its pursuit of its own design for détente, must constantly be aware of the special role of East Germany.

Today the FRG has resumed Germany's traditional *Ostpolitik* with great vigor and dynamism, the ultimate consequences of which cannot be accurately perceived at the moment. The term *Ostpolitik,* used daily in official statements and the press, is not a fortunate one. It revives forbidding memories of the same terminology, heard during each period of German expansionism since Frederick the Great: Bismarck, William II, Stresemann's revisionism, and the apocalyptic crimes of Hitler.

East Germany has her own concept of *Westpolitik,* the goal of which is to achieve universal recognition as an independent state. She has already established regular diplomatic relations with twenty-three countries, consular relations with fifteen, and trade representations with twenty-two.[1] In comparison with the FRG, which entertains world-wide diplomatic contacts, the East German regime has still a long way to go to reach its goal, but it has already achieved a respectable measure of recognition and should the two countries normalize relations between themselves, all other countries (including West Europe), would undoubtedly fully or partly recognize the GDR.

AN OSTPOLITIK

A stabilized relationship between West Germany and the countries of Central and Eastern Europe is essential to a policy of détente over the whole of Europe. This reality not only rises from such familiar concerns as peace, national security, stability and trade, but is also deeply embedded in history. For good or for bad, Germany has always understood better than any other big power the complex problems of the nations in this area, and their relations with Germany have been, in the memorable words of František Palacký, a history of contacts and conflicts.

For centuries the priceless heritage of Gothic, Renaissance, and Baroque architecture has come to Central Europe from

---

[1] In addition to diplomatic representation in all communist countries, the GDR has embassies in Iraq, Cambodia, Sudan, South Yemen, Somalia, Syria, Egypt, the Republic of Central Africa, Congo (Brazzaville), and Ceylon; consulates in Burma, Guinea, Indonesia, The Arab Republic of Yemen, Tanzania, and India. (Mitteilugen des Bundesministeriums für innerdeutsche Beziehungen, *Gesamtdeutsche Fragen,* No. 11, April 21, 1970, pp. 2-4.)

or through the German states; German philosophy, music, and literature have left a lasting mark on the region. These richly creative contacts have tragically and persistently been eclipsed by the conflicts, originated more often than not by Germany. No computer will ever be able to measure the enormity and the depth of suffering of the people of the East at the hands of Hitler's Germany, and this unforgotten trauma will assuredly haunt even Willy Brandt in his efforts at rapprochement. For even though some communist leaders and newspapers express an understanding for Brandt's policy, the memory of Nazi horrors is still there, ready grist for the communist propaganda mill, a powerful weapon in the hands of the Soviet Union and her satellites. Be that as it may, West Germany has certainly regained a position of power.

West Germany's *Ostpolitik* can be properly evaluated only in the light of the significant changes that have taken place in the last twenty years, not only in Europe and the world at large, but also in the international position of the Federal Republic. These years witnessed the period of the Cold War (1946 to the middle 1950's), peaceful coexistence (to the beginning of the 1960's), and its more constructive corollary, détente. The FRG has passed through political impotence, through immobility and disorientation, to become finally an active, powerful force in European politics. Its *Ostpolitik* is a reflection of these changes.

The Adenauer-Erhard Era: Inflexible Idealism

Konrad Adenauer's policy toward Eastern Europe was governed by the harsh realities of the Cold War, which affected Germany with particular intensity. In the first years after the war, with hatreds vastly aggravated, no one gave a thought to the possibility of reconciliation. Germany was an occupied country and her political moves depended entirely on the will of the Big Four. On the one hand, the Soviet government preferred to keep its allies isolated from the West, and its own position toward West Germany remained rigid and hostile even after it had entered into diplomatic relations with Bonn. On the other hand, Adenauer was not anxious to normalize his government's policy toward East Europe; he insisted, according to the preamble of the FRG Basic Law, that the Bonn government was the sole representative of greater Germany as that nation had existed within the boundaries of 1937. He also endorsed the Hallstein Doctrine, according to which recognition of the GDR by a third nation would be viewed as a hostile act by Bonn. This position not only marred any prospects of opening contacts with these countries that had no direct dispute with West Germany (Hungary, Rumania, and Bulgaria) because of their obligation to support the notion of an independent East Germany; it also further aggravated Bonn's relations with Poland and Czechoslovakia. Adenauer emphatically refused to recognize the Oder-Neisse boundary and as to Czechoslovakia, although he advanced no territorial claim against her, he was not willing to denounce the Munich Agreement. To compromise on these issues would have undermined his policy and weakened his strategy of forcing German unification through diplomatic pressures *before* an accommodation with the East could be considered and negotiated. He thus became and remained the prisoner of his own inflexible concepts. Moreover, he could not ignore the role in German politics of the powerful Union of German Refugees and Expellees who claimed the right to their homeland. Even his successor had to assuage their bitter feelings.

Erhard's government preserved the basic principles of Adenauer's *Ostpolitik* (the Hallstein Doctrine and exclusive representation), but it did shift the emphasis from outright hostility to the cautious opening of contacts with the countries of Eastern Europe. The general mood of East-West relations encouraged this trend as the Cold War slowly gave way to a "cold armistice" and later to proclamations of a mutual desire for détente. The official policy of Washington, London, and Paris continued to support the fundamentals of Bonn's position. However, as the Western nations—particularly France and Great Britain—showed such preponderant interest in trade and in the exchange of visits with the communist states, Bonn realized the danger of its negative stance, particularly that of being left behind in trade relations with the East. Indeed, Erhard launched a policy of "trade diplomacy," and in 1963 and 1964 trade missions were exchanged with all East European countries except Czechoslovakia.

In political matters, Erhard's government on many occasions expressed the wish for an improvement of relations short of diplomatic recognition, which in his words was "not at present an instrument [*instrumentarium*] of practical policy." [2] However, on the question of the Polish boundary, it remained adamantly opposed to any discussion before a freely elected government of a united Germany could meet with Poland at a peace conference. In the case of Czechoslovakia, Bonn was not willing to renounce the Munich Pact except to restate that the agreement had been "torn apart" by Hitler and that Germany did "not assert any territorial claims against Czechoslovakia." [3]

At the same time, within the Federal Republic, opposition elements, including political parties, business circles, and influential religious groups, pressed for a shift away from the immobilism of government policy. Some leaders of the SPD and FDP visited East European countries and subjected the Hallstein Doctrine to severe criticism. Industrial concerns became nervous about the unhappy prospects of French, British, and Italian penetration of East European markets.

[2] *Die Internationale Politik, 1965,* Zeittafel, Register, Erganzungsband II zu dem Jahrbuch 1966, Munich, R. Oldenbourg, 1966, p. 102.
[3] *Die Bemühungen der Deutschen Regierung und ihrer Verbündeten um die Einheit Deutschlands, 1955-1966,* Bonn, Auswärtiges Amt, 1966, p. 560.

In October 1965 the Synod of the Protestant Church published a long memorandum that approached the problem of German-Polish relations and the Oder-Neisse boundary in a conciliatory way.[4] In December the Catholic Church accepted an invitation from the Polish bishops to attend the celebrations of the millennium of Catholicism in Poland. Although the intervention of the Warsaw government made the trip impossible, the correspondence exchanged between the representatives of the church bore witness to the warm sympathy of German Catholics toward the Polish nation.[5]

The German daily press and periodicals opened a "great debate," advocating in general a fundamental change in the government's *Ostpolitik*. Even some prominent CDU members, sensitive to the danger of estrangement from the populace, advanced new ideas for Bonn's relations with Eastern Europe. Rainer Barzel, the parliamentary leader of the CDU, in a speech in New York in June 1966, suggested that Soviet troops might be stationed in a united Germany.[6] Two months later, Gerhard Schroeder, Bonn's Foreign Minister, suggested a veiled allusion to possible recognition of the East European countries in a carefully but artificially balanced statement to the effect that the opening of diplomatic relations would not imply giving up the principle of exclusive representation.[7]

For some time, Erhard resisted pressures from without and within his own party. However, on March 25, 1966, he sent a peace note to 115 governments, including those of Eastern Europe, stating that while his government still considered reunification its greatest national task it was prepared to make sacrifices to achieve this goal. He proposed to exchange with all East European governments a declaration not to use force

---

[4] For the text, see *Deutschland und die östlichen Nachbarn,* Stuttgart, Kreuz-Verlag, 1966, pp. 176-217.

[5] *Ibid.,* pp. 218-230.

[6] *Frankfurter Allgemeine Zeitung,* June 16, 1966.

[7] *Die Internationale Politik, 1966, op.cit.,* 1967, pp. 149-150.

in settling international disputes and offered to exchange observers to attend military maneuvers. The note addressed some special conciliatory words to Poland and Czechoslovakia.[8] The proposals signaled progress in Erhard's thinking, but they nevertheless met with opposition from the recipients. They came at a time when the Soviet attitude toward West Germany had once again stiffened; moreover, the peace note had not been sent to Ulbricht's government at all; and, in any case, it was considered to be too vague and noncommittal.

By the close of 1966, it became clear that Erhard's *Ostpolitik* had run into a dead end. The Western allies, busily engaged in cultivating correct diplomatic relations with the East European countries and broadening trade, cultural, and scientific contacts with them, lost active interest in German reunification. Instead of isolating the GDR from the rest of the world, the FRG faced the prospect of being isolated itself.

The German people began to realize West Germany's impotence in matters of European politics. Dependent on the United States, paternalized by France, neglected by Great Britain, checked by the Soviet Union, the official policy was boxed into a position of immobility. "Economically we are a giant, politically a dwarf," Willy Brandt had stated on one occasion. A general malaise, also caused by some domestic fiscal and military problems, produced some nervous reactions. One author pleaded for greater adaptability which ". . . is best defined with reference to the example of Bismarck." [9] Another publicist advocated a policy of German independence from the United States and of patient negotiations with the Soviet Union, concluding that "today, when [Germany] wants to overcome her division, she needs the

---

[8] *Die Bemühungen. . .* , *op.cit.*, pp. 559-562.
[9] Fritz Baade, "Neugestaltung unserer Politik in Nah- und Mittelost," *Aussenpolitik,* November 1965, p. 743.

147

opening to the East more urgently than in Stresemann's times." [10]

The references to Bismarck and Stresemann would not call up pleasant memories among students of European history. For Bismarck's fundamental concept was to keep France isolated, "the wires to St. Petersburg open," and to continue in collusion with Russia in the policy of the division of Poland. As for Stresemann, his policy cannot be reduced to the simple formula of seeking an opening to the East. He did not conceal that his goal was peacefully to revise Germany's boundary with Poland, and it became known after his death that, according to his diary, he "never thought more about the East than during the time [he] was looking for an understanding in the West." [11]

Clearly, references to Bismarck or even to Stresemann were out of date in the 1960's, due in part to the new political sophistication of the German people and in part to a configuration of forces in Europe far different from what was the case in the 1870's or the 1920's. Such allusions to these men were principally due to the general disenchantment of the public with Erhard's (and Adenauer's) futile attempts to achieve progress in Bonn's *Deutschland Ostpolitik*.

Public polls in West Germany reflected this change. In October 1954, 39 percent of interviewees had considered the West German foreign policy "successful"; in May 1966, the percentage dropped to 9 percent. In October 1954, 19 percent had expressed the opinion that the German position had "deteriorated"; in May 1966, the percentage rose to 38.[12]

The Kiesinger-Brandt Era: Adjustment to Reality

There is a certain wisdom in changing the leadership of any

---

[10] Paul Seethe, "Oeffnung nach Osten," *Die Zeit*, October 4, 1966.

[11] Gerald Freund, *Unholy Alliance*, New York, Harcourt, Brace, 1957, quoting from Stresemann's *Nachlass*, 3167/163659.

[12] Elizabeth Noelle and E. P. Neumann, eds., *The Germans: Public Opinion Polls*, Allensbach, Verlag für Demoskopie, 1967, p. 522.

institutional structure from time to time. The old establishment frequently runs out of ideas or it becomes a prisoner of its own fixed concepts, losing thereby at least some of the respect of its followers. The Adenauer-Erhard establishment was no exception to this rule. It took a new regime to create new opportunities.

The Kiesinger government of the CDU-SPD coalition, established in December 1966, inspired hopeful expectations for Bonn's *Ostpolitik.* The Grand Coalition came to realize not only that reunification can be pursued by way of a general détente rather than by isolating the GDR, but also that a rapprochement with Eastern Europe must be based on constructive proposals. One may safely assume that Brandt's membership in the government as Minister for Foreign Affairs materially influenced Kiesinger's thinking; Brandt's past record as leader of the SPD opposition testified to his advanced views about West Germany's *Ostpolitik.*

The new Chancellor's first official declaration, on December 13, 1966, struck a somewhat refreshing note. He expressed "a keen wish for a reconciliation with Poland" whose "claim to live finally in a state with assured boundaries . . . [Germany] understands better than in times past." He did, however, insist on the old demand of a reunited Germany as a precondition to a boundary settlement, which was in his opinion the only way to establish "lasting and friendly relations of good neighborliness" between the two nations.

As to Czechoslovakia, Kiesinger recognized that the "Munich Agreement was no longer valid." At the same time, he pointed out certain problems, such as his government's obligations toward the Sudeten Germans.[13]

In a general diplomatic offensive, Kiesinger's government offered the hand of friendship to the Soviet Union and the

---

[13] Kurt Georg Kiesinger, *Entspannung in Deutschland, Friede in Europa,* Reden und Interviews 1967, Bonn, Presse- und Informationsamt der Bundesregierung [n.d.], p. 4.

East European countries by advancing a number of proposals for improved relations with them.[14] The first reaction from the East was in the main negative, though subtly so. However, as early as January 1967, Bonn scored a significant achievement by opening diplomatic relations with Rumania. Separate statements issued by the two governments to accompany the official announcement about mutual recognition were meant to save face by reaffirming both Rumania's solidarity with the Warsaw Pact countries as well as West Germany's insistence on exclusive representation.[15]

Nevertheless, the event itself was of remarkable significance to both countries: for Rumania (which, in fact, had initiated the move on the occasion of the visit of Bonn's Minister of Economic Affairs, Karl Schiller, in Bucharest), it represented an eloquent manifestation of her independent foreign policy and a dissociation from the other members of the Warsaw Pact in their hostile attitude toward West Germany. For West Germany, it was not only the first breakthrough in her *Ostpolitik* but also clearly a relaxation of her hitherto inflexible policy.

Ulbricht was fully aware of this danger. *Neues Deutschland* first reminded Rumania of the agreement reached at the Warsaw Pact meeting in Bucharest in July 1966—that recognition of the two German states was a condition of peace and security—and then openly branded Bucharest's recognition of the FRG as "deplorable" because it had not insisted on Bonn's recognition of the GDR as a precondition.[16] After a flurry of nervous contacts with the other East European governments and an abortive attempt to convene a meeting in East Berlin,

---

[14] *Texte zur Deutschlandpolitik,* Vol. 1, Bonn, Bundesministerium für gesamtdeutsche Fragen, 1967.

[15] *Europa-Archiv,* Vol. 22, No. 5, pp. D 115, 116.

[16] February 2 and 3, 1967. For the text of the Bucharest communique, see *The Current Digest of the Soviet Press,* Vol. XVIII, No. 27, pp. 3-8.

the Warsaw Pact countries met on February 8 in Warsaw, where Ulbricht succeeded, with full Soviet support, in lining up behind his policy all member states except Rumania. This rebuff to Bonn nipped what might soon have been a *fait accompli*. In January a representative of Kiesinger's government had inquired discreetly in Prague and Budapest under what conditions Czechoslovakia and Hungary would consider entering into diplomatic relations with the FRG; even though they raised the familiar questions, their responses had not appeared altogether negative.[17] However, after the Warsaw meeting, all East European nations except Rumania resumed, each in its own way, their attacks on West Germany, insisting on her recognition of the GDR, on the principle of the inviolability of their boundaries, and on her acknowledgment of West Berlin as a special state entity.

Another meeting of the communist European countries, at Karlovy Vary, toward the end of April 1967, resulted in a declaration "For Peace and Security in Europe" that made the recognition of the GDR and the defense of its sovereign rights one of the main tasks of the struggle for European security.[18] At this meeting the Soviet Union, East Germany, and Poland presented a united front in opposing West German "militarism and revanchism"; Czechoslovakia and Hungary once again took a slightly less hostile position (Rumania, Yugoslavia, and Albania were not represented). A similar pattern was followed when the East European countries renewed their treaties of mutual assistance in the spring and summer of 1967.[19]

---

[17] "Eastern Europe and the Kiesinger Offensive," Research Departments of Radio Free Europe, February 4, 1967.

[18] *Europa-Archiv,* Vol. 12, No. 11, p. D 261.

[19] The East German-Polish treaty was signed on March 15, 1967; the East German-Czechoslovak treaty March 17, 1967; the Polish-Czechoslovak treaty March 1, 1967; the Polish-Bulgarian treaty April 4, 1967; the Czechoslovak-Rumanian treaty August 8, 1967.

Meanwhile, however, in spite of East Berlin's protests, Rumanian-West German relations continued a conciliatory trend. Brandt paid an official visit to Bucharest in August 1967 and on that occasion signed a treaty on trade and cultural contacts. The newly established relations were accompanied by some delicate issues. When, for instance, tourists from East Germany besieged Bonn's Embassy in Bucharest, asking for visas to West Germany, their applications were politely declined in order to avoid embarrassing Rumania. Thus, curiously, the principle of sole representation was temporarily shelved by Bonn itself out of consideration for Bucharest. In another instance, Rumanian authorities cancelled, apparently at the request of Ulbricht's government, an exhibition of books published in the FRG that included works by authors who had defected from East to West Germany.[20] Such episodes were indicative of the difficulties that West Germany was to face in her relations with East Europe as long as she refused to establish normal relations with the GDR.

Meanwhile, Bonn's repeated statements about its sincere wish for cooperation were ignored by the communist governments, which remained unimpressed even by Brandt's assurance that West Germany "always emphasized that [she did] not play the East European countries one against the other, nor [did she] want to isolate any country of the area— even the other part of Germany." [21]

In February 1967, the FRG government submitted to Moscow a draft declaration renouncing the use of force

---

(The Soviet-East German treaty had been signed June 12, 1964.) The texts of the treaties differed in some significant details, reflecting varied attitudes of the individual countries toward West Germany.

[20] *The Observer,* Foreign News Service, No. 24833, February 15, 1968; Radio Free Europe, Research, *Rumania/100,* November 17, 1969, p. 4.

[21] Willy Brandt, "Entspannungpolitik mit langen Atem," *Aussenpolitik,* August 1967, p. 450.

between the two countries and subsequently expressed readiness to enter into the same commitments with all other East European governments, including East Germany. The Soviet government seemed to be interested in the proposition, a number of diplomatic notes were exchanged, and the Soviet Ambassador to Bonn held frequent talks with Kiesinger and Brandt. The contacts were understood to be confidential until *Izvestiia,* on July 11, 1968, published one of Moscow's notes to Bonn, which then felt compelled to make the correspondence available to the public.[22] The note revealed that the Soviet government had attached to the proposed treaty the familiar conditions: that West Germany also renounce access to nuclear weapons, recognize West Berlin as a special political entity, invalidate Munich *ab initio,* recognize the inviolability of existing European boundaries (including the GDR's), and normalize relations between the two Germanys. In addition, Moscow, in an obvious threat, reminded Bonn of the Soviet right, under Articles 107 and 53 of the UN Charter, to intervene in West German internal affairs under the pretext of growing militarism and nazism on FRG territory.

After the publication of these diplomatic notes, the Soviet government unleashed another campaign of denunciation against Bonn's policy. Any further probing of the prospects for détente was suspended for some fifteen months, until Willy Brandt became Chancellor. One may speculate that Moscow's change in strategy was designed to divert Western Europe's attention from the mounting crisis in its relations with Czechoslovakia that culminated in her occupation by Soviet-led forces in August 1968. But whatever the Soviet motivation was, the disclosure of the notes triggered off an

[22] *The Policy of Renunciation of Force,* Documents on German and Soviet Declarations on the Renunciation of Force, 1949 to July 1968, Bonn, Press and Information Office of the Federal Government, July 1968.

153

intensive reaction in the West German press, ranging from exasperation and frustration to calls for patience. Even such persons in official positions as Defense Minister Gerhard Schroeder, who had previously advocated a policy of rapprochement, now maintained that hopes for an understanding between East and West had "proved to be illusory." [23]

Despite the fact that of all the East European countries, other than the GDR, Poland demonstrated the most uncompromising attitude toward the FRG, nevertheless West Germany was anxious above all else to normalize her relations with Poland. Willy Brandt again took the lead in formulating an *Ostpolitik,* but this time as Bonn's Foreign Minister. He spoke at the SPD Congress in Nuremberg in March 1968 about the "reality" that 40 percent of the people living in Poland's former German territory had been born since World War II and concluded that this reality demanded "recognition of, or respect for, the Oder-Neisse line until a peace treaty settlement." [24]

Chancellor Kiesinger, too, made a step forward as he called on "the Polish people and the Polish government not to reject the hand we stretch out to [them]" and, while admonishing Brandt for an "unhappy" choice of words, suggested cautiously to Warsaw an "exchange of thoughts" on a future solution of the boundary problem. [25]

However, profound differences, over and above age-old hatreds, kept the two countries apart. Poland is more interested than any other country of the area in maintaining a divided Germany. Her boundary with East Germany is not internationally guaranteed; her communist regime is shielded from the direct political influence of West Germany by the East German buffer state; the division of Germany eliminates the nightmare of being crushed for the fifth time between a

---

[23] *Le Monde,* July 9, 1968.
[24] *Frankfurter Allgemeine Zeitung,* March 19, 1968.
[25] *Ibid.,* March 26, 1968.

united Germany and the Soviet Union; and a divided Germany makes Poland a more useful and, therefore, more influential ally to Moscow. For all these reasons, Gomulka unleashed a ferocious attack on West Germany, identifying himself unreservedly with East Germany, his closest ally among the communist nations.

Poland, during the last twenty years, has not always taken such an uncompromising position toward the problem of Germany. When all interested parties were nominally in favor of a united Germany, Gomulka declared in April 1948 that "only politically naive people might think that a divided Germany [was] less dangerous than a united Germany. . . . A divided Germany between West and East means the unlimited power of monopolist American capital in the Western part of Germany, and that is a preparation for new German aggression." According to him, only a united, demilitarized, and democratic Germany assured Europe of peace. Ten years later, he still expressed himself in favor of a unified German state and considered it "a reasonable and just right" of the German nation.[26] But, when the Soviet Union opened a campaign for the recognition of two separate German states, Gomulka allied himself fully with East Germany, insisted with growing intensity on an unqualified recognition by West Germany of the Oder-Neisse boundary, and rejected Erhard's and Kiesinger's feelers for at least a discussion of the question.

In the spring of 1969 Gomulka unexpectedly struck a different tone. On May 17 he delivered a speech that received careful analysis in Bonn. He still repeated the old demands on the FRG, but he also recognized that changes in West Germany's political posture, and in particular Brandt's statement about the Oder-Neisse boundary, represented a step forward, the subtle indication being that Warsaw no longer wanted to identify itself with East Berlin's inflexible attitude. There was growing evidence that Poland was disappointed

[26] *Le Monde,* March 11, 1970.

with East Germany's sluggishness in supporting Poland's economic growth, a need that could be materially improved by increased imports from West Germany. More importantly, Gomulka could not be unaffected by Moscow's interest in direct negotiations with Bonn, to the disregard of Ulbricht's feelings. Nor, according to some analysts, could he ignore the danger of Poland's isolation as a result of her participation in the invasion of Czechoslovakia, a brutal act in which only the Polish and East German governments eagerly rallied behind the Soviet Union, the other allies being merely reluctant accomplices. Though he did reject Brandt's idea of respecting the Oder-Neisse boundary until a peace treaty could be arrived at, Gomulka did not close the door to further approaches.

Brandt did not miss the opportunity to slip a message to Gomulka through the half-open door. Characterizing his speech as a constructive step, he immediately offered Poland a treaty of renunciation of force and proposed to enter into negotiations on the boundary that would precede a final peace treaty. Kiesinger expressed a similar though more cautiously formulated view.[27]

Klaus Schuetz, Mayor of West Berlin and a leading politician in SPD, after an official visit in Poland, went even further. "The Polish nation must have the certainty that nothing will change in its own reality," he wrote, expressing the hope that boundaries would lose their current importance in a European settlement; meanwhile, West German-Polish relations should be improved "not tomorrow but today." In his opinion a legalistic position, based on the Potsdam Agreement and awaiting a regular peace treaty, in which no one is interested, had been outdated by more than twenty years of reali-

[27] "A New Phase in Polish-West German Relations," Radio Free Europe, Research, *Poland, Part II,* July 13, 1969; *Part III,* August 14, 1969.

ties. Such a position, he felt, only hindered the development of normal Polish-German relations.[28]

The three statements—Gomulka's speech, Brandt's reaction, and Schuetz's article—spurred another wave of public debate about Bonn's *Ostpolitik.* Some CDU and in particular CSU politicians were critical of Brandt's position about the Oder-Neisse boundary and rejected Schuetz's approach. The expellees organizations, as might be expected, took a negative position. The newspapers saw in Gomulka's speech an attempt to influence the forthcoming election campaign in favor of SPD, but were divided about the merits of the case. For instance, *Christ und Welt, Rheinischer Merkur,* and *Münchner Merkur* were critical, while *Handelsblatt, Süddeutsche Zeitung, Frankfurter Rundschau, Frankfurter Allgemeine Zeitung,* and even the otherwise skeptical *Die Welt* expressed various degrees of enthusiasm about the prospects of reaching an understanding with Poland. At any rate, the tangled and delicate events of West German-Polish relations appeared to be inching toward a denouement. Bonn was now ready to discuss the question of the Oder-Neisse boundary before a peace treaty was signed and Warsaw now separated the question from the demand for a recognition of East Germany.

The impact of this new thrust of Bonn's *Ostpolitik,* which had found expression in the Kiesinger coalition government from its inception, was not lost upon the West German populace. Public opinion polls indicated that an increasing number of West Germans considered the former eastern territories lost forever: in 1953, 11 percent; in 1959, 32 percent; in 1965, 46 percent; in 1967, 61 percent; and in November 1969, 68 percent. The same trend was registered for the Oder-Neisse boundary. The number of respondents in favor of accepting the present frontier rose from 8 percent in 1951

[28] *Die Zeit,* July 1, 1969.

to 26 percent in 1962, to 46 percent in 1967, and 51 percent in November 1969. In both cases, it was particularly those interviewees between sixteen and forty-four years of age who accepted the current situation. When asked whether they would return to the lost territories should they rejoin Germany, an overwhelming majority of respondents answered in the negative. The answer to the emotional question as to whether they liked or disliked Poles indicated an encouraging tendency—25 percent liked them in 1967 and 36 percent in 1969 as against only 25 percent in 1969 who "did not like them in particular." [29]

A study of elite groups in West Germany, made in the summer of 1967, gave support to this trend: 85 percent of the respondents either did not desire reestablishment or were more or less resigned to the loss of Germany's territory. More specifically, the recognition of the Oder-Neisse boundary was strongly supported by the academic elite (70 percent), by labor (58.3 percent), by significant minorities of journalists (43.5 percent) and members of miscellaneous elite groups (42 percent). Members of the Parliament, in contrast, were critical and cautious: only 20 percent of SPD, 13.3 percent of FDP, and no members of CDU came out in favor of giving up the land east of the boundary. Nevertheless, large minorities of SPD and FDP members of parliament (48 and 40 percent, respectively) were, somewhat inconsistently, of the opinion that "it would help West Germany if she would make territorial concessions [even] in advance of the peace conference." However, on this question, favorable reactions were received from only 18 percent of the CDU members of parliament. On the other hand, in non-political circles, 87.5 percent of the academicians, 46.2 percent of the students, and 71.5 percent of the members of the Curatorium for an Indi-

[29] Noelle and Neumann, *op.cit.,* pp. 482, 483. Some data were provided through the courtesy of Inter Nationes, Bonn, by the Allensbach Institute for Demoscopy. Tables 1, 3, 4, 5.

visible Germany favored such concessions. Curiously enough, only 25 percent of the labor group were so inclined.[30]

Thus, by the end of 1969, both the Bonn government and the West German people were moving toward a settlement of the problem of their relations with Poland. Concrete achievements, however, had to wait for the new government of Willy Brandt.

Czechoslovakia is another country with which the FRG faced a special problem. It is the problem of Munich, which for its signatories—France, Great Britain, Germany, and Italy—may be only a matter of history, but for the Czecho-slovak people it will remain a nightmare for decades. They will not soon forget the memory, the humiliation, and the lessons of Munich. Czechoslovakia insists that her govern-ment succumbed to the Munich dictate under pressure and that it never received a constitutional sanction. The Czecho-slovak government, therefore, demanded that Munich must be declared invalid *ab initio*. France and Italy satisfied their request by a declaration on September 29, 1942, and Sep-tember 26, 1944, respectively; Britain declared Munich null and void with the explanation that it had been violated by Hitler, but she has refused to declare it non-existent "from the beginning." Though this stand has not complicated rela-tions between these two countries, in the case of West Ger-many it became a real obstacle because Prague continued to insist on Bonn's invalidation of Munich *ab initio* as a pre-requisite to normalization of Czechoslovak-West German relations. Adenauer, Erhard, and Kiesinger, as was indicated, moved slowly toward the Czechoslovak position, but declined to meet it fully, asserting that such a step would open such delicate and complex questions as the citizenship of the Sudeten Germans, their military duty, property, the validity

[30] John W. Keller, "German Elites and Foreign Policy" (mimeo. n.d.), pp. 4, 12, 13.

of marriages, and many others. Since the government was under constant pressure from the organizations of the Sudeten Germans, some government officials stated from time to time that indeed the expellees could not give up their right to the fatherland and to self-determination. Even Herbert Wehner, a leading member of the SPD opposition, spoke in the same spirit.[31]

Nevertheless, on August 3, 1967, West Germany and Czechoslovakia at long last signed an agreement on exchange of trade missions—an event of considerable political significance. According to West German sources, in an unpublished letter attached to the agreement, Czechoslovakia conceded that, for the purposes of trade, West Berlin would be treated as part of West Germany—a factor responsible for the refusal of the Soviet Union to renew a trade agreement with Bonn. Though Prague declined to accept the FRG proposal to permit the mission to cover some diplomatic assignments, the mission was granted diplomatic status and the right to issue visas. In the last minutes before signing the trade agreement, a linguistic dispute, with a political accent, developed when the Prague negotiators declined to have Bonn sign the agreement on behalf of the Federal Republic of Germany (Federální Republika Německa) because it would have implied an acceptance of Bonn's position of being the sole representative of the whole Germany; it insisted that in the spirit of the Czech language the official name of West Germany should read the German Federal Republic (Německá Federální Republika). The problem was solved by using the

---

[31] *Wiedervereinigung und Sicherheit Deutschlands, op.cit.,* Vol. II, pp. 13, 40. For an analysis of Czechoslovak-FRG relations, see Eberhard Schulz, "Prague und Bonn, Politische Belastungen in Deutschtschekoslovakischen Verhältnis," *Europa-Archiv,* Vol. 22, No. 4, pp. 115-125.

term demanded by the Prague delegation in the Czech text of the agreement.[32]

The "Czechoslovak Spring" appeared to be a turning point in relations between Bonn and Prague. These developments in Czechoslovakia were followed with intensive and friendly interest in Bonn, but the charge that the federal government gave support to "counter-revolutionary" elements in Czechoslovakia, as Moscow subsequently alleged, is, of course, nonsense. Contacts between West Germany and Czechoslovakia increased considerably at every level—political, cultural, scientific, and economic. The borders' electrified fences and tank barriers were removed and the mayor of a Czech border town visited his counterpart on the other side of the frontier, the first visit of its kind since World War II.[33] Travel was free and Czechoslovak officials, scholars, writers, and artists made full use of the opportunity. One official, referring to Mrs. Brandt's visits to Prague for the annual music festival, remarked that "Herr Brandt would find and hear many pleasant things [there], more than just good music. . . ."[34] Indeed, rumors were spreading in July that Willy Brandt would shortly pay a visit to Prague, as the troublesome question of Munich appeared to be near solution. One German official put it this way, "If we can start negotiations with the Czechs from a zero balance we can, then, talk about Munich as non-existent."

Then, just as there was a chance to put Czechoslovak-West German relations on a normal basis, came the Soviet occupation of Czechoslovakia. Czechoslovakia's interests once again were to be subjected completely to the broader interests of the Soviet Union.

[32] Research Department of Radio Free Europe, "Czechoslovak-West German Accord," August 7, 1967.

[33] *International Herald Tribune,* April 5, 1968; *New York Times,* July 19, 1968.

[34] *The German Tribune* (Bonn), Vol. 7, No. 327, July 13, 1968.

Even after the invasion, cultural and trade (but not political) contacts between Czechoslovakia and the FRG continued for a few months. With the arrival of Gustav Husák to power in April 1969, the Prague regime resumed the policy of utter subservience to Moscow and parroted its campaign against West Germany. Cultural contacts were reduced to a minimum. The *New York Times* correspondent, for instance, reported that the Frankfurt Book Fair, which two years previously had greeted Czech writers and publishers as "political and literary heroes," treated them on the same occasion in September 1970 with "the mixed emotions often displayed to a fallen champion—respect, apathy and pity." Two German authors of reknown, Günter Grass and Heinrich Böll, who paid homage to the heroic Czechoslovak writers, spoke before an audience of barely 200 persons.[35] Even after Brandt had become Chancellor a resumption of political contacts with Prague had to wait until 1971.

All in all, an incongruous situation developed in East-West European relations. While the rest of Western Europe was engaged in fostering a policy of détente, including official visits at high state levels, the West German-East European contacts continued to be exposed to the lingering hostilities of the Cold War. This was exactly the intent of the Soviet government: to welcome Western Europe's initiative for a détente and to reciprocate by giving the appearance of a friendly policy; but, at the same time, to isolate West Germany and single out the Bonn government as the continuing disturber of the peace.

Kiesinger's approach to Eastern Europe produced no tangible political results (with the exception of Rumania), but it would be unfair to give exclusive credit for subsequent developments to SPD and FDP. The Grand Coalition had laid down the foundations for the current progress in West

[35] September 23, 1970.

German-East European relations. These were in part facilitated by Kiesinger's remarkable achievements in trade and cultural contacts—which have always been viewed by Bonn as avenues toward political goals.

In the interwar period, a most significant part of the export trade of the East European countries had been with Germany. It had ranged from some 20 percent in the case of Czechoslovakia to close to 70 percent in the case of Bulgaria. Under Hitler's regime, Schacht's "aspirin diplomacy" did "wonders" in contributing to the political dependence of Eastern Europe on Nazi Germany. However, this trade still represented only a small part of Germany's total foreign trade, ranging in 1937 from 1.2 percent in imports from Poland to 3.3 percent in imports from Rumania and from 1.2 percent in exports to Bulgaria to 2.6 percent in exports to Czechoslovakia.

The picture is not much different today. In 1969, imports from Bulgaria (the lowest in the range) accounted for only 0.2 percent of West Germany's total imports and those from Czechoslovakia (the highest) for only 0.6 percent. Export to the same countries, again lowest and highest, reached only 0.2 percent and 0.7 percent respectively.[36] However, even this trickle of trade with the East is not only a matter of German businessmen's traditional eagerness to penetrate the vast Eastern markets but also of the government's unconcealed instrument in its *Ostpolitik*. Particularly in the case of the intra-German trade, Bonn's offers to extend generous credits to the GDR were openly tied to demands for political concessions.[37]

In the period following the end of World War II and during Adenauer's first years, trade with Eastern Europe was practically zero. Later, particularly in Erhard's time, trade began to grow. Still later, developments in Eastern Europe—political

[36] See chart in *New York Times,* December 14, 1969.

[37] For a depth study, see Robert W. Dean, *The Politics of West German Trade with the Soviet Bloc, 1954-1968,* a dissertation, Graduate School of International Studies, University of Denver, 1970.

liberalization in some countries and growing economic needs in all—facilitated Kiesinger's moves to fill the economic vacuum. Because of attempts at economic reforms in the communist states, a more diversified trade with the industrialized and technologically developed West was necessary; the FRG became the leading prospect and before long the leading partner. Periodically, trade negotiations ran into the obstacle of West Berlin: was it or was it not a "separate political entity?" However, ways were found that permitted the Bonn negotiators to act on behalf of West Berlin.

Kiesinger moved swiftly to exploit these trade potentials. In January 1967 he lifted the embargo on several thousand items hitherto excluded from trade. The following July, the Western allies abolished the visa requirements for East European visitors to West Berlin. West Germany quickly saw an advantage in a new design in East-West economic and technological cooperation—the coproduction scheme—and joined with several East European countries in such mutual ventures as the complementary production of machine parts and arrangements to build factories for such countries in exchange for their products.

Between 1958 and 1969, the FRG led all other continental West European countries in trade with Eastern Europe, both in export and import; in only five exceptional instances did Italy take first place.[38]

In the period between 1960 and 1969, exports from East Europe to West Germany rose remarkably. From Bulgaria, for example, they increased by about 250 percent; from Czechoslovakia by close to 300 percent; from Hungary by over 200 percent; from Poland by close to 200 percent; and from Rumania by about 300 percent. Imports to Bulgaria grew by about 200 percent; to Czechoslovakia by about 300 percent; to Hungary by close to 200 percent; to Poland

[38] Office statistique des communautés européennes, *Bloc Oriental* 1-1969, No. 4, pp. 28-30.

by over 200 percent; and Rumania by over 500 percent.[39] In spite of an accelerated rate of export to, and a declining rate of imports from, West Germany, all East European countries continued to experience the problem of trade deficits. However, Bonn does not appear to be worried about this indebtedness. Apparently, with its strong economy it is willing to pay the price for the political effects West Germany earns from her trade policy toward East Europe.[40]

Tourism serves as another indicator of the progress of West Germany's contacts with Russia's allies. One must, however, approach statistical data in this field with considerable caution, partially because figures concerning travel from the East European countries to the West are for the most part not available, nor do the individual governments apply the same methods in checking the number of travelers. To the extent that information is supplied, there is no special identification of tourists. Instead, it includes all types of visits, ranging from official and business trips to truck drivers.

Nevertheless, with this *caveat* in mind, the effects of travel on détente must be considered, not only for its direct effect on economic aspects but also for its indirect effects in political affairs. Trips to West Europe suffer under severe limitations, for both political and economic reasons. Prospective travelers from the East are subjected to cumbersome procedures: as a rule they have to be invited to visit the West, and they are allocated either no foreign currency or only very modest amounts. Hungary and Poland appear to be more liberal, while Rumania and Bulgaria are rather restrictive in granting exit permits. Czechoslovakian travel had been spurred by a most liberal policy in 1968 and the first three months of 1969,

---

[39] See Table x.

[40] Pages 143-165 are an adapted and enlarged version of the article, Josef Korbel, "West Germany's Ostpolitik: II, A Policy Toward the Soviet Allies," *Orbis*, Vol. xiv, No. 2, Summer 1970, pp. 327-344. Permission is gratefully acknowledged.

but since then has become the most retrogressive country in permitting travel to the West.[41]

Statistics about travel from the East to the four West European powers—France, West Germany, Italy, and Great Britain—are too meager to draw any conclusions. We do know only that in the period between 1958 and 1968 the highest number of Poles who visited West Germany amounted to a mere 15,770 in 1967 and that the number of visitors from Czechoslovakia grew from 8,000 in 1958 to 37,000 in 1967, and the following year, due to the Czechoslovak Spring, it jumped to 62,000. We also know that, in spite of political hostility, the visits from these two countries to West Germany exceeded those made to Great Britain.

The picture is more complete and more telling in regard to trips to the east by citizens of the major Western powers. In most cases, West German travelers take the leading position by comparison with those from the other countries, with France, Great Britain, and Italy following, in that order. As to the individual East European countries, some 232,000 West Germans visited Czechoslovakia in the peak year of 1968; about 152,000 were in Hungary in 1968; 120,000 in Bulgaria the same year; and about 66,000 in Rumania the preceding year. Surprisingly, the number of West German visitors in Poland had fallen from 37,000 in 1958 to 23,000 in 1968.[42]

The East European countries earned considerable benefit from this travel, acquiring currency from tourism coming from all Western countries. In 1969 alone this represented an equivalent of over 300 million dollars. However, the West German visitors to Bulgaria's summer resorts on the Black Sea attracted severe criticism. They were accused of spying, provoking unrest, and attempting to discredit the socialist

[41] Radio Free Europe, Research, *East Europe/4,* October 31, 1969.
[42] For details, see Table xv.

166

system. A sociological study, undertaken in Burgas district, called for a struggle against "bourgeois influence" to which its populace was exposed from contacts with Western holiday makers.[43]

If tourists on the Black Sea beaches are sometimes accused of subversive activities, then cultural and scientific visits from West Germany almost inevitably carry political implications. These contacts were close to zero during the first ten years after the war. Hatred of everything German had produced even such absurdities as the elimination of even German classical music from the programs of some state-owned radio stations. However, historic ties cannot be ignored indefinitely, and since about 1960 these contacts have been cautiously resumed. Again, as in the case of tourism, no complete statistics exist about the number and purpose of the visits, and many scholars and performing artists travel individually and sometimes without any publicity. Besides, as a West German official said, "The number of students who come to West Germany on scholarship from communist countries is fantastically high—but secret." The reason for secrecy lies in the fact that the East European countries do not coordinate such programs and the programs could be endangered if their true scope were known.[44]

Information, scattered through the West German press, is indicative of a steady growth of cultural and scientific contacts. Thus, as recently as 1963, only thirty-nine East European representatives of culture and science visited West Germany, but the next year the number nearly doubled and the following year it rose to 276. By 1967 it had grown to ten times the 1963 figures.[45]

East Europeans have participated in West German book

---

[43] *Le Monde,* September 13-14, 1970; *Neues Deutschland,* June 18, 1968; Radio Free Europe, Research, *Bulgaria/5,* February 4, 1971.

[44] *Christian Science Monitor,* January 5, 1968.

[45] *Die Welt,* March 9, 1968.

and art exhibitions and in music festivals; they have exported films to West Germany and their literary works have been translated into German in growing numbers. Their compositions have been presented in concern halls and on the radio.[46]

In addition, contacts have been maintained through press reporters, athletic competitions, the exchange of trade union delegations, and youth organizations. Since 1964 the Bonn government and various state and private agencies have followed the principle of reciprocity, and the number of exchanges has grown steadily, though at a faster rate from East Europe to West Germany than vice versa. The latter continues to be hampered by political considerations. Even so, West German literature in Czechoslovakia, for instance, ranks second only to American literature.[47]

Kiesinger's Grand Coalition achieved an undeniable success in economic and cultural contacts, due not only to the systematic endeavors and interest of West German businessmen and representatives of culture and learning but also to the growing receptivity of East Europe. In politics, its achievements were more modest and during the election campaign such efforts were marred by increasing dissension between the coalition partners, the CDU and SPD. After three years of common efforts, the time was ripe for a change.

INTRA-GERMAN RELATIONS:
FROM REUNIFICATION TOWARD SEPARATION

Intra-German relations are to the whole problem of Germany what that problem is to the future of détente in Europe. West Germany's *Ostpolitik* has been motivated by a number of considerations, but a solution to the question of a divided

---

[46] IN-Press, Inter-Nationes (Bonn), *Ost-West Echo,* publishes regularly reviews of the West German press about East Europe's cultural activities in West Germany.

[47] "Cultural Relations between West Germany and Czechoslovakia," *The German Tribune,* February 3, 1968.

Germany is paramount in Bonn's concept of détente. It is, however, an equally cardinal factor in the prospects for European peace.

Many Anglo-Saxon scholars trace the origins of Hitlerism to the injustices of the Versailles Peace Treaty. Germany lost territories to France, Belgium, and Poland; she was stripped of colonies and ordered to pay heavy reparations; her conscience was burdened with war guilt. German people viewed the Treaty as a grave humiliation and retaliated, these scholars maintain, by giving support to Hitler.

The circumstances following the cessation of hostilities of World War II were entirely different from those of World War I, and it would be folly to draw analogies. One can only hope that the cruel experience of the last war and the political, economic, and social development of Germany since the war have imbued its people with enough political wisdom to give them a sense of satisfaction and national self-fulfillment anchored not in a desire to revenge this last defeat but rather in a dedication to peace. But the wounds of this war are far deeper than those from the last. Not only did Germany lose more territory to Poland, not only did she pay reparations, but she was also divided into two separate countries. Thus the motivations for deep trauma leading to emotional upheaval exists. This time, however, there are evidences of very different responses.

Reunification of Germany was for twenty years—from 1949 to 1969—the primary publicly professed goal of the governments of the FRG. Since the coalition government of Willy Brandt came to power, the term "reunification" has virtually disappeared. On the occasion of the signing of a treaty with the Soviet Union in August 1970, Brandt merely mentioned in a letter, addressed to the Soviet government, that the treaty did not preclude an eventual reunification.

West Germany's position on the problem of the division of the country has undergone a profound change—from open hostility toward East Germany to *de facto* recognition of the East German state, from the indivisible unity of Germany to an acceptance of the existence of two German states. There has been a steady decline in the interest and expectations of West Germany in reunification.

Conversations conducted in the spring of 1968 and 1970 with scholars, government officials, and young people appear to confirm this trend. They see the FRG prospering, free of social disturbances, politically stable, and enjoying the fruits of close association with the West. They have only a vague notion about their responsibility for their co-nationals in the GDR, and some believe that twenty-five years of its communist system have so estranged its citizens that they have lost their sense of identity with West Germans and their positive interest in reunification.

Even Bonn officials have stopped making stereotyped pronouncements on reunification. Such statements, after a quarter of a century of unproductive efforts, have lost both their conviction and their realism. As one official put it: "The separation is not an unnatural development. For most of their history Germans have been used to living in a number of independent states. In this capacity they served the peaceful purpose of connecting the West and East. When they were united, for a brief period of less than one hundred years, they brought only havoc upon themselves and Europe and the rest of the world. Now, we have peace and prosperity. Look at me: the suit I wear is from France, the tie from Belgium, the shoes from Italy; only my shirt is German made."

Yet appearances and trends may be misleading in any hard evaluation of the future. One reason for Germany's aggressiveness in the past lies in the fact that she did not experience an evolutionary growth of nationalism, a gradual maturation into statehood. Rather, Bismarck suddenly welded her together in the fires of three wars. It is therefore difficult to imagine that a nation endowed as it is with a unique capacity for orderly organization, with a long administrative tradition, with a high level of technological expertise, and with remarkable achievements in literature, music, and arts could resign itself for long to an imposed division in an age when a surging nationalism has given the right of self-determination to so many other nations, ill-equipped for statehood.

On the other hand, though many Germans still speak about a future federation of the two Germanys, it is hard to foresee any meaningful arrangement (one that inevitably presupposes such elements as a common foreign policy and a parallel economic and social development) between two countries that are by now so clearly identified with two different power systems, profess to two mutually exclusive world outlooks, and whose economies are based on mutually incompatible principles. Nor can one expect for a long time to come that one or the other part of Germany would change its system to such an extent as to make federation feasible.

Still, even if one assumes a certain stabilization of forces between West and East Germany, a sudden eruption of long-buried emotional elements cannot be altogether excluded as a possibility. Such events as an economic depression in West Germany or a brutal oppression in East Germany could yet unleash hidden forces that would shatter the foundations of the present political and economic structures and destroy the tenuous equilibrium of peace. Nothing in the current situation in the FRG is indicative of such a trend, but the enthusiastic welcome that Willy Brandt received from East German youth in Erfurt in March 1970 intimated East Germany's real feelings and the potential dangers to both the tranquility and the permanency of German division.

Adenauer's Strategy: Through Strength

Konrad Adenauer was profoundly convinced that Germany could be rehabilitated from the moral ravages of Hitlerism only in close association with the West. This Western-directed orientation would, in his opinion, launch Germany on the path of real democracy and a peaceful pursuit of her political goals. He therefore became a fervent supporter of every idea that would tie his country, at every level, to the West, particularly to France. He led it into the Council of Europe, the European Coal and Steel Community, the Western European Union, NATO, OECD, EEC, and Euratom. West Germany's national interests—political, economic, and military—are today identified with the interests of the rest of Western Europe and the United States, and her internal development has been a remarkable demonstration in democratic stability. This is the lasting value of Adenauer's leadership and his historical contribution to the growth of democracy in Germany and prospects for peace in Europe.

However, the coin of Adenauer's political concept also has an obverse side. Although the reunification of Germany was his primary publicly professed goal, yet every step he undertook in the process of integration with West Europe led the FRG farther away from his plan for reunification. His plan proved to emanate from wrong assumptions. He expected that the close cooperation of the West European countries and the firm ties of the NATO states would lead to such a position of strength that the Soviet Union would be forced to concede free elections in Germany. He refused to enter into any normal relationships with the satellites of Moscow, and he succeeded for many years in keeping East Germany isolated from all other countries. He did establish diplomatic relations with the Soviet Union in September 1955, because he saw in this move not only a confirmation of Moscow's responsibility for the solution of the German problem (and for East Germany's satellite status) but also because he intended to and succeeded in negotiating with the Soviet government the repatriation of German prisoners of war.

Legally, Adenauer based his policy on the Potsdam Agreement, which envisaged Germany as an economic entity and charged the Big Four with the responsibility of signing a peace treaty, sometime in an undefined future, with the freely elected government of a united Germany.

None of these basic stipulations of Potsdam were implemented. In the economic sphere, East Germany was treated from the outset as a Soviet satrapy; in the political sphere, every measure taken both by the Soviet Union and the West only deepened the division of the two parts of Germany. If Stalin had ever nurtured the idea of a unified Germany, as he publicly professed in a speech delivered after the end of hostilities, he appeared to have abandoned it some time in the early 1950's when domestic developments in West Germany offered little prospect for the communization of the whole country. All attempts of the Western Allies at numerous conferences of the Big Four and through a number of diplomatic notes to agree on the modalities and processes of free elections faced and were defeated by the unrelenting opposition of the Soviet Union, which insisted on exercising a veto power over the circumstances, supervision, and results of the envisaged elections.

The summit meeting in Geneva in July 1955 and the subsequent meeting of the four Foreign Ministers in October 1955 marked a watershed in the protracted attempts to solve the problem of German division. The Soviet government advanced the idea, which had been advocated by Ulbricht since 1950, that reunification is primarily a problem for the German people; to pave the way for free elections, it proposed the establishment of an All-German Council and the drafting of a new constitution by representatives of both parts of the country. The proposal was turned down by the West because it would have implied giving equal representation to the GDR and because the Western powers were skeptical that the Soviet Union would actually permit the last step— free elections.

Formally, the East and West continued to insist on the

173

validity of the Potsdam Agreement, still binding its signatories to responsibility for the fate of Germany. In fact, however, both sides have moved farther away from that Agreement's spirit as well as its letter. By the end of the 1950's, the
Soviet leaders demanded the recognition of two separate
German states and of West Berlin as an independent political
entity; the Western countries individually and collectively,
through NATO communiques, continued to speak in favor
of unification. However, their pronouncements faded into
empty phrases as they themselves became increasingly aware
of their powerlessness to reverse the tide of events. Thus,
Adenauer's fundamental assumption that he would be able
to accomplish his goals through a reliance on strength proved
to be an illusion.

The Bonn government has always attached importance to
trade with East Germany. Adenauer, though he consistently
pursued a policy of the political isolation of the GDR from the
FRG and the rest of the world, did not conceal the belief that
to him trade was a political weapon meant to contribute to an
erosion of communist authority in the Soviet zone of occupation. West Germany was prospering and her industry was
working at full capacity to provide for both domestic and
foreign markets. Adenauer knew that East Germany, on the
other hand, was in need of the advanced technology and
industry of West Germany as her own resources were depleted
by reparations due to the Soviet Union and Poland. He rea-
soned that increased exportation of West Germany's refined
products to a demoralized East German populace, with its low
productivity system and its labor and resources exploited by
the Soviet Union, would be a continuing demonstration of the
superiority of the free market society over the state monopoly
system.

But, as it turned out, there were many problems and few
substantial results. For one thing, the economic clauses of
the Potsdam Agreement were not implemented and trade

exchanges between the zones of occupation were necessarily on an ad hoc basis. The Berlin blockade brought even this limited experience to an almost complete standstill. Then, in October 1949 and in September 1951, two arrangements— the Frankfurt Agreement and Berlin Agreement respectively —established a procedure regulating trade between the two parts of Germany as barter deals, determined from year to year by quotas and balanced by a technically complex accounts in value units. The annual agreements on imports and exports were negotiated by the Trusteeship Office for Interzonal Trade on the part of West Germany and by East Germany's Ministry for Foreign and Interzonal Trade. The two agreements and the system of negotiations remain in force to this day.

However, interzonal trade during Adenauer's era, as well as during subsequent periods, encountered serious trouble. It was difficult to reconcile trade practices between a free market and state monopoly. Moreover, East Germany was in default in meeting her export obligations; this resulted, particularly since 1966, in a deficit in her balance of payments. In addition, political tensions, aggravated by intermittent crises concerning Berlin, inescapably affected trade. Thus, in the period between 1950 and 1960 interzonal trade increased five times and then, for the next three years, it dropped. For West Germany, with her worldwide commercial interests, such trade represented only 1.8 percent of her total volume of trade; for East Germany, however, it constituted from 8.5 percent to 11 percent of her world trade.[48] In contrast to other East European countries (and for that matter, all other countries outside the European Common Market) East Germany has enjoyed the privilege of exemption from the restrictive measures imposed by the Treaty of Rome upon imports of agricultural products to EEC members. This ex-

[48] *Neue Zuercher Zeitung,* October 22, 23, 1965.

emption stemmed from a special protocol attached to the Treaty that acquiesced in the Bonn government's claim that all of Germany must be viewed as an economic entity. East Germany has taken full advantage of the opportunity, but on the whole Adenauer's concept of trade as an effective weapon proved to be impotent against the GDR political armor.

Erhard's Strategy: A Long and Thorny Road

Chancellor Erhard's policy (October 1963 to December 1966) toward East Germany continued to pursue the concept framed by his predecessor. His chief goal was still Germany's reunification, though he recognized that the "road would be long and thorny." Within a broader context of Bonn's *Ostpolitik,* he developed some new initiatives designed to further undermine Ulbricht's international position. His moves were motivated by several considerations: NATO was undergoing a process of internal disruptions as protracted negotiations on a multilateral nuclear force in Europe (MLF) demonstrated a lack of coherence among its members on a number of vital matters of strategy as well as the degree of their continuing distrust of West Germany. France reduced her military commitment to NATO and her relations with West Germany cooled visibly. On one occasion, General De Gaulle questioned the value of the French-German Treaty of Friendship of January 1963, because "preferential contacts ceaselessly developed by Bonn with Washington have deprived this French-German agreement of inspiration and substance." [49] On the other hand, the process of liberalization in some Central and East European countries encouraged Bonn to attempt an additional isolation of the GDR by inconspicuous contacts with the other members of the Warsaw Pact.

Ulbricht reacted with a counter-offensive. Reunification, he

[49] *New York Times,* October 29, 1966.

stated, was not a national but a social and class question; he advanced the idea of a confederation of the two German states that would be based on an understanding of the workers' organizations in both parts of Germany and preceded by social changes in the western part. This was, of course, an utterly unrealistic proposition; Ulbricht was fully aware of its character. But he undoubtedly intended to compel the Bonn government to first recognize and then to reconcile itself to the existence of a separate, communist German state. Moreover, he answered Erhard's attempts to isolate the GDR with a series of notes, addressed to the United Nations and to all European governments, in which he asked for recognition of East Germany and then proposed that both Germanys renounce the acquisition of atomic weapons, disarm, and that Europe should guarantee German security.[50] In fact, of course, his regime was no longer as isolated from the rest of the world as in the first period of its existence or as Erhard would have desired. It had developed close economic aid contacts with some African states, and it had become an attractive partner in trade and in cultural activities with France, England, and Italy. East Germany was still officially recognized only by the other communist states, but she was well on the way toward international respectability.

In regard to trade, the Bonn government registered marked progress. Erhard's "trade diplomacy" reversed the downward trend in the exchange of goods and by 1966 its volume rose by more than 21 percent.[51]

Kiesinger's Strategy: Practical Steps

Kiesinger's Grand Coalition, composed of CDU/CSU and

---

[50] For the text see *Die deutsche Ostpolitik 1961-1970, op.cit.,* pp. 120-124, 134-137, 185-186, 200.

[51] For details, see *Statistisches Amt der Europäischen Gemeinschaften, Ostblock,* No. 1, pp. 5-6; Department of Economic and Social Affairs, Statistical Office of the United Nations; *Yearbook of International Statistics 1966,* New York, UN, 1968, pp. 294, 299.

SPD (December 1966 to October 1969), signaled a new approach to the German problem. True, it continued to view reunification as the cardinal task of FRG policy and it re-iterated its predecessors' stand on the Hallstein Doctrine and the right of exclusive representation. However, in contrast to the previous governments, its strategy as well as its attitude toward East Germany changed. It recognized that reunification could be achieved only with the approval of the Soviet Union and as a result of a general détente in Europe. It abandoned the proposition that reunification was a pre-condition to détente and could be achieved only as a con-sequence of the West's posture of strength. East Germany was not to be isolated, but induced into a closer association with her western counterpart by a policy of "practical steps," specifically by the lure of trade and cultural contacts. More-over, the inhuman separation of the German people would be alleviated by measures facilitating and increasing visits in East Germany. Brief visitations of Berliners had been granted be-fore by special arrangements at the Christmas and Easter holidays but, since 1967, they had not been renewed because Ulbricht became aware of their political connotation.[52]

Thus, in Bonn at least, a fresh breeze began to permeate the musty atmosphere of intra-German relations. For almost twenty years, the governmental spokesmen and the press had referred to East Germany as the Soviet zone of occupation, or Middle Germany, or the "so-called" GDR. Letters that Willi Stoph addressed to the Chancellor of the FRG were returned unopened. Kiesinger acknowledged the receipt of the letters and his answers were directed to the Chairman of the Council of Ministers of the GDR. The official name of East Germany began to be used by some members of the Bonn government and some mass media. Kiesinger advanced a

---

[52] From October 1, 1964, to January 31, 1967, 76,498 Berliners were permitted to visit their relatives in East Berlin. (Siegler, *op.cit.*, Vol. II, p. 219.)

number of proposals for the resumption and intensification of technical, trade, and cultural contacts, for dealing with the division of Berlin, and for the reunion of families. In August 1968 the Bonn government issued a permit for all East German newspapers to enter West Germany freely, without waiting for reciprocity, and it eased restrictions on the travel of East Germans. Bonn modified the Hallstein Doctrine when it opened diplomatic relations with Rumania in January 1967, when it resumed them with Yugoslavia one year later, and reacted to the recognition of the GDR by Syria, Iraq, Sudan, Southern Yemen, and Cambodia in the first half of 1969, not by an application of the Doctrine, but by calling the recognition only an "unfriendly act."

Then came the Soviet occupation of Czechoslovakia. The Soviet Ambassador warned Kiesinger that "no one will ever be allowed to break as much as a single link away from the community of socialist countries." When the Chancellor raised the question as to whether this included Bonn's peaceful attempts at reunification, the Ambassador retorted that the federal government would have to recognize the present situation in Europe.[53] This statement not only implied another reaffirmation of the persistent Soviet demand for recognition of the GDR, but it also meant that, according to the Brezhnev Doctrine, attempts at cooperation between the two Germanys could be interpreted as incitement to a "counter-revolution" in East Germany. In spite of these ominous portents, Kiesinger nevertheless renewed his proposal that representatives of both parts of Germany cooperatively establish all-German commissions on a parity basis to prepare agreements on matters of common interest, including mutual renunciation of force.[54]

Aware of Kiesinger's efforts by way of "practical steps" to make some inroads into the isolated fortress of his regime,

[53] *The Bulletin* (Bonn), October 1, 1968, p. 5.
[54] *Ibid,* June 24, 1969.

Ulbricht undertook a number of measures to make the fortress impregnable. In February 1967 his government adopted a new Nationality Bill. Cultural and scientific contacts were reduced to a minimum. New regulations on telephone, telegraph, and postal services made contacts even more frustrating than before. In April 1968 a new Constitution proclaimed the GDR a "socialist state of the German people." In June 1968 the East Berlin government issued an ordinance demanding presentation of passports and visas from all FRG citizens and West Berliners who wished to cross into GDR territory. In addition to the old demands for normalization of relations between the two Germanys, Ulbricht appealed to the working class in West Germany to join the SED in a class struggle against Bonn's capitalism, which must be destroyed before any negotiations on reunification could be considered.[55]

In one respect, however—trade—Ulbricht continued to cultivate contacts with West Germany. Somehow, even his ideological passion could not blind him to the importance of imports from West Germany's highly developed industry to East Germany's economic growth. Over a period of ten years, from 1960 to 1969, trade doubled in value, with a particularly notable increase in 1969.[56] Toward the end of that year, the two countries signed a long-term agreement that envisages another doubling of trade by 1975. In spite of critical political relations, West Germany remains the leading trading partner of the GDR, though other West European nations have also been anxious to increase their trade with East Germany. The Leipzig Fair, with a long tradition of international reknown, has for years been a place of competition among industrial concerns. West German firms first participated in the exhibits on a private, individual basis. In March 1967, however, the

---

[55] For details, see Josef Korbel, "West Germany's Ostpolitik: I. Intra-German Relations," *Orbis,* Vol. XIII, No. 4, winter 1970, pp. 1,053-1,056.

[56] Table XIII.

FRG Minister of Economics, Karl Schiller, urged business-men to present their goods in Leipzig and for the first time an offical of the Bonn government visited the fair.[57]

If statistical data provide a fairly accurate picture of intra-German trade and of the success of Bonn's trade efforts, one cannot draw similar conclusions about Bonn's endeavors in the field of cultural and scientific contacts. Official information is either not available or incomplete; however, it is known that the two parts of Germany have been engaged in arts and book exhibitions, exchange of films, scholarly conferences, and visits of theatre groups, orchestras, and choirs.

But the fortunes of cultural and scientific exchanges have been subject to the shifting winds of politics. In Adenauer's time they were almost non-existent; in Erhard's period they picked up momentum since Ulbricht was anxious to demonstrate that culture was not neglected in a country of former remarkable cultural achievements. When, however, visits of East German groups to West Germany (and vice versa) met with demonstrative applause from audiences, the Ministry of Culture in East Berlin confessed that such visits were "not safe." [58]

Kiesinger's somewhat conciliatory approach to the GDR encountered three difficulties in the area of cultural contacts. First, Ulbricht, aware of their importance, hampered the development of such contacts as a matter of policy. Second, as the number of similar visits from France, England, and other West European countries increased, many of them publicly praising East Germany's achievements, the interest of the government in cultivating such contacts with West Germany slackened. Third, the Bonn government, in reaction to the invasion of Czechoslovakia, cancelled a number of planned visits.

On the broader scene of personal intra-German contacts,

[57] *Frankfurter Allgemeine Zeitung,* February 7, 1967.
[58] *Die Welt,* February 3, 1966.

Bonn's official figures disclose considerable traffic, both ways. Since November 1964 the GDR government has permitted four-week visits to relatives in West Germany by East German pensioners: women of sixty and men of sixty-five years of age or older. According to FRG statistics, by the end of 1968 there were in East Germany over 3.2 million persons in this category and over 6 million visits were made by such persons to West Germany in the period between 1964 and December 1969. Obviously, many visited several times. Some of them—10,061, to be exact—did not return to East Germany. In addition, over 100,000 persons from East Germany traveled each year to West Germany on matters of business, for cultural and scientific conferences, and in sports exhibitions, etc.[59]

It is apparent that in the case of travel by pensioners the East German regime can afford this privilege because the visits do not entail the danger of defections that would drain its labor force and because they bring some economic advantages to East Germany. In addition, they alleviate to some extent the discontent created by the enforced division of families.

It is not generally known that about the same number—over one million—of West Germans visited East Germany each year in the period between 1967 and 1969.[60] West Berliners, however, were excluded from any travel to East Germany, with the exception of occasional visits on holidays.

All in all, however, the balance sheet of Kiesinger's policy toward the GDR is not too substantially on the credit side. In matters of culture, his efforts were entirely dependent on Ulbricht's political caprice. In trade, East Germany continued to profit from West German trade without permitting any

[59] Das Bundesministerium für innerdeutsche Beziehungen, "Flucht von Bewohnern der DDR in das Bundesgebiet," 11/3-35-214, Bonn, January 15, 1970, p. 1.

[60] *Ibid.*, 11/3-34-180, Bonn, January 19, 1970, p. 3.

tangible effect on her political stance. In politics, any over-tures from Bonn that would launch the two parts of Germany on the path to at least initial negotiations were answered in East Berlin by an ever-more-intense insistence on recognition of the GDR and by firm refusals to consider reunification with a capitalist, militarist, and revanchist West Germany.

In spite of the intransigent position taken by the East German government over a period of years, the West German government persisted in its approach to the problem of intra-German relations, as it was described, in an evolutionary way. This shift from Adenauer's inflexible, maximal demand for reunification to Kiesinger's strategy of "practical steps" did not develop in a vacuum; it reflected, though to a limited extent, the changing political opinions of West Germans themselves.

West German public opinion appears to have vacillated in its attitude toward the problems of reunification. A survey, conducted regularly by the *Institut für Demoskopie,* shows that over a period of fourteen years there has been an upward curve of answers to the question: which, in your opinion, is the most important question we in West Germany should at present occupy ourselves with? In 1951, a year of economic difficulties, only 18 percent of the respondents gave prefer-ence to reunification, giving a top priority (45 percent) to economic problems. Later, the percentage indicating reuni-fication as of the highest priority varied from 23 in 1952 to the high point of 47 in 1965. In 1969 it dropped to 44 per-cent. Curiously, the perservation of peace and East-West détente was rated most important by a rather small but fairly steady minority ranging between 10 percent (1965) and 26 percent (1962).[61]

In 1956 the partition of Germany was considered "intoler-

[61] Noelle and Neumann, *op.cit.,* p. 459; *The Bulletin* (Bonn), June 18, 1969.

able" by 52 percent; in 1962 by 61 percent; and in 1963 by 53 percent.[62] Then, a sudden drop occurred: in 1965 the proportion finding it intolerable declined to 38 percent, and in 1966 to 26 percent.[63]

Between 1952 and 1965 about half of the respondents believed that reunification would be achieved by peaceful means, and around 40 percent were of the opinion that there was no prospect of reunification.[64] In the period between 1952 and 1959 the majority thought security vis-à-vis the Russians was more important than German unity.[65]

In 1966 only one-tenth of the population considered recognition of East Germany "unavoidable" as a means to unification, and the thesis that unification would come through a hardline policy was supported by only 19 percent. In the fall of 1967, 90 percent of the population were in favor of initiating and continuing direct negotiations with the GDR; 50 percent expressed the belief that one day the GDR would be recognized by the FRG, and 53 percent expected reunification within thirty years.[66]

Another study, undertaken in the summer of 1967 and concerned with the attitude of German elite groups, showed that an overwhelming majority agreed that reunification depended on better relations with the Soviet Union and East European states. Some 90 percent, on the other hand, attached as much importance to defense as to détente. A majority favored an economic union between East and West Germany (with the exception of a strong CDU opposition), and all categories of respondents favored an exchange of

[62] *Ibid.*, p. 460.
[63] *Die Zeit,* March 28, 1967.
[64] Noelle and Neumann, *op.cit.*, p. 461.
[65] *Ibid.*, p. 462.
[66] *Deutsche Presse-Agentur,* December 7, 1967.

speakers, representing the various political parties, between the two countries.[67]

As moods changed and policies shifted over the years, the questions submitted to the interviewees also changed, and the answers reflected an awareness of the realities of the situation on the part of West Germans. Such questions as whether they gave preference to economic problems over reunification disappeared from the surveys for the obvious reason that the booming economy was no longer a problem as compared to that of the unsolved division of Germany. Nor was it considered necessary to repeat the question of whether the respondents considered the partition of Germany intolerable; quite obviously it had become a fact of life. Instead, they were asked whether they believed that they would live to see reunification. In November 1967, 49 percent answered the question in the negative and 21 percent in the positive. Two years later, 62 percent replied in the negative and 11 percent in the positive. When asked whether they would prefer to wait fifty years for unification without a détente in Europe, or whether they would prefer not to wait any longer and recognize the existence of two German states, thus gaining a general détente, an increasing number expressed themselves in favor of the latter: 36 percent in November 1967, and 50 percent in November 1969; 34 percent and 24 percent respectively preferred to wait. In a similar vein, an increasing number of respondents were in favor of recognizing the GDR as a state: 27 percent in November 1967, and 34 percent in March 1969; though, surprisingly enough, two months later, in May 1969, the percentage dropped to 28. However, a considerable majority continued to be against formal recognition: 61 percent

[67] John W. Keller, *op.cit.*, pp. 9, 11. Pages 184-186 are taken in a slightly adapted form from Josef Korbel, "West Germany's Ostpolitik: I," *op.cit.*, pp. 1,062-1,063. Permission is gratefully acknowledged.

185

in November 1967, 57 percent in March, and 52 percent in May 1969.[68]

Thus it appears that by the end of 1969 the majority of West Germans, if not reconciled, could see no viable alternative to an indefinite existence of two German states and, for the benefit to a détente in Europe, they were not willing to press for reunification. At the same time, however, an even larger majority was not yet ready to go as far as full recognition of East Germany as a state. This position was taken just at a most important juncture of German contemporary history, when Willy Brandt advanced the idea of "two German states of one German nation."

Nor did the German people believe any longer that the Western big powers were in favor of reunification. According to the polls, in 1955, 58 percent felt that the United States desired reunification and 10 percent felt she wished to prevent it. As to Great Britain, the percentages were 36 and 20; in the case of France, they were (without illusion) 15 and 50. When asked in November 1969 whether they believed that these powers were in favor of reunification, there was a marked change. Thirty seven percent of the respondents thought the United States favored reunification and 42 percent thought it did not. As to Great Britain, the percentages were 32 and 43; as to France (with some illusion and strangely enough), 28 and 50, respectively.[69]

Aware of this change in German public opinion, the coalition of SPD-FDP, established in October 1969, opened an entirely novel chapter in Bonn's *Ostpolitik* in general and in its policy toward the GDR in particular. Whether it succeeds or fails—and its effects will mature only after several years— Brandt's policy is undoubtedly one of historical significance.

---

[68] Data supplied through the courtesy of Inter Nationes by the Allensbach Institute for Demoscopy, Tables 7, 9, 11.

[69] *Ibid.*, Table 8; Noelle and Neumann, *op.cit.*, p. 463.

CHAPTER 5

Brandt's Detente

THE new coalition government brought to an end the dream of reunification that had persisted for twenty long years. In place of the illusion, it substituted the reality of a policy of reconciliation.

Neither Willy Brandt nor Walter Scheel, the leader of the FDP, were to be embarrassed by their past when they inaugurated their new version of *Ostpolitik,* which differed materially from their CDU/CSU predecessors. The SPD, as the opposition party, had been against rearmament of the FRG and its membership in NATO, convinced as it was that these steps would hamper efforts for reunification. In March 1959 it published its own plan for reunification, which resembled in many aspects Ulbricht's proposals, including reduction of armaments, denuclearization of both parts of Germany, and their mutual withdrawal from NATO and the Warsaw Pact.[1] However, after the Berlin Wall had been constructed, the SPD renounced its plan and basically approved the CDU Western oriented policy.

On the other hand, in the belief that its progressive domestic program would not be entirely repulsive to the SED, it sought to maintain contacts by an exchange of views between the two parties. Toward the end of 1964 it published a program proposing a solution of such practical questions as visits, local traffic, and exchange of newspapers. Then, in the spring of 1966, it engaged in correspondence with the SED, this time at the latter's initiative, in an attempt to arrange two meetings, one in Hanover and another at Karl-Marx-Stadt, but the plan was called off by Ulbricht.[2]

When the SPD formed a coalition government with the

[1] Siegler, Vol. 1, *op.cit.,* pp. 322-325.
[2] For the text of the letters, see *Die Internationale Politik, 1966, op.cit.,* 1967, pp. D 177-188.

CDU in December 1966, its leaders immediately proposed some fresh ideas about intra-German relations. Brandt was regularly one step ahead of Kiesinger, much to the latter's displeasure, and Herbert Wehner, Minister for All-German Affairs, was, probably by mutual agreement, one step ahead of even Willy Brandt.

Soon after the new government had taken over, Wehner declared that people in the other part of Germany had the right to determine their social system and, should the GDR government "receive from the people a democratic mandate" on the basis of "free and secret elections," he did not see any "reason why the Federal government could not reconsider its currently justifiable policy of non-recognition." [3] The call for free and secret elections was, of course, more of a gambit than an expectation, but it was subsequently modified when Wehner stated that he would be satisfied even with elections modeled after those of Yugoslavia.[4] Brandt himself, toward the end of 1967, questioned the wisdom of Bonn's stand on its exclusive right of representing the whole German nation and urged the government to start "from the current facts," such as "an existing government" in East Berlin.[5]

At its annual congress, in March 1968, the SPD advocated the policy of bilateral and multilateral cooperation in Europe, with the goal of establishing a new security system in Europe without, however, disturbing the balance of power. It was in favor of negotiations with East Germany, maintaining, however, that both parts of Germany belonged to one nation and, therefore, could not treat each other as foreign countries.[6] Brandt alluded for the first time publicly (he had been saying it privately since 1964) to the theory of two German states of one German nation. The logical consequence of this posi-

---

[3] *Europa-Archiv,* January 10, 1967, p. 3.
[4] *Washington Post,* February 1, 1967.
[5] *Frankfurter Rundschau,* November 15, 1967.
[6] *Die deutsche Ostpolitik 1961-1970, op.cit.,* pp. 245-247.

tion was, as he put it, that "Bonn has taken cognizance of the existence of the GDR" and was ready to enter into various engagements with it but it "would not recognize, even in one-hundred years that the Germans on the other side [were] anything else than Germans. They don't belong to another nation. . . ." [7]

The FDP's position developed along analogous lines. Originally, it advocated a policy of bilateral talks with the Soviet Union and disengagement from the West. By 1962 it fully subscribed to West Germany's integration with the West, but in 1965 Erich Mende, then the Chairman of the FDP and a member of the government, reminded his CDU senior partner in the government that for years the FDP had been in favor of full diplomatic relations with the East European countries and against a strict implementation of the Hallstein Doctrine. [8]

During the election campaign in 1969, the positions of the contending parties were further clarified, but they also became mutually inflexible. The CDU/CSU, although taking a positive stand on questions of *Ostpolitik*, was cautious and, addressing itself particularly to conservative voters, it stressed the need for West German security, which in its view was being threatened by the East. The SPD, on the other hand, spoke about "regulated coexistence" with East Germany and normalization of relations with all East European countries. The FDP advanced some even more specific ideas, such as a complete abolition of the Hallstein Doctrine and renunciation by the Federal Republic of the right of sole representation of the whole German nation. "No German territorial claims must be allowed to stand in the way of a peaceful order between East and West Europe," stated one of its proclamations. [9] Representatives of the two parties made unofficial trips

---

[7] *Le Monde,* July 7, 1968.

[8] Siegler, Vol. ii, *op.cit.,* pp. 66-67.

[9] *German International* (Bonn), July 7, 1969, p. 15.

to Moscow during the campaign while Kiesinger declined an invitation for a similar visit.

The Soviet press did not conceal its bias about the course of the campaign. It referred to the process of "progressive" forces in West Germany, separating them from "capitalist" and "imperialist" elements. The Soviet government gallantly sent to the socialist President of the FRG, Gustav Heinemann, on the occasion of his seventieth birthday, fifty red roses, caviar, Crimean champagne, and vodka.[10]

When the two parties, the SPD and FDP, won a majority of the votes (though a slim one), it was then possible to form a new government and to begin the business of giving Bonn's *Ostpolitik* a new look.

Two States, One Nation

For the first time since the foundation of the Federal Republic of Germany and, in fact, since the early interwar period, the Chancellorship passed into the hands of the Social Democratic Party. Assisted by its junior partner in the coalition, the Free Democratic Party, it moved with impressive speed to implement its political program. In his first declaration before the *Bundestag* on October 28, 1969, Brandt outlined in rather concrete terms the government's foreign policy. Without mentioning reunification, on which every preceding government had insisted as its primary goal, he spoke about the preservation of the "coherence of the German nation" and expressed the conviction "that the Germans [had] a right to self-determination just as any other nation," and that "this right and the will to defend it are not negotiable." However, he recognized the existence of two German states and wished to achieve a regular *modus vivendi* between them, without discrimination on either side. This, he hoped, would lead "to contractually agreed cooperation." Nevertheless, he declared,

---

[10] *New York Times,* July 29, 1969.

"international recognition of the GDR by the Federal Republic is out of the question," since the two Germanys "are not foreign countries to each other; their relations with each other can only be of a special nature." He reiterated the old offer to sign a treaty on renunciation of force with West Germany's neighbors to the East, including the GDR, and stressed the government's respect for territorial integrity. In the light of this new concept of a new relationship between the two Germanys, he announced that the Ministry for All-German Affairs had been renamed the Ministry for Intra-German Relations. On a broader scene, among other matters, he emphasized Bonn's firm solidarity with NATO, its close relations with the United States, and expressed the intention to open negotiations very soon with the Soviet Union and Poland.[11]

The Declaration obviated the Hallstein Doctrine and Bonn's previous insistence on being the sole representative of the whole German nation. According to *Neues Deutschland,* the new Foreign Minister, Walter Scheel, sent to all West German embassies an instruction indicating that the recognition of the GDR was no longer to be considered by Bonn as an "unfriendly act" but only a move that should be discouraged in that it would interfere with intra-German relations.[12]

The significance of Brandt's program was not lost on East European governments. Brezhnev had already called the result of the West German elections an "unambiguous success," and the whole East saw in the new Bonn government an opportunity for progress in normalizing their relations with the FRG. East Germany was the sole exception, for Ulbricht

[11] *The Bulletin* (Bonn), Vol. 17, No. 39, November 4, 1969. A Supplement, p. 3, 11. For the text of the Declaration, see *Texte zur Deutschlandpolitik, op.cit.,* Vol. IV, pp. 9-40.
[12] Radio Free Europe, Research, *GDR,* November 5, 1969. Also see *Bulletin* (Bonn), No. 134, November 5, 1969, p. 1,141.

feared such actions would weaken his position. After the elections he still maintained that nothing had changed in the policy of the capitalist and revanchist Germany; he continued to insist on "full, internationally legal recognition" of the GDR. He branded Brandt's formula on two German states of one German nation as a "mischievous maneuver." However, exposed to the danger of isolation from his allies and acting undoubtedly under Moscow's pressure, he later reluctantly recognized that some positive changes had occurred in West German policy and expressed readiness to enter into negotiations with Bonn. But this attitude was by no means the end of his struggle for the international recognition of East Germany.[13]

Meanwhile, the new government in Bonn developed a feverish activity that has no parallel in contemporary diplomatic history. It entered simultaneously into negotiations with the Soviet Union, Poland, and the GDR. As expected, these negotiations were closely interconnected, but the key to their progress was to be found in Moscow.

Bonn-Moscow Reconciliation

Before the end of 1969, only six weeks after his government had been installed, Brandt renewed his predecessors' offer to sign a treaty with the Soviet Union on the renunciation of force. Brandt's close associate, State Secretary (*Staatssekretär*) Egon Bahr held thirteen meetings with Gromyko out of which came what was to be known as the "Bahr Paper." It was to serve as a basis for the envisaged treaty. *Bild Zeitung,* a paper that belongs to Springer's newspaper chain, which was highly critical of Brandt's *Ostpolitik,* published the confidential document at the beginning of June,

---

[13] East Germany's position on Brandt's policy is explained in detail in Ulbricht's speech at the meeting of the Central Committee of the SED, delivered December 12, 1969. (*Texte zur Deutschlandpolitik, op.cit.,* Vol. IV, pp. 96-142.)

triggering off an intensified campaign by the CDU/CSU opposition against the government. They had criticized Brandt's program from its inception, objecting to the fact that it omitted the goal of reunification, was vague on the question of self-determination, implied recognition of East Germany, did not seek sufficient assurances on the future of West Berlin, did not mention a possible elimination of sanctions against West Germany according to articles 52 and 107 of the UN Charter, and weakened the NATO alliance.[14] The Bahr Paper confirmed the opposition's worst suspicions. Its intent went far beyond the strictly bilateral questions of Soviet-West German relations, dealing also with the old Soviet demands on boundaries and on East Germany. It was more significant in what it failed to include than what it contained. The criticism was only heightened when *Die Welt,* another spring paper, published next to the Bahr Paper what was alleged to be a "Gromyko Paper," which differed in some substantial points from the Bahr document.[15] However, the government denied the existence of such a paper.

The Bahr Paper was published on the eve of the elections in three states, North Westphalia, Lower Saxony, and the Saarland, presumably to influence their outcome. Indeed, the Foreign Minister Scheel's FDP suffered a serious defeat, failing to qualify in two states for representation in the local legislature. However, at the congress of the party, held a few days later, Scheel won a vote of confidence. A failure would have seriously threatened both Brandt's policy and even the existence of his coalition government, which could not exist without the support of FDP. Even so, three members later defected and Brandt's majority became precarious indeed. However, he was not deterred from audaciously pursuing his

---

[14] For the statements of Rainer Barzel in the *Bundestag,* see *Texte zur Deutschlandpolitik, op.cit.,* Vol. IV, pp. 74-85; of Kurt Kiesinger, *ibid.,* Vol. V, pp. 222-232.

[15] July 23, 1970.

goal, despite growing problems that were not limited to domestic opposition.

Though the Western powers officially gave support to Bonn's endeavors, many observers reported that they were worried about the speed and thrust of Brandt's policy. In France, his action, it was said, "has come as a bombshell." President Nixon addressed a letter to Brandt in which he tried to dispell rumors about U.S. concern but, while expressing confidence in Bonn's serious efforts to contribute to the cohesion of West's community by attempting to reduce tensions in the East, the letter contained a telling sentence: "Like you, I believe that the first is the indispensable condition for success in the second." Similarly, the British Foreign Secretary, Michael Stewart, welcomed Brandt's efforts as a "recognition of reality" but reminded Bonn, as did Paris and Washington, that the question of Berlin was a prerogative of the Big Four and the question of German boundaries was that of a peace conference.[16] These claims and rights were to be repeated on many occasions since then. When Scheel visited the Western capitals shortly before his trip to Moscow, an identity of allied views on Brandt's *Ostpolitik* appeared to have been established.

The West's concern and the CDU opposition were certainly not entirely unjustified. According to preliminary reports about the draft treaty between Bonn and Moscow, the latter's demands were to be satisfied while some basic aspects of Brandt's program were ignored. Specifically, the future of West Berlin was separated from treaty negotiations as the Soviet government insisted that the issue was in the sovereign domain of the Big Four. It was legally right, but one may add

[16] *Times,* December 10, 1969; *International Herald Tribune,* December 8, 1969; *Süddeutsche Zeitung,* November 7, 1969. For other reports on the West's critical attitude, see *New York Times,* December 14, 1969; *Frankfurter Allgemeine Zeitung,* April 4, 1970; *Le Monde,* May 13, 1970, July 3, 1970.

that the same was true of Germany's boundaries, which were to be determined at a peace conference and not by a bilateral treaty between Moscow and Bonn.

Nor could the West be pleased with the East's enthusiastic support of the negotiations. Its representatives and press obviously expected they would produce a formal confirmation of the status quo and, in particular, recognition of the GDR. Moreover, as if it wished to revive the ghost of the Rapallo spirit, the Soviet press at the beginning of 1970 published articles on the history and great significance of the 1922 Rapallo Treaty. An East German weekly, *Horizont,* even described it as an example for treaties between states of different social systems and as a model of peaceful co-existence.[17]

However, the die was cast. At the beginning of August, Walter Scheel journeyed to Moscow to initial the treaty. The CDU declined the government's invitation to have its representatives accompany the Foreign Minister. It took the position that it was not adequately informed, that it was critical of the Bahr Paper, which it considered a basis for the forthcoming negotiations, and it repeated its insistence on a conclusion of negotiations on Berlin before negotiations at Moscow had reached the final stage. Finally, it declared it was convinced that, in spite of Brandt's assurances to the contrary, this was also the position of France, Britain, and the United States.[18] However, Scheel's trip proved to be more than just a formal state visit, putting the final touches on a prepared text. Rather, it was an occasion to press for some substantial changes and additions to the Bahr Paper. These had been presumably negotiated before the trip itself since Scheel departed from Bonn with a six-point governmental

---

[17] Radio Free Europe, Research, *USSR,* March 19, 1970; *GDR/5,* March 11, 1970.

[18] *Frankfurter Allgemeine Zeitung,* July 21, 1970.

desiderata that had been made public.[19] The treaty was initialed August 8, but its signature and publication was postponed until August 12, in order to reserve the historical event for Brandt, whose determined efforts appeared to have been crowned with success.

Thus, on that day it seemed that Moscow and Bonn, twenty-five years after the end of war, had reached a reconciliation of momentous consequences for the two countries, for détente in Europe, and, indeed, for the peace of the whole world.

The treaty consists of only five articles. Article One speaks of the endeavors of the signatories to foster normalization of the situation in Europe, an effort that would proceed from the realities of that situation. Article Two commits them to conduct their mutual relations according to the aims and principles of the UN Charter and to solve their disputes exclusively by peaceful means, with the obligation to refrain, pursuant to Article 2 of the UN Charter, from the threat of force or the use of force in questions that affect security in Europe and international security. Article Three expresses their agreement that peace in Europe can be maintained only if present boundaries are declared inviolate. Thus, they oblige themselves to respect without reservation the territorial integrity of all states in Europe within their present frontiers, including the Oder-Neisse line and the frontier between the FRG and GDR, and declare that they have no territorial claims against anyone now, nor in the future. Article Four stipulates that the treaty does not affect agreements, concluded previously by the contracting parties. According to Article Five, the treaty becomes effective upon ratification.[20]

It is obvious that the treaty legally confirms the Soviet goal to have West Germany recognize the status quo: the East

[19] *Le Monde,* July 25, 1970.
[20] For the text of the treaty and other related documents, see *Bulletin* (Bonn), August 17, 1970.

German-Polish boundary and the frontiers between West and East Germany thus implicitly achieving de facto recognition for East Germany. On the other hand, but only indirectly, the reference to Article 2 of the UN Charter signifies that the Soviet Union now considers its Articles 53 and 107 obsolete and would presumably not claim the right to interfere in West German internal affairs.

Other of Bonn's political goals were met in a different legal manner—in the form of letters. One, addressed to Gromyko, ascertains that the treaty does not stand in contradiction to the FRG's aim "to work toward a condition of peace in Europe in which the German nation attains its unity again in free self-determination." The other letter, sent to the Western three powers, states that the signatories agree that the treaty does not affect the rights and responsibilities of the Big Four concerning Germany as a whole and Berlin. This question has no connection with the treaty, is not affected by the treaty, nor was it a subject of negotiations.

Thus it is equally obvious that Bonn's claim for reunification was met in a vague way, as a general acceptance of necessary conditions for peace in Europe and in a form that is not legally binding on the Soviet government. However, although such a one-sided exchange indicates a bleak prospect for reunification, it is also apparent that the documents are both a testimony to and a product of undeniable and incontestable realism.

Brandt recognized this situation in a moving and frank speech that he addressed from Moscow to Germans at home over radio and television stations. He told the listeners that now, twenty-five years after the German capitulation, the time had come to establish German relations with the East on a new foundation, and continued, "Our national interest does not permit us to stand between the East and West. Our country needs cooperation and harmony with the West and understanding with the East." The treaty, he stated, is a success of

German postwar policy and a decisive step toward improving Germany's relations with her eastern neighbors—"one quarter of a century after the catastrophe that demanded even greater, more unspeakable sacrifices from the nations of the East than of the West. . . . Russia is insolubly tied to the history of Europe, not only as an adversary but also as a partner. . . ." Then he realistically and with a sense of resignation added, "With this treaty nothing is lost that had not been lost long ago. We have the courage to open a new page in history." [21]

The treaty was a new page in the history of both Germany and of all of Europe. It was, as Brandt also said in Moscow, the end of one era and the beginning of a new one.

When he appeared before the *Bundestag* on September 18 to report about the treaty, Brandt made some very important points. First, he announced that "the Soviet government was forcefully advised. . ., that in the view of the Federal government a détente in Europe [was] not possible without an improvement of the situation in and around Berlin. The government of the USSR knows that the treaty cannot become effective without a satisfactory Berlin settlement." Thus, making the ratification of the treaty conditional upon the "satisfactory" solution of the Berlin problem—as vague as is the meaning of the term "satisfactory"—he put Moscow under pressure to seek an agreement on Berlin if it wishes the treaty to come into force.

Second, Brandt referred to the Bahr Paper as a document that Bahr and Gromyko "had formulated" together, the last five guiding principles of which were "the declarations of intent of both governments." Accordingly, they refer to: the "oneness" of all treaties with the Warsaw Pact countries; the readiness of the FRG to sign a treaty with the GDR "on the basis of equality, non-discrimination, and independence and with the same binding force as with other third countries";

[21] *Die Welt,* August 13, 1970.

the furtherance of both German states joining the United Nations at a time of a settlement of relations with the GDR; the solution of the invalidity of the Munich Agreement; further development of German-Soviet relations; furtherance of the plan of a European security conference.[22]

The CDU/CSU opposition reacted to the treaty and to the Chancellor's speech with restrained criticism. In contrast to past accusations of "sell out," "adventurism," and even "treason," its position was now expressed in a carefully balanced, though still reserved manner, aware as it was of the historical significance of the moment and of its consequences for the future of Germany and Europe. Dr. Rainer Barzel, the parliamentary head of the CDU, expressed the fear that the treaty made the solution of the Berlin problem no easier but rather more difficult, and his party would have preferred to see this problem solved first. He was concerned about the future of NATO; he declined to view the treaty as an instrument that would lead to reduction of tensions; he saw the right of self-determination of the German people threatened; he expressed the worry that the treaty cemented the boundaries, strengthened the predominance of the Soviet Union, threatened the balance in Europe, and would lead to new tensions because of its different interpretations (the Russian text, for instance, spoke about "immutability" and the German text about "inviolability" of European frontiers). He emphasized that for the CDU the unification of free Europe and the Atlantic alliance was the basis of its *Ostpolitik*. Although most of these points were shared by the government and although Barzel admitted that the treaty met some of his party's expectations, he declared that it would now wait for deeds.[23]

Strong reservations regarding Brandt's policy were not

---

[22] *Bulletin* (Bonn), No. 125, September 19, 1970, pp. 1,289-1,290.
[23] *Ibid.*, pp. 1,290-1,293. For other voices of opposition, see *Die Welt,* August 11, 24, 27, 1970.

limited to West German political circles. Bonn's allies officially expressed agreement, but their repeated insistence on Big Four responsibility for Berlin and comments of the press about the undue haste with which the treaty had been negotiated and signed revealed the misgivings and the discomfort of the West. In the United States an official remarked that it would take time to see whether the pact was a genuine instrument "in reducing tensions or a cynical swindle." Henry A. Kissinger and the former U.S. High Commissioners in Germany, Lucius D. Clay and John J. McCloy, were reportedly suspicious of Brandt's policy. Dean Acheson viewed it "with great alarm" and George Ball expressed concern that it might lead to "diplomatic adventures." [24]

President Pompidou and Foreign Minister Schumann on several occasions—with a somewhat conspicuous emphasis —gave their full approval to Brandt's policy, and the President of France even expressed admiration for his courage. Sir Alec Douglas-Home stated that Brandt had the British government's support and that "he handled the matter with considerable skill." [25] However, the communique, issued on the occasion of a meeting between the French and British Foreign Ministers three weeks before the signature of the treaty, revealed some official anxiety. It spoke about the two governments' "complete concordance of views" on the Bonn-Moscow negotiations while following Bonn's efforts with a "vigilant sympathy." [26]

The reaction of the French press was mixed. While recognizing that France had in the past taken the lead in the policy of détente and that jealousy would be out of place when West Germany now followed in Paris' path, many newspapers shared common concerns. They saw in the treaty an instru-

[24] *New York Times,* August 13, 1970; December 20, 1970; December 29, 1970.

[25] *Times,* December 9, 1970.

[26] *Le Monde,* July 17, 1970.

ment that would facilitate Soviet influence in West Europe, weaken NATO, make Bonn's position in the Western alliance uncertain, endanger West Europe's unity and its further growth, and increase FRG trade with the Soviet Union at the expense of French commercial interests.[27]

Of all official sources, the Secretary-General of NATO, Manlio Brosio, expressed most clearly the West's concern about the treaty. He maintained that as a consequence of the treaty the importance of accelerating West European unification increased, although it was apparent that Soviet space for maneuvering had also increased. He cautioned, "Should . . . an error in evaluation of the Moscow treaty induce the allied countries to a hasty engagement in bilateral accords with the Soviet Union or its allies for the purpose of finding political or economic advantage, we would play the game of Soviet diplomacy and the effects of the treaty would turn to our complete disadvantage." [28] Mr. Brosio exonerated West Germany, whose "loyalty remained intact," but his message was clear: the treaty opens an avenue to developments that may endanger the West's security.

Chancellor Brandt was not unaware of his allies' reservations, nor did he underestimate the arguments of his powerful opposition in the *Bundestag.* Yet he was determined to carry the negotiations through, and he proceeded with all proper speed. There were a host of motivations for his new look in both policy and implementation.

First, looking back at twenty years of effort by his predecessors, he understood the futility of these endeavors; the goal of reunification had been based on and subsequently became an apparent fiction. On the other hand, he realized that Soviet insistence on recognition of the status quo emanated from the reality of Soviet power. Moreover, the dimin-

---

[27] For the position of the French press, see *Le Monde,* August 13, 14, 23, 24; September 13-14, 17, 24, 1970.

[28] *Ibid.,* September 22, 1970.

ishing support received by the federal government from its NATO allies made its fictitious policy all the more bankrupt. This conflict between German fiction and Soviet reality stripped Bonn's original *Ostpolitik* of its effectiveness. As long as she remained burdened by memories of the past, refusing to recognize the grim consequences of defeat, West Germany could not play the role that truly represented her power and influence in European and world politics. In addition, France had developed close contacts with Moscow and her leaders as well as those of Great Britain freely exchanged state visits. West Germany remained aloof, out of step with the movement toward a general détente in Europe and in danger of estrangement from her own allies.

Second, Brandt could not ignore a change in the orientation of U.S. foreign policy. This was not a matter of a sudden switch; it was in the making for years and it concerned in particular West Germany's security. No sooner had the Eisenhower administration proclaimed the policy of massive nuclear retaliation—highly controversial from its outset— than its credibility became questionable when, in 1953, Moscow detonated the first H-bomb. From then on, Allied strategy was in a process of change, always materially affecting West Germany. Whether it was the new concept of "forward strategy" or of "flexible response," including use of tactical nuclear weapons, or of "graduated" deterrent, West Germany—due to her geographical position—would inescapably carry the first brunt of war. In order to remedy the growing gap in the credibility of the United States commitment to contribute to the defense of Europe from the beginning of a conflict, West Europe, and the FRG in particular, first welcomed another idea that would establish a European nuclear striking force, with the European powers sharing with Washington in the control of atomic weapons. However, this plan of multilateral nuclear force (MLF) was scrapped by the end of 1965, mainly because some European powers had serious misgivings about the prospect of West Germany's having her finger anywhere near the atomic trigger. Bonn finally found herself the sole protagonist of the MLF, and its apprehension and sense of isolation only grew.

These developments were accompanied by Soviet-American negotiations which led to the treaty on banning atomic tests in 1963 and later, in 1968, together with Great Britain, to the treaty on the non-proliferation of atomic weapons. The treaties contributed to some controls of atomic weaponry but they only intensified Bonn's concern with the danger of a separate U.S.-USSR "deal" affecting West Germany's security and her still much publicized quest for unification. Bonn, therefore, resisted for some time the pressure of adding its signature to the non-proliferation treaty.

As the United States was increasingly torn by the war in Vietnam, and less concerned with European problems; as NATO's homogeneity was weakening and its strategy constantly changing; as President Johnson in his October 1966 "building bridges" speech failed to mention the problem of Germany; and, in particular, as Senator Mansfield continued to press for a partial and unilateral withdrawal of U.S. troops from West Europe, the Bonn government felt compelled to prepare itself for the possibly grave consequences of this American neo-isolationism. Brandt's gambit was to accelerate the FRG *Ostpolitik* and to seek an understanding with the Soviet Union.

Third, Brandt considered the moment for reaching an agreement with Moscow propitious because he sensed that the Soviet government was also now interested in finding an accommodation with West Germany. Not only would the treaty confirm and solidify Soviet power in East Europe, not only would it permit Moscow to guard against the danger of another "Czechoslovak Spring" in any country of the area; it would also make possible a new trade relationship with Bonn, capable of supplying the Soviet economy with urgently needed capital goods and technology. However, if Brandt contemplated that this latter economic factor would materially strengthen his hand in the political aspects of Bonn's negotiations, he may have misjudged. As one highly placed official in Bonn put it at the time of preliminary contacts with Moscow, "We have learned from experience that we cannot extract political concessions from the Soviet government by attractive economic offers." Moscow, though the assets of an agreement were great, must have had some forebodings, knowing that it also contributed to the growth of Bonn's prestige and influence, not only in the West but also in East Europe—a byproduct that Brandt undoubtedly anticipated and welcomed.

Last but not least, the developments on the domestic scene led Chancellor Brandt to proceed quickly. His government, facing an economic recession and growing inflation, watched critically by the CDU/CSU, and existing on a narrow majority in the *Bundestag,* was eager to impress the nation with its courageous leadership and to take fullest advantage of a favorable public opinion. According to a poll taken a few weeks before the treaty was signed, 92 percent of the Germans were in favor of reconciliation with the Soviet Union. According to another poll, taken one week before Brandt's trip to Moscow, 47 percent expected Bonn's relations with Moscow under the present federal government to improve, 40 percent did not expect any change, and only 2 percent expected a worsening of these relations. Still another poll, conducted a few days before the Moscow visit, indicated that 81 percent approved the envisaged treaty and 78 percent expected an easing of tensions as its result.[29]

However, public opinion and the motivations of political leaders cannot be the sole index of either the wisdom or the

[29] *Le Monde,* July 26-27, 1970; *Die Welt,* August 4, 1970; *New York Times,* August 15, 1970.

complex consequences of an issue. Such consequences must be evaluated in both their short-term and long-term significance.

There is little doubt that the treaty brings a sense of immediate relief to West Germany and to the whole of Europe. It has opened the door (in fact, it has been prerequisite) to settling Bonn's relations with all East European nations, including East Germany. It has substantially contributed to détente since the major political question of Europe—the place of West Germany in European politics—has been for the time being clarified if not fully answered. The principal source of tension—Bonn's quest for reunification—has been removed. In its place is now the clear confirmation of Germany's division, and this fact alone is expected to bring about a reduction if not an elimination of tensions. The treaty is supposed to set Europe on the path of normalcy and peace.

However, all these short-term achievements and expectations carry farreaching, long-term connotations that are at best uncertain and that inescapably hinge upon the Soviet's real intentions and Bonn's perception of Soviet goals in Europe. We know what the Soviets say but not what they think. It is only logical to expect that Moscow will take advantage of this new situation and play the Western powers against each other. Only a few months after the treaty had been signed in May 1970, Kosygin appealed to the West European nations to seek independence from the United States. Using the treaty as an instrument, the Soviet government may thus exercise similar kinds of pressure on the federal government that may be difficult for Bonn to resist, particularly since the treaty itself was greeted with some displeasure in Western capitals. Although they may have full trust in Brandt and his determination to uphold the solidarity of NATO (which is in any case not very firm), they are aware that politics are not, or at least ought not to be, tailored to the person or political lifetime of one specific leader. The consequences of his decision will survive Brandt and may prove to be either a burden or blessing to his successors. The treaty that today gives West Germany a sense of confidence and even security may turn into a cause for alarm and increased peril tomorrow.

The confirmed division of Germany may, in the changing environment of East European politics and with the emotional potential of the German people, produce serious conflicts. Brandt himself, in his State of the Union message in January 1970, in connection with the problem of divided Germany, described the concept of nation as a matter of "historical reality and political will. The term nation implies," he stated, "more than a common language or culture, more than state and society. The nation is rooted in the peoples' lasting sense of solidarity. . . . As long as the Germans do not abandon this political will and do not give up this demand [for self-determination], the hope remains that future generations will live in a Germany in whose political structure all Germans can take part." [30] It is this "political will" that the treaty undoubtedly exposes to severe pressures, and the question as to whether or not historical and social forces in the long run will prevail over political forces, or vice versa, remains unanswered. Therein lies the Faustian dilemma of Brandt's treaty.

Furthermore, Brandt's government was committed to submit the treaty for ratification to the *Bundestag* only after a "satisfactory" solution of the Berlin problem had been achieved. Here is a paradoxical situation that points to its disproportionate obligations. On the one hand, Bonn commits itself to most significant concessions. On the other, the Soviet government has conceded nothing beyond its willingness merely to confirm what have been the rights of the Western Big Three since 1945 in the question of Berlin, a question that President Eisenhower characterized in 1959 as an ab-

---

[30] *Texte zur Deutschlandpolitik, op.cit.,* Vol. IV, p. 203.

normal situation. The imbalance is apparent; the Soviet-West German reconciliation rests on recognition of a "normal" situation in East Europe and an "abnormal" situation in Berlin. However, one should recognize that such are the "normalities" of international affairs.

Although the Soviet Union was advised at the time of the signature of the treaty of the link between its ratification and a solution of the Berlin problem, by February 1971 it had begun to have second thoughts. *Pravda* criticized those in West Germany who were trying to hamper the implementation of the treaty by insisting on the precondition and indirectly chastized Brandt by commenting that "those who are devoid of courage to face facts honestly and with dignity cannot be trusted." [31]

At the CPSU Congress, Brezhnev warned that delay in the ratification of the treaty "would give rise to a new crisis of confidence in the FRG's entire policy and would worsen the political climate in Europe and the prospects for an easing of international tensions." [32]

However, by the fall of 1971 such a crisis of confidence was averted. The Big Four reached what appeared to them and to Brandt to be a "satisfactory" agreement on West Berlin. Thus, the prerequisite for submitting the treaty for ratification was met and the FRG Chancellor presumably regained in Moscow's eyes the qualities of courage, honesty, dignity, and trust. At any rate, as soon as the agreement on Berlin had been signed, Soviet and West German activities were resumed once again at an accelerated speed, carrying both some promising and some ominous connotations.

For reasons that are not quite clear, Brandt accepted Moscow's invitation to meet Brezhnev during the latter part of September at the Crimean resort Oreanda. According to the communique, the two leaders "acting in complete loyalty

[31] *New York Times,* February 14, 1971.
[32] *The Current Digest of the Soviet Press,* Vol. XXIII, No. 12, p. 12.

to their alliance partners," expressed the conviction that the early implementation of the treaties, signed by the FRG with the Soviet Union and Poland "will make possible a decisive turning point in the relations between these countries." They considered the agreement on Berlin "a major step on the way to European and international détente." They noted that the "developments in Europe were conducive" to convening a European security conference and proposed to conduct consultations "in order to expedite the holdings of such a conference." They were persuaded that the solution of the difficult problem of the reduction of troops and armaments in Europe "would effectually secure the foundation of European and international peace." They saw it to be possible to achieve "the general normalization" of relations between the two Germanys, and stated that, "one of the most important steps in this direction will be the entry of the two states, in the course of détente, into the United Nations Organization and its special agencies"; they agreed to "promote such a solution of these questions in appropriate form." They further agreed on broadening trade, cultural, and scientific contacts. They concluded that "the emerging practice of exchanges of views and of consultations . . . is useful and should be continued." [33]

The visit itself and the communique immediately raised a number of questions. It appears that Brandt journeyed to Crimea without prior consultation with the Allies. President Pompidou, although welcoming Brandt's trip, added, "Maybe, the treaty on French-German cooperation or, moreover, the French-Soviet Protocol would have justified a bit more advance information." [34] However, the FRG government's

---

[33] *The Bulletin* (Bonn), Vol. 19, no. 32, September 21, 1971, pp. 241-242.

[34] Ambassade de France, "Conférence de Presse de Monsieur Georges Pompidou, Président de la République," September 23, 1971, New York, Service de Presse et d'Information.

spokesman resentfully rejected such criticism when he retorted that Bonn "did not have to consult anyone about invitations from foreign governments." [35] This would be the case indeed if the Chancellor had paid a visit to some such country as Oman; but when it concerned a power like the Soviet Union, an antagonist of NATO, which, along with its leading individual members, was engaged in complex and diplomatically delicate negotiations on a number of questions, such an attitude on the part of Bonn, a key member of NATO, was puzzling and such a reaction was, to say the least, brusque. It might be argued, of course, that Bonn thus only repaid its several allies in kind; their top representatives have gone to Moscow without prior consultations with the West German government, or announced planned visits (without consultation with Bonn or anyone else) to the Chinese capital. At any rate, it was with some justification that Brandt declared, after his visit in the Soviet Union, that while not becoming its friend the FRG has "become partners in a businesslike contract just as other Western States. . . ." [36]

But it is not entirely convincing that Brandt acted "in complete loyalty to [his] alliance partners" when he agreed with the Soviet position to "expedite" the security conference, when it is known that some of the FRG allies continue to have doubts about Soviet intent. But, again, other members of NATO were eager to have such a conference, without careful preparation, at a time when Brandt was still rather cautious about it.

These two instances illustrate only some of the risks that NATO solidarity may be weakened by this wooing of the East and indicate that Moscow proceeds, not without success, toward one of its principal goals for détente: the disruption of the Western alliance.

[35] *Frankfurter Allgemeine Zeitung,* September 24, 1971; *New York Times,* September 16, 1971.

[36] *New York Times,* September 20, 1971.

The communique's allusion to the possibility of the FRG and GDR entering the United Nations was only an opening shot in Moscow's ultimate intent. Gromyko, speaking before the General Assembly, characterized their absence as a "political anomaly"; since the GDR "has firmly established itself as a real and active component of the European system of states . . . and modern Europe is already inconceivable without it," the time has come to admit both Germanys to the United Nations.[37] (One wonders why he does not use the same argument in favor of the admission of South Vietnam and South Korea, or to refuse to expel Taiwan.) However, in this case, the Bonn government attached a different interpretation to the Oreanda communique; it stated officially that both German states "joining the world body" could not "be considered until relations between the Federal Republic and the German Democratic Republic have been normalized." [38] Bonn was apparently aware of the danger that such a premature move would not only strengthen East Germany's international position but would also work to her advantage in intra-German negotiations.

However, if the Bonn government feels that, with the signing of the agreement on Berlin, the initiative in proceeding with its *Ostpolitik* has passed into their hands, Gromyko made it clear that the event in no way weakened Moscow's pressure on the FRG to speed up the ratification of the Soviet-West German and Polish-West German treaties by the *Bundestag*. Just as the FRG, prior to the Berlin agreement, refused to submit these treaties for ratification before a "satisfactory" agreement had been reached on West Berlin, so the Soviet Foreign Minister established a *junktim* between the ratification and implementation of the Berlin agreement, indicating that the Soviet government may not sign the latter before the

[37] *Ibid.,* September 29, 1971.
[38] *The Bulletin* (Bonn), Vol. 19, no. 33, September 28, 1971, p. 255.

first takes place.[39] Indeed, the Soviet government made it clear to Scheel when he was in Moscow toward the end of November 1971 that it would insist that the two treaties take effect simultaneously.

The CDU/CSU opposition did not take kindly to this question, nor to Brandt's visit in the Soviet Union. Rainer Barzel, the newly elected successor to Kiesinger in the party leadership, stated that Soviet pressure would only increase his party's determination. On another occasion, he threatened that the CDU would vote against ratification because the heart of German *Ostpolitik,* "the self-determination of Germans in Germany," had not been achieved. Upon the Chancellor's return from the Crimea, he considered the results of the trip not yet evident, commenting that while "new demands of the Soviet Union were to be met, our vital questions were not discussed. . . ."

Two other opposition leaders, Gerhard Schroeder and Helmut Kohl, had been critical of Brandt's trip before he undertook it. The first did not see the conditions for the trip "particularly favorable"; the latter characterized the methods of his *Ostpolitik* "dilettantish and too hectic." [40]

As the Bonn government, toward the end of the year, submitted the treaties with the Soviet Union and Poland to the Parliament, the voices of opposition continued unabated. After Barzel's visit in Moscow, the CDU/CSU unanimously decided to reject ratification. But it was not apparent what role the Upper Chamber, the *Bundesrat,* in which the CDU has a majority, would play in the process of ratification, i.e., whether it will claim it as *zustimmungspflichtig,* requiring its concurrence with the vote in the *Bundestag.* Beginning in February 1972, the FRG Parliament opened a debate on the ratification and as this book reached publication the outcome was not known.

[39] *Frankfurter Allgemeine Zeitung,* October 8, 9, 1971.
[40] *Ibid.,* October 9, 6; September 20, 13, 1971.

Nevertheless, whatever the attitude of the opposition may be, Brandt's achievements appear at present to be spectacular and impressive. They certainly were most convincing to the Nobel Peace Prize Committee that bestowed this coveted honor upon him for 1971. However, one cannot abstain from adding that what appears to be a convincing achievement in 1971 may carry a different connotation in 1981. Only history can say.

If and when the treaties with the Soviet Union and Poland are ratified and the Berlin agreement comes into force, a giant step in détente apparently will have been made. On the other hand, although many persons in Europe will be jubilant, the outlook for the future, riddled as it is with vast uncertainties, invites a sober evaluation of the nature of the détente achieved by the pacts. The day may yet come when Germany's *Ostpolitik* may fail to be identified with West Europe's policy and Moscow's own *Westpolitik* may develop a thrust beyond the present ideological and political status quo. Should this happen, the Soviet-West German pact would then ultimately have served not as an instrument of peace but as a spearhead of Soviet disruption of West European strength.

However, it is even more appalling to contemplate future developments should the treaties fail the test of ratification. Then, Pandora's Box would certainly be open and forces set in motion that might all but destroy the years-long efforts for détente while another Cold War swept over the European continent.

The Berlin Quandary

In international affairs, abnormal situations have a tendency to be defended with obstinate persistency as they develop into questions of power and prestige. Once that happens, the governments concerned translate their predicaments into principles and thus make it impossible to extricate themselves from their follies. Berlin is such a case: a divided city, one sector of it an integral part and the capital of the GDR, the other an equally integral part of the FRG but separated from it by 110 miles of communist territory. Had those who were responsible for this situation deliberately attempted to create a dangerously inflammable international situation, they could not have invented a better arrangement.

The wartime planners for postwar Germany had different designs in mind. By dividing Berlin into four zones of occupation and administering it through the Allied *Kommandatura,* the Big Four wished to present a vivid demonstration of their complete victory by their continuing presence in the citadel of Prussianism. During the war the European Allied Council in London had prepared arrangements for access to and administration of the city. However, it was meant to be a temporary arrangement that was to last only until Germany was united and when Berlin would have again become the capital of Germany.

Events took an entirely different trend. Berlin became a fierce battlefield of the Cold War. The *Kommandatura* functioned smoothly until October 1946 (although to this day it is nominally in existence), when the municipal elections gave an overwhelming majority to non-communist parties. In June 1948 the Soviet representative walked out of the *Kommandatura;* three months later the Soviet administration in the eastern sector brought the SED into being as the single political party in that sector. The division of Berlin became an accomplished fact. The Berlin blockade, from June 1948 until May 1949, demonstrated Soviet plans to force the Western Allies out of the city. The Allied air lift, on the other hand, testified to the Allies' equal determination to defend their rights and position in Berlin. What followed was an extension of the irreconcilable stand of the two adversaries, intensified and complicated by the hostilities between the two Germanys. Fundamentally, the situation was still the same until the fall of 1971, twenty-six years after the war.

The Constitution of the FRG designated Berlin as the capital of Germany and incorporated it as a federal "district" that sends delegates to the *Bundestag,* but without voting rights. The Western Big Three did not formally approve this but acquiesced in it and eventually (at first individually and then collectively through NATO) extended to West Berlin their commitment to defend it against any attack.

The Soviet government permitted the Ulbricht regime to integrate East Berlin into the GDR, send its representatives to its parliament (also without voting rights), and designate it as the capital city. Thus East Berlin received the defense guarantees of the Soviet Union and the whole Warsaw Pact. The whole city became a powder-keg. The fact, however, that in spite of periodical crises the explosion has not taken place and that the Big Four, including the Soviet Union, have repeatedly insisted on maintaining and invoking their responsibilities over Berlin, testifies to their mutual desire to keep this dangerous situation under control.

However, no political situation is ever static, nor has been the Berlin quandary. In November 1958 Khrushchev issued a near-ultimatum that West Berlin must be demilitarized, neutralized, and turned into an independent political entity, possibly under an international guarantee. The West resolutely rejected the idea. It is regrettable that it was presented in such a crude form, and that the West refused to give the proposal careful thought. A variation of it conceivably could have preserved the city's economic ties with West Germany and assured it of at least the same degree of safety it enjoys under current circumstances.

It must be recognized, however, that such an attempt would have run counter not only to the position of the Bonn government but also to public opinion. West Germans have consistently clung to their ties with Berlin; the Berliners themselves take a perverse pride in the plight of their exposed and isolated city. They have never vacillated in their fierce desire to maintain the special status of Berlin. In public polls (including West Berliners), conducted in the month of Khrushchev's proposal, 80 percent expressed themselves in favor of retaining Berlin as compared with 70 percent in June 1953; only 3 percent were in favor of relinquishing Berlin as compared with 5 percent on the previous date. They trusted the Western powers to stand "solidly" behind them—37 percent in December 1958 and 41 percent in December 1959. On both dates, 34 percent responded that they could not rely on the Western powers "absolutely," though interestingly enough they had a greater trust in the United States. Forty-two percent of all respondents in December 1958, 46 percent in December 1959, and 51 percent in November 1962, felt that the United States was "solidly" behind them on the Berlin issue, while on the same dates 31 percent, 20 percent, and 27 percent respectively were of the opinion that they could not rely on the United States "absolutely." In November 1958 an equal percentage (37) believed (a) that the United States would defend the city and (b) would not risk a war. Impressively enough, in the period between February 1959 and September 1962, in nine polls taken in that time, only 7.3 percent, on average, expressed much fear that West Berlin would be turned over to the East; 35.2 percent were "pretty sure" that West Berlin would not be left to the East; 25.7 percent were "quite sure" about it.

In June 1959, 62 percent of the interviewees were against turning Berlin into a free city, 15 percent were in favor, and 23 percent were undecided. Three years later the percentage "against" rose to 69; in favor dropped to 14; 17 percent remained undecided. However, in February 1961, half-a-year before the Wall, 53 percent felt that the Berlin situation could

215

not remain as it was and that all concerned must make a compromise, while 24 percent believed that any new arrangement would only cause the situation to deteriorate.[41]

In fact, it was the old arrangement that led to an aggravation of the problem of Berlin. Ever since Khrushchev's proposals were rejected, the Soviet Union and the GDR have repeatedly stated that West Berlin was a political unit, separate from West Germany, and the government in East Berlin has considered it as a part of East German territory. The access to the city from the west has been exposed to periodical harrassment and convoys; military and civilian trucks and cars have been stopped for hours and days whenever West Germany staged any political activity in West Berlin to demonstrate the city's status as a part of the FRG. To the east, the disruption of traffic was to serve as a different demonstration: Berlin's encirclement by the communist camp.

The ultimate provocation was the construction of the Berlin Wall by the Soviet and East German government, begun on August 13, 1961. Eventually, this physical and political separation was extended to the entire 1,346 kilometers of the West-East German boundary—an unsurmountable obstacle erected to divide the people of one nation, now forced to live in two separate countries. The Wall became an ugly monument to the "popularity" of Ulbricht's regime. Until then close to three million East Germans, 74 percent of them under forty-five years of age, had fled from East to West Germany. Ulbricht saw no other way to stop this process of depopulation, a serious drain on the labor force, than to plug up this escape hatch to freedom. From 1961 until December 1969, only 28,711 East Germans succeeded in penetrating the Wall, and many met death on the electrified barbed wires or from bullets.[42]

[41] Noelle and Neumann, *op.cit.,* pp. 485, 486, 488, 489.

[42] Ministry for Intra-German Relations, 11 3035-214, January 15, 1970, p. 1.

West Berliners have stoically and courageously adjusted themselves to life in this beleaguered city. Of the 2.2 million inhabitants, one-fifth of them are over sixty-five years of age; every fourth person came there as a refugee after the war; and every third has relatives in East Berlin whom he can visit only on special occasions.

Almost one-half of the West Berliners are gainfully employed. Until the Wall, 76,300 East Berliners crossed the "border" daily for work in the Western sectors of the city, while only 13,000 West Berliners had jobs in the Soviet sector. The resultant shortage in the labor force is partly alleviated by foreign workers, who come in increasing numbers. Economically, the situation would be intolerable if West Berlin did not receive considerable aid from the federal government in such forms as industry subsidies, tax privileges, and social assistance.[43]

According to a popular saying, "one gets accustomed even to the gallows," and the desires of West Berliners are modest. Public polls conducted in June 1971 indicated that they considered free access to the city their most important goal (74 percent), followed by the right to visit East Berlin (69 percent) and by Soviet recognition that West Berlin belongs to the political structure of the FRG (63 percent). Only 24 percent wished to see the *Bundestag's* committees continue to meet in their city [44]—a minority small enough to give Brandt the idea of making some concessions on this point to which the Soviet government has attached great importance.

It has mattered little that all of these desires of the West Berliners had been embodied in the wartime agreements. The Soviet and the East German governments have simply abrogated them and insisted on treating West Berlin as an

---

[43] *The Bulletin* (Bonn), Vol. 19, No. 1, March 9, 1971, p. 51; *Texte zur Deutschlandpolitik, op.cit.,* Vol. IV, pp. 193-200.

[44] *The Bulletin* (Bonn), Vol. 19, No. 22, June 29, 1971, p. 163.

independent territory. They have disregarded the inconsistency of their own position, asking for recognition of the status quo in East Europe but refusing to accept the same for Berlin. Ever since the policy of détente developed, the Western Big Three, while willing to make concessions regarding Soviet goals for East Europe, have tried with little success to receive from the Soviet government a binding assurance on Berlin.

In December 1969 they proposed to the Soviet Union negotiations that would improve the situation in Berlin and assure a free access to the divided city. After some delay, Moscow reacted positively, realizing that the outcome of its negotiations with Bonn was closely related to a solution of the Berlin question. Toward the end of March 1970 the British, American, and French Ambassadors to West Germany and the Soviet Ambassador to East Germany opened a series of meetings to negotiate a number of political and technical problems concerning the city. Basically, the West aimed at assuring West Berlin of its legal, political, and economic ties with West Germany and of freedom of access to and from the city, and of travel between West and East Berlin. The Soviet Union demanded severance of these ties but appeared willing to grant some concessions on matters of traffic.

Ulbricht tried hard to undermine the negotiations on Berlin. He was altogether critical (though understandably obliquely so) of Moscow's contacts with Bonn and its willingness to discuss the Berlin situation, concerned as he was with the danger that his own insistence on full international recognition for the GDR might at first suffer a setback. In January 1970 he declared the Big Four had no responsibility for the GDR. "Since 1945, we have heard nothing from the Soviet Union about it," he stated and as to West Berlin it "is under a status of occupation." [45] To prove the point, the East German government suspended traffic to West Berlin on several occasions when President Heinemann visited the city and when the West German political parties organized meetings there. It also continued to refuse West Berliners permission to visit East Berlin during the Christmas and Easter holidays; this had been forbidden since 1966. In an attempt to sabotage the Big Four negotiations, it offered to discuss directly with the Bonn government the question of transit through East German territory and with the West Berlin Senate the question of West Berliners' travel to East Berlin. Bonn and the West Berlin's mayor, Klaus Schuetz, declined, pointing to the responsibilities of the Big Four for such questions. The East German government also continued to insist on the special independent status of West Berlin and on the elimination of the presence of West German authorities and of all other "provocative" activities in the city. The day the four ambassadors met for the first time, East Germany raised by 30 percent the tolls on goods delivered on highways and canals passing through East German territories to West Berlin. [46] The only concession it extended was the resumption—after nineteen years—of direct telephone communications between the two parts of the city, but one year later increased eight times the telephone fees. [47]

On the other hand, the West German government and the Big Three indicated a willingness to retreat from their original position. Soon after the signing of the Soviet-West German treaty, the organizations of refugees were to hold their annual "day of the homeland" in West Berlin, as they had done in the preceding ten years. This time governmental funds were withdrawn and the West Berlin mayor explained the decision by reference to the danger that the meeting

[45] *Neues Deutschland,* January 29, 1970.
[46] *Neue Zürcher Zeitung,* April 15, 1970.
[47] *Frankfurter Allgemeine Zeitung,* July 7, 1971.

could turn into a militant demonstration.[48] More importantly, when asked which forms of the Federal Republic's presence in West Berlin he could give up, the mayor answered, "There are forms of ties between Berlin and the federation that exist as an ingredient of our belonging to the economic, legal, and financial system of the Federal Republic of Germany as well as [its] contribution to the viability of West Berlin. . . . There are other forms, such as the demonstrative presence of the federation, that we have provided in the past years and decades to make it clear where this city belongs. When the Soviet Union will finally accept [our] belonging to the economic, legal, and financial unity of the federation, it will not be necessary to maintain these forms which we must use to show where we belong." [49]

In a similar vein and indicating the thoughts of the Bonn government on this question (crucial to the outcome of the Big Four negotiations), its Foreign Minister, Walter Scheel, seven months later stated that the current form of the federal presence in Berlin was "not normal." As he said, the Federal Republic does not appear in other states and cities as it does in West Berlin. It is not the federation but the Western powers that have a right in Berlin and the federation has "simply borrowed" this right. Since, he continued, today there is no legal basis for this, the Western allies try to insure these ties juridically.[50] Then, an article in *Frankfurter Rundschau* (which is close to SPD circles) raised doubts about Bonn's legal claim that West Berlin was a state of the FRG. Since it was widely believed that the article was written by someone in the government, its publication only intensified the critical attitude of the CDU toward Brandt, his *Ostpolitik* in general, and his Berlin policy in

[48] *New York Times,* August 19, 1970.
[49] *Die Welt,* August 17, 1970.
[50] *Ibid.,* March 20, 1971.

particular.[51] For the first time in years, the budget committee of the *Bundestag* did not meet in Berlin, although its absence was strongly protested by the opposition.

Meanwhile, the Big Four continued their meetings. According to meager reports they were prepared to forego the claim that West Berlin was an integral part of West Germany if the Soviet government would recognize that the city, through "accumulated ties," had special cultural, economic and political connections with West Germany.[52] Kosygin in August 1970 gave assurances to Brandt that the Soviet Union would seek ways to relax tensions in Berlin, and Brezhnev expressed later the belief that it was possible to achieve an improvement in the Berlin situation: "It is necessary only that the interested partners show good will and work out decisions that correspond to the wishes of the West Berlin people and the legitimate interests and sovereign rights of the German Democratic Republic." [53]

Finally, after eighteen months of secret and hard negotiations, the four ambassadors on September 3, 1971 signed a document of historical importance, "The Quadripartite Agreement on Berlin." The preamble and first part of the document confirm the rights and responsibilities of the four powers in Berlin, based on wartime and postwar agreements. This is a significant statement in that the Soviet government has maintained for years the position that East Germany (including East Berlin) was a sovereign entity and that West Berlin was an independent unit.

In the same vein, the Soviet Union made the "concession" that in fact is a confirmation of the West's rights dating back to 1944: that transit through the GDR territory "will be unimpeded," "conveyances sealed before departure," and inspection limited to "inspections of seals and accompanying

[51] *New York Times,* June 7, 1971.
[52] *Ibid.,* February 15, 1971.
[53] *Die Welt,* August 14, 1970; November 30, 1970.

documents." In case of suspicion that unsealed conveyances contain "either material intended for dissemination along the designated routes or persons or material put on board along these routes," content may be inspected. Detailed arrangements "will be agreed upon by the competent German authorities."

These provisions of the agreement signal a marked step forward in comparison with past practices, assuming that the "competent German authorities" (the West and East German governments) clarify in mutually satisfactory detail the implementation of the Berlin document. It is of particular importance that the provisions renew the Soviet government's direct responsibility for the issue of traffic—a position that it pretended to have transferred to the East German authorities in 1955—and offer the possibility that the East German regime will be restrained from resuming its policy of harrassing these communications.

Another weighty part of the agreement concerns the relations between West Berlin and the FRG. No longer can Bonn claim that, according to article 23 of its Constitution, the city is an integral part of the Federal Republic; no longer will its individual official representatives and its bodies be permitted to perform in West Berlin any "constitutional or official acts," except for single committees of the Federal Parliament when dealing with matters related to the ties between the city and the FRG. Nor will parliamentary parties (*Fraktionen*) be permitted to hold meetings there simultaneously. Thus, though "the ties between the Western sectors of Berlin and the Federal Republic of Germany will be maintained and developed" and the latter will be represented in the former by a permanent liaison agency, West Berlin continues "not to be a constituent part of the Federal Republic of Germany and not to be governed by it." The three Western allies and the West Berlin Senate presumably govern the city though "established procedures" about the applicability of the FRG legislation "shall remain unchanged." This stipulation, designed to reconcile the positions of the negotiating parties, would appear to be fraught with many juridical and pragmatic problems, bound to create frictions and protests.

In another part of the agreement the Soviet Union declares that communications between West Berlin and East Berlin and East Germany "will be improved" and that "permanent residents of West Berlin will be able to travel to and visit such areas for compassionate, family, religious, cultural, or commercial reasons, or as tourists, under conditions comparable to those applying to other persons entering these areas." Whatever this qualification may entail (for what are comparable conditions of permission to travel to a communist country?), the Soviet declaration seems to represent great progress because West Berliners have been denied the opportunity of visiting East Berlin since 1966 and East Germany since 1952. Nothing in the agreement suggests that the ambassadors of either side were particularly intent on facilitating visits by East Berliners to West Berlin and West Germany. The Berlin Wall will thus remain impregnable from East to West—a sad reminder, in the midst of current euphoria, of the real meaning of détente. And, indeed, East Germans understand that the agreement has not altered their situation; the number who have escaped to West Germany or have been killed while attempting to escape has increased considerably since its signature.

As a result of another compromise, the international position of West Berlin remains cryptic. While the United States, Great Britain, and France "maintain their rights and responsibilities relating to the representation abroad of the interests of the Western sectors of Berlin, and their permanent residents, including those rights and responsibilities concerning matters of security and status, both in international organizations and in relations with other countries," the FRG "may perform consular services" for West Berliners, its international agreements "may be extended" to West Berlin, it may represent its interests "in international organizations and in international conferences," its residents may "participate jointly" with West German participants in international exchanges and exhibitions, and international conferences and exhibitions may be held in West Berlin. This oddly formulated concession to the West is balanced by its authorization of the Soviet Union to establish in West Berlin a Consulate General, which will be accredited to the authority of the Western allies in the city, and to expand the activities of Soviet commercial organizations, whose personnel, however, will be limited in numbers, as stipulated in "Agreed Minute II." To preserve further the quasi-autonomous status of the city, its permanent residents shall present, in order to receive a Soviet visa, a passport, stamped, "issued in accordance with Quadripartite Agreement of September 3, 1971," as well as an identity card. This stamp will appear on all passports of West Berliners "for journeys to such countries [communist] as may require it." The provisions are meant to underline the special status of West Berlin.

The "Final Quadripartite Protocol" stipulates that special agreements to be concluded between "competent German authorities" that will determine numerous details of the Agreement "shall enter into force simultaneously with the Quadripartite Agreement and any serious difficulty in implementing them will call for quadripartite consultations."

These are the main points of the Berlin agreements. In addition, the Bonn government published, together with a German translation, an elaborate statement explaining its individual paragraphs.[54]

---

[54] For the English text of the Quadripartite Agreement, see *The Bulletin* (Bonn), special edition, Vol. 19, no. 4, September 4, 1971, pp. 225-231. For the German translation and the Bonn government's

No sooner was the Agreement signed than the first difficulties about its German translation arose. Although the two German governments had agreed on the German text, the East German press slipped in an inconspicuous but significant change: in the paragraph of the Agreement which speaks of West Berlin's "ties" (*Bindungen*) with the FRG it used the word *Verbindungen* (connections), which implies loose relationship between the two entities. The GDR government immediately attempted to draw a practical conclusion from this difference, insisting at first that the question of travel through and communications with East Germany was a matter for the West Berlin Senate, not for Bonn, to negotiate with East German authorities. After a few days of such skirmishing, however, the East German regime gave in when it signed with the representative of Bonn (not the Senate) an agreement on improved postal, telephone, and telegraph communications, complying thus with the stipulation that Bonn has the right to negotiate on behalf of West Berlin.[55]

Another indication of forthcoming troubles, stemming from controversial interpretations of the Quadripartite Agreement, was the protest of the East German press against a conference held by Bonn's Minister of Culture in West Berlin that was condemned as a continuation of "political demonstrations." [56]

One of the most politically and humanly delicate problems that will probably cloud the results of the negotiations on Berlin concerns possible misuse of the transit routes as GDR citizens try to flee to West Germany. According to at least one newspaper, the Bonn government, in such cases, would have to agree to the punishment of such refugees (or possibly

---

explanatory statement, see *Bulletin* (Bonn), No. 127, September 3, 1971, pp. 1,368-1,395.

[55] *Frankfurter Allgemeine Zeitung,* September 6, 10, 11, 17, 1971; October 1, 1971.

[56] *Ibid.,* September 25, 1971.

their return to East German authorities), whereas the FRG Constitution guarantees freedom of travel to all Germans.[57]

These few instances are indicative of the difficulties that lie ahead in the implementation of the Quadripartite Agreement, and the CDU/CSU opposition has not been slow to voice its criticisms. It pointed to the concessions, made to the Soviet Union and the GDR "partly because of the federal government's pressure." These caused them "special doubts" and Strauss branded the Agreement a "rubber treaty." [58] However, according to a poll taken in West Berlin, the percentage of the CDU respondents who, after the Agreement had been signed, considered the situation still "serious" dropped from 58 (in 1968) to 48, while the percentage of the SPD interviewees dropped drastically from 62 to 13. Between April 1968 and September 1971 the "hopeful attitude" of all respondents toward the question of Berlin increased from 39 to 64 percent, while the "skeptical judgment" decreased from 62 to 25 percent.[59] Moreover, the elections in Bremen, held in October, gave an impressive victory to the SPD, an indication that not only the West Berliners but also the West Germans were satisfied with Brandt's policy and the Berlin Agreement.

The East German government as a result of the agreement found it necessary to swallow an assortment of bitter pills. It was required to recognize the "ties" between West Berlin and West Germany, to renounce the claim that the city was an independent entity, to liberalize traffic through its territory (especially that of West Berliners), and in particular to give up the illusion of being solely responsible for matters that were originally and are now once more declared to be within the purview of Soviet rights and duties.

The GDR government, in an effort to minimize or ignore

[57] *Ibid.,* October 2, 1971.
[58] *Ibid.,* September 4, 1971; *New York Times,* September 5, 1971.
[59] *Frankfurter Allgemeine Zeitung,* September 22, 1971.

these obvious drawbacks, focused on other aspects of the Agreement. Honecker stated, "The three Western powers, the USA, Great Britain, and France, have, through the four-power agreement, for the first time bindingly expressed themselves about the German Democratic Republic as a sovereign state, about its boundary and its relations with the Federal Republic of Germany and with West Berlin." They have also for the first time stated "in an internationally binding way" that West Berlin was not a part of the Federal Republic and was not governed by it.[60] On the latter issue he was correct, but as to the matter of the GDR sovereignty he clearly not only overstated the case but also spoke prematurely. The American ambassador to the FRG set him right when he declared "unequivocally" that the Agreement did not "in any way provide recognition by the three Western allies of the sovereignty of the GDR, *de facto* or otherwise." [61] For that achievement, the GDR will have to wait until intra-German relations have been settled.

At any rate, after three months of intensive negotiations, the West and East German representatives on December 17 signed an accord which elaborates in great detail the Quadripartite Agreement that now was ready to enter into force. This step was postponed, however, because the Soviet government linked it with the ratification of the treaty with the FRG.

The Quadripartite Agreement closes one chapter of negotiations on the problem of West Berlin, but it also opens a new one; it solves some problems, but creates some new ones. It is a tenuous compromise, acceptable under the circumstances to the parties concerned, but, stemming as it does from an unnatural situation, its effectiveness depends on the good intentions not only of its signatories but also of West and East Germany. Legally, it creates a strange suzerainty

[60] *Ibid.,* September 6, 1971.
[61] *The Bulletin* (Bonn), Vol. 19, no. 33, September 28, 1971, p. 255.

over West Berlin, with Bonn having authority in matters of legislation and limited representation abroad, but with the sovereign rights vested collectively with the Four Powers. This itself is an oddity since these powers may not agree on controversial issues that may be brought before them and the Agreement makes no procedural provision for solving their own mutual disagreements. The real value of the Agreement will have to stand the test of its implementation; this will require time. Thus, as in the other areas of Brandt's *Ostpolitik,* the immediate prospect for a solution of the Berlin problem is "satisfactory," but the distant future is open to serious concern. No agreement can find a satisfactory and lasting solution for the geopolitical abnormality of West Berlin—a democratic island surrounded by a rough communist sea.

Warsaw-Bonn Reconciliation

No other country in Europe is more exposed to geopolitical factors than Poland. Nestled between Germany and the Soviet Union and never able to forget her four partitions by these two powerful neighbors, she finds her very existence dependent not only on her relations with them but also on their relationships to each other. In the period between the last two wars, the Polish government, motivated by a profound and justified distrust of both Germany and the Soviet Union, assumed first a position of hostility toward both and sought a guarantee of her national security in a close alliance with France, while her neighbors, cooperating in "the spirit of Rapallo," were secretly scheming against her. In the 1930's, with her distrust unabating but the credibility of her French alliance diminishing, she tried to balance the terrible odds of her precarious situation by seeking an accommodation with her traditional enemies (whose own relations had become tense) through treaties of non-aggression. Neither concept proved to be effective. Thus, the first political consequence of World War Two was the fourth partition of Poland. Enemy military action and occupation exposed her to incomparable suffering.

Such experiences cannot be forgotten by any nation; indeed they command a thorough reexamination of basic policy. Thus postwar Poland, under entirely new circumstances, led by communists and controlled by the Soviet Union, moved toward assurance of at least a dubious independence through alliance with Moscow. However, in so doing, her relations to the other traditional enemy, West Germany, remained unsettled, indeed hostile. It took more than a quarter of a century to regularize these relations, though in no sense were they as complete as with the Soviet Union. This new situation, however, is a most significant contribution to détente in Europe though at the same time it reveals détente's true meaning. The reconciliation between Poland and West Germany does close a painful chapter of past hostilities and symbolizes the final step in the cleansing process of the German nation from its Nazi heritage. It therefore represents not only a fresh political attitude but also a purification of moral values. Indeed, the steps that led to the reconciliation and the speeches that Chancellor Brandt made during the Bonn-Warsaw negotiations reflect this peculiar moral dimension of the issue.

The opening of contacts was tenuous and distant. Brandt began by expressing "respect" for the Oder-Neisse boundary until a peace treaty was signed. For Prime Minister Cyrankiewicz, however, "the starting point" for opening of the "process of normalization of relations [was] the recognition of Poland's western boundary as final and incontestable." He also spoke in favor of recognition of the GDR according to international law, although he no longer made the process of the normalization of relations between Poland and West Germany dependent on this step.[62]

---

[62] *Frankfurter Allgemeine Zeitung,* December 23, 1969.

Moreover, the Polish leadership was reported not to be of one mind about a proper response to Brandt's proposition for negotiations. Some "hardliners," among them allegedly Edward Gierek, took the position that nothing was to be gained since the Oder-Neisse boundary was already fixed beyond any threat. On the contrary, they saw in the negotiations an opening for imperialist diversion.[63]

Nor did Brandt, on the other hand, receive a clear-cut mandate from the West Germans to reach a final agreement on the question of frontiers. Although in the public opinion poll taken on the eve of the negotiations, in November 1969, 68 percent expressed the belief (as against 57 percent in November 1967) that the Poles had acquired home rights to the disputed territory, 47 percent considered it wrong if the Chancellor recognized beforehand the finality of the border, while 31 percent considered it right to do so. Young interviewees (between 19 and 29), however, held a different opinion: 47 percent were in favor and 41 percent were against such an action.[64]

Circumstances did not appear propitious when the State Secretary, Georg F. Duckwitz, journeyed to Warsaw at the beginning of February 1970 to open first contacts. Simultaneously, his colleague Egon Bahr negotiated in Moscow. Duckwitz held a series of six meetings, lasting until October, and was cautious to call them an "exchange of views," not negotiations. Meanwhile, however, there were more and more signs of good will on both sides. The Polish Minister of Foreign Trade, J. Burakiewicz, visited Bonn, and his West German counterpart, Schiller, reciprocated. Both visits were "firsts" by a member of one government to the other after the war. Carlo Schmid, Deputy President of the

---

[63] *Le Monde,* November 23, 1969, February 5, 1970; *Le Figaro,* April 7, 1970.

[64] Data supplied through the courtesy of *Inter Nationes* by Allensbach Institute für Demoskopie, Tables 2, 6.

Bundestag and a leading member of SPD, was in Warsaw in November; groups of politicians of both the SPD and CSU at various periods spent several days in Poland; in October a five-year trade agreement between the two countries was signed in Warsaw.

Finally, on November 2, Foreign Minister Walter Scheel left for Warsaw to bring the negotiations to a conclusion. It took nine sessions and eleven days to work out the differences, which were related not only to the question of boundary but also to the problem of the German minority in Poland whose nationals would wish to move to West Germany. On November 18 the two parties initialed the Treaty on the Foundation of the Normalization of the Mutual Relations between the FRG and the Peoples' Republic of Poland.

The awkward name of the treaty suggests that it has not solved all the problems between the two countries. Indeed, as important as it is, it only creates a basis for further constructive developments. Its substance confirms the commitments already undertaken in the Soviet-West German treaty. Accordingly, the signatories "state in mutual agreement" (West Germany thus avoided the term "recognition") that "the existing boundary line . . . shall constitute the western state frontier of the Peoples' Republic of Poland." Further, they "reaffirm the inviolability of their frontiers now and in the future and undertake to respect each other's territorial integrity without restriction." Their mutual relations would be guided by the UN Charter; accordingly, they would settle their disputes exclusively by peaceful means and refrain from any threat or use of force.

The Bonn government sent the United States, Great Britain, and France identical notes advising them that it had made it clear to the Polish government that the treaty did not affect their rights and responsibilities (concerning a final decision about boundaries), nor did it those of the Soviet Union.[65]

To meet the stipulation of Article IV of the treaty (that both governments "shall take further steps towards full normalization and a comprehensive development of their mutual relations") the Polish government communicated to Bonn "information on measures for a solution of humanitarian problems." Declining to commit itself in a contractual form, it did advise the FRG government that persons of indisputable ethnic German origin who wish to leave for either of the two German states may do so and that consideration would be given also to mixed and separated families.[66]

The promise was of substantial importance to the Bonn government, not only for the humanitarian aspect of the issue but also because it was one of the major points of criticism raised by the opposition against Brandt's policy. However, while Warsaw maintains that only "some tens of thousands of people" might meet the required criteria, Bonn thinks in terms of some 200,000 persons. The Polish government began to fulfill its promise and by January 1971 had released 3,300 emigrees; it is expected that some 90,000 will have been granted exit permits by the end of 1972.[67]

The Polish-West German treaty was signed on December 7, 1970. Willy Brandt, accompanied by prominent representatives of industry and of cultural life, went to Warsaw to put his name on the historical document. The opposition leaders, as in the case of his trip to Moscow, declined to participate in the ceremony, raising similar (but less vehemently expressed) dissatisfactions to those they had

---

[65] For the text of the treaty and related documents, see *Bulletin* (Bonn), Special Edition, No. 171, December 8, 1970, pp. 1,815-1,816.

[66] *Ibid.,* p. 1817.

[67] *Die Welt,* February 26, 1971; *New York Times,* December 7, 1970.

expressed about the treaty with the Soviet Union. The speeches and ceremonies were conspicuously solemn, appropriately so, reflecting as they did the burden of the past. However, Brandt's apparent sincerity and emotion somewhat relieved the somber atmosphere as he spoke about the evil past, about the indescribable suffering of the Polish people, and as he fell on his knees before the memorial to the Jews, expressing in a subdued tone hope for a better future.

Thus Brandt added a second stone to the edifice of his *Ostpolitik,* although it too, as in the case of the Soviet-West German treaty, was implanted on somewhat shifting soil because it too was to be ratified only after a "satisfactory" solution is reached on Berlin. This is a surprising condition because Poland has no responsibilities for the city. However, as Scheel put it, on the solution of the Berlin problem depends "the ratification of the whole range of the East European treaties. For the entirety is after all an attempt to achieve an effective détente in Europe"—and one cannot speak at all about détente as long as tensions about Berlin are not solved.[68] Luckily for the final fate of the Polish-West German treaty (as well as of the Soviet-West German treaty) an agreement on Berlin has been reached.

To complete the circle of his *Ostpolitik* Brandt now turned to the minor problem of settling FRG relations with Czechoslovakia and the major problem of finding a solution to the relationship between "two German states of one German nation."

The Munich Tangle

To Brandt, normalization of the relations between Czechoslovakia and the FRG took a subordinate place to the more important solution of Bonn's relations with Moscow and Warsaw. In his first governmental declaration, on October 28,

---

[68] *Die Welt,* November 30, 1970.

1969, which happened to be the anniversary of Czechoslovakia's Independence Day, he simply wanted to make it clear that West Germany was "ready to reach with [her] immediate Czechoslovak neighbor an agreement that would surmount the past." [69]

Gustav Husák, the Moscow-controlled new leader of the communist party of Czechoslovakia, appeared eager not to remain behind his Soviet and Polish colleagues. As Bonn's negotiations with Moscow and Warsaw were about to open, he proposed to Bonn an economic and technological cooperation and an understanding on a number of practical questions. At the same time, however, he stressed that West Germany's relations with the whole socialist camp depended on the FRG's relations with the GDR. "We guarantee our absolute solidarity with the German Democratic Republic, we support its [claim] for a full *de jure* recognition," he stated.[70] Obviously he did not realize that Moscow and Warsaw were about to separate themselves on this issue from the wishes of East Berlin.

Brandt was not in a hurry to open negotiations with Prague, for he rightly expected that, once the negotiations with Moscow succeeded, Husák would dutifully follow the Soviet policy; nor was he sure as yet of the security of Husák's political position; nor did he want to create the impression that Bonn "was undertaking too much, concerning the number of negotiations, or that [it] was pushing." [71]

The Munich Agreement was, of course, the chief stumbling block to a Czechoslovak-West German understanding. In contrast to the problem of the Oder-Neisse boundary, of the international position of East Germany, and of Berlin (which are related not only to West Germany's *Ostpolitik* but also to the Big Four responsibilities for a final settlement of the

---

[69] *Texte zur Deutschlandpolitik, op.cit.,* Vol. IV, p. 38.
[70] *Die Welt,* December 11, 1969.
[71] *Ibid.,* December 13, 1969.

problem of Germany), the Munich question belongs strictly in the domain of Czechoslovak-West German relations. However, Prague saw it primarily as a political problem, while Bonn was concerned principally with the legal consequences of its solution.

As the Czechoslovak government continued to express interest in bringing the question to a solution (and began subtly to deemphasize its intransigent attitude) and as West Germany meanwhile signed treaties with the Soviet Union and Poland, contacts were quietly opened between Bonn and Prague. After a preliminary conversation in Prague, which was conducted in October 1970 by Counsellor Jürgen von Alten, State Secretary Paul Frank in March 1971 opened a series of exploratory conversations that received little publicity but that will probably lead to an agreement. It would be based on Brandt's formula that would presumably satisfy both sides: Munich is "invalid and from the beginning unjust." [72]

Thus, another pillar will be erected in Brandt's *Ostpolitik* and then normalization of relations with Hungary and Bulgaria will presumably follow. It is a most impressive achievement, indeed, but even with these astonishing results of Brandt's two years of effort, his imposingly designed structure will remain incomplete as long as still another and larger problem remains unsettled—the relations between the two Germanys.

The Intra-German Syndrome

Intra-German relations are for both West and East Germany (and in the final analysis for the whole of Europe) a witches' brew of factors and forces, a cauldron of ideologies and power politics and national pride and prejudice that on the one hand is appalling to contemplate and on the other

[72] Radio Free Europe, Research, *Czechoslovakia/19*, May 26, 1971.

demands an ultimate solution if enduring détente in Europe is to be achieved.

As in all other aspects of Brandt's new *Ostpolitik,* his policy toward the GDR is heavy on short-run plans and hopes but filled with uncertainties for the distant future. As long as the reunification of Germany was the principal goal of West Germany's *Ostpolitik,* Ulbricht could continue with his intransigent demands for full recognition of the GDR and could rely on the unqualified support of his allies. In fact, he thrived on tensions in Europe, on her division into two irreconcilable camps; he was an implacable enemy of détente. Now that Brandt has found a course that may lead to a reconciliation with the Soviet Union and Poland, and now that the Big Four have reached an understanding on the normalization of West Berlin, a "regulated coexistence" (a term used by Brandt) may prove to be not at all to East Germany's liking. No wonder that the East German government has tried from the outset to undermine Brandt's *Ostpolitik.* But it could not resist it too vigorously because the other members of the Warsaw Pact were determined to make the best use of the policy of détente and East Berlin had no choice but to adjust itself to the new situation.

When Brandt proposed to Ulbricht negotiation on the basis of equality, recognizing the existence "of two German states of one nation" (a formula which Ulbricht had used as late as April 1967), states that are not "strangers to one another," and the establishment of relations "of special nature," though "without discrimination," he was indeed going more than halfway to compromise. The GDR first rejected the proposition, continuing to beat the drum of full recognition according to the norms of international law. However, as it became apparent to Ulbricht that, like it or not, his allies were actually engaged in a variety of treaty negotiations with West Germany, his vocabulary concerning recognition

236

slowly changed. It was not just a matter of semantics; it was a change, though a subtle one, in substance.

Reacting to Brandt's public invitation for opening negotiations, Ulbricht sent a letter to President Heinemann on December 17, 1969, attaching a draft treaty on which the relations between the two countries ought to be established. It was the first official contact at the level of Heads of States since 1951; the draft contained the same points that the GDR government had once before submitted to Bonn in September 1967. It contained articles on establishing normal state relations, on the inviolability of frontiers, on forbidding any discrimination between the two countries, on renunciation of acquiring atomic weapons and on the possession of chemical or biological weapons, on mutual disarmament, on recognition of West Berlin as an independent political entity, and on admission of both Germanys to the United Nations.[73]

President Heinemann politely answered the letter and referred the draft treaty to the government. Some of its points were acceptable to Bonn; others were open to negotiations; still others were not negotiable at all. However, feeling that the time was not ripe to open negotiations on such far-reaching aspects as were contained in the draft, Bonn declined to pursue it further. Nevertheless, after twenty years of the existence of two German states, the two sides were for the first time ready to enter into official contact and to discuss the problems that had separated them for so long. It was to be a difficult road that might one day lead them to a normalization of their relations.

Characteristic of the difficulties the two adversaries were to face was such a seemingly insignificant arrangement as to where they were to meet. The East German government proposed East Berlin; the West German government, while

---

[73] *Texte zur Deutschlandpolitik, op.cit.,* Vol. IV, pp. 144-147.

accepting, insisted that Brandt make a stop in West Berlin. Ulbricht rejected the idea because the visit to West Berlin would once again demonstrate the city's ties with the FRG, this time with the obvious implication that Ulbricht was condoning Brandt's demonstration. Finally, the ancient towns of Erfurt in East Germany and Kassel in West Germany were selected as the places for the meetings.

The historical significance of these occasions does not lie in what was achieved but rather in the notion that a new era had started in relations between the two Germanys, that thereafter they would never be the same. Neither of the two meetings produced anything new; nor did they yield any positive result. Willi Stoph in Erfurt (March 19) repeated the old demands and proposed to conduct the negotiations on the basis of (1) creating normal and equal relations between the two countries in conformity with international law and without any discrimination; (2) non-intervention in the external affairs of the other state and clear rejection of the Hallstein Doctrine; (3) reaching an agreement on renunciation of force; (4) recognition of the juridical existence and territorial integrity and inviolability of boundaries; (5) candidature of the two countries to the United Nations; (6) renunciation of production and possession of nuclear, chemical, and bacteriological arms, and reduction of the defense budgets by fifty percent. He also advanced the demand for 100 billion marks in reparation as a reimbursement for the losses that East Germany suffered before the construction of the Berlin Wall.[74]

[74] *Ibid.*, pp. 327-349. The request for reparations was not quite new; it had been raised before by Ulbricht, shortly after the Wall had been erected and again in April 1968. The figure of 100 billion marks was composed of 33 billion as an indemnity for loss of manpower of over 3 million persons who fled East Germany and of 66.4 billion, which represented a proportionate part of the reparations that the GDR had paid, supposedly on behalf of all Germany, to the Soviet

Brandt's speech at Erfurt only confirmed the profound abyss that separated the two parties. He advanced the equally well-known position of his government. He asked for détente instead of tensions, for peace instead of confrontation. He spoke about humane relations, pointing in particular to such cases as the separation of children from their parents, of affianced persons awaiting each other and separated by boundaries. On the more political and substantive problems he stressed again "the lasting and living reality of one German nation," which although now in two states, must exist next to each other, find a regulated form of peaceful coexistence that would not prejudice the right of self-determination of future generations. Under no circumstances, he stressed, could the negotiations abrogate the rights of the Big Four concerning Germany and Berlin. Brandt then summarized his government's position as a foundation for negotiations: (1) both states have an obligation to preserve the unity of the German nation, for they are not foreign countries; (2) their relationship must be based on the recognized principles of international law, without discrimination, with respect for territorial integrity, the peaceful solution of disputes, and respect for boundaries; (3) each is obligated not to try to change by force the other's social structure; (4) each must develop efforts toward neighborly cooperation; (5) each must respect the rights and responsibilities of the Big Four; and (6) each must support the Big Four efforts on Berlin.

As one can see, there were points in the position taken by the representatives of the two otherwise hostile countries that were either identical or similar. Brandt also agreed with Stoph on the question of renunciation of force and was close to him on the question of the membership of both states in the United Nations and on limitation of armament. He asked,

Union and Poland. (Radio Free Europe, Research, *GDR/7,* April 10, 1970.)

in addition, for an enlarged trade and for the opening of personal contacts. Against Stoph's accusations, he also defended Bonn's policy of peace and alliance with the West. However, on one issue, the crucial issue, Brandt could not satisfy Stoph's demand: recognizing East Germany as a "foreign" country.[75]

Obviously, for both sides, the purpose of the Erfurt meeting was to state their position, a position which, in the case of the GDR, had been known for years and, in the case of the FRG, since Brandt had become Chancellor. Its importance lies in the fact that it did take place.

The second meeting, at Kassel (May 21), was of the same nature, only more tense and, on the part of Stoph, bellicose. To him Brandt's idea on "special intra-German relations" was "absolutely unacceptable."[76] The stand taken by each side appeared as irreconcilable as ever. However, some important facts emerged from the meetings. First, the continuous existence of East Germany was recognized by Bonn not only as a prerequisite to a solution of the German problem but also as an integral assumption of efforts toward détente. Moreover, West Germany had taken the problem of Germany into her own hands, a position which, according to a view expressed privately by a high official in Bonn, was alarming to France, received without enthusiasm in England and with reservations in America.

The meetings caused some dissension also in both East and West German domestic politics. According to the same source, the SED Politburo was split into two factions; Stoph represented a pragmatic position, in favor of contacts with Bonn, while Ulbricht, Honecker, Winzer, and Norden saw in the negotiations a threat to the building of socialism in East Germany. One day, a high official in Bonn remarked,

---

[75] *Ibid.,* pp. 350-364.
[76] *The Bulletin* (Bonn), Vol. 18, No. 17, May 26, 1970.

they will emerge as followers of the best Prussian tradition and advocate reunification—on their own terms.

As to CDU/CSU, Brandt's actions caused divisions in the ranks of its leadership, with Strauss seeing "the shadow of Moscow growing more and more over Europe," Schroeder supporting the government's policy and Barzel taking a middle position, trying to preserve party unity.[77]

However, public opinion appears to have accepted and supported Brandt's policy. Soon after he had announced the government's program, 74 percent of respondents to a public opinion poll thought it right for him to meet with a representative of the GDR, 10 percent were against; and almost every second interviewee (47 percent) was ready to accept the recognition of the GDR. In May, 1970, 77 percent were in favor of bringing about some practical advantages to Germans in both parts of the country before international recognition could be considered, and 14 percent supported Stoph's demand. In February, 1971, however, the percentage of those in favor of recognition dropped to 40 percent. Nevertheless, 46 percent "trusted most" SPD, 26 percent CDU, and 6 percent FDP; and in April, 84 percent expressed satisfaction with the government's work. Still later, in October 1971, according to a poll taken by the Allensbach Institute for Demoscopy, 70 percent of the population believed that the SPD was the party doing most for German reunification (as against 52 percent in 1969) while the CDU scored only 10 percent and the FDP 4 percent. This is rather a surprising view, for it may be said that while Kiesinger's and Barzel's party failed to advance the goal of reunification, Brandt's party, it would appear moved away from it. Scheel's party, as one would expect, riding on the crest of Brandt's popularity, recorded only an embarrassing fraction of recognition.

However, the poll also indicated another aspect of West

[77] *Frankfurter Allgemeine Zeitung,* March 26, 1970.

Germany's political thinking, one that may be significant in terms of her future international position. In the fall of 1969, 39 percent of all respondents expressed themselves in favor of neutrality; two years later the percentage rose to 50 percent. In the fall of 1969, 48 percent had been in favor of a firm military alliance with the United States; by 1971 the percentage dropped to 39—an ominous sign for the West but a welcome indicator to the Soviet Union that its concept of détente was working.[78] It was obviously Brandt's success in negotiating the treaties with Moscow and Warsaw and the agreement on Berlin that caused such a marked change in West German public opinion.

These events also influenced the position of the East German government on intra-German relations. While the treaties were still in a negotiating stage the GDR came to realize that its policy toward the FRG was being charted in Moscow and it quietly but quickly retreated from the ultra-intransigent position that it had taken at the Erfurt and Kassel meetings. In July 1970, in the midst of Soviet-West German negotiations, Ulbricht, and after him Norden and Winzer, anticipated the inevitable and stated that the relations between West and East Germany must be based on the principle of peaceful coexistence, without insisting on full international recognition.[79] Subsequently, when the text of the Soviet-West German treaty was made public, Ulbricht could find at least partial satisfaction in Bonn's recognition of the existence of the GDR, the inviolability of its boundary, and the integrity of its territory. The Council of GDR Ministers, however, went beyond the meaning of the treaty when it stated that it made the establishment of normal diplomatic relations between the two Germanys necessary, that Wash-

---

[78] *Le Monde,* December 24, 1969; *International Herald Tribune,* May 23, 1970; *Die Welt,* January 16, March 13, 31, April 16, 1971; *Frankfurter Allgemeine Zeitung,* October 21, 1971.

[79] *Frankfurter Allgemeine Zeitung,* July 14, 17, 1970.

ington, London, and Paris—which approved the pact—would now also normalize their relations with the GDR and would not put obstacles to the entrance of both Germanys into the United Nations; and that other third countries would not delay opening diplomatic relations with the GDR. Interestingly (and eloquently) enough, the Soviet newspapers, when reproducing East Berlin's statement, abstained from quoting its interpretative sentences.[80]

Some difficult situations awaited Ulbricht. When the Warsaw Pact countries met in Moscow on August 20 he had no choice but to join in welcoming the pact without reservations, amplifications, or clarifications. Once the Soviet-West German relations were put on a treaty basis, the East German leaders' course was determined. From time to time, Ulbricht and others still raised their wounded heads, refusing to discuss "intra-German relations," insisting on separation (*Abgrenzung,* a new term in the East German political dictionary) of the two Germanys, rejecting Brandt's notion of "one German nation," and accusing Bonn of American-supported imperialism. But in decisive moments they followed the Moscow line. On the occasion of the Warsaw Pact meeting in East Berlin on December 2, 1970 they had to be satisfied with the broad meaning of the declaration which called for "equal relations, based on generally valid norms of international law" between the GDR and FRG.

Then, something unexpected but significant occurred in May 1971: Walter Ulbricht resigned as First Secretary of the SED, giving as his reason old age and ill health. This man, who had helped found the GDR, who had run its affairs for over twenty-five years with an iron hand, who had proved to be the most skillful operator in complex international situations, who survived all the many purges in communist ranks before and after the war, who always could bend

---

[80] *Die Welt,* August 14, 21, 1970.

(happily or unhappily) to the changing directions of Soviet politics and dictates, disappeared with neither ceremonial nor sadness just on the eve of the party's Eighth Congress. He was rewarded for his lifelong services with the dubious honor of the nomination as the party's chairman, keeping the function of head of state.

This event, as well as Ulbricht's absence from the Congress in June, triggered off a chain of speculation about the causes and circumstances of the change. On the one hand, convictions were expressed that Ulbricht was removed because his stubborn attitude had become inconvenient to Moscow, which in its familiar merciless way reached the conclusion that "the Moor has done his work, the Moor can go." On the other hand, the maiden speech delivered by his successor, Erich Honecker, did not provide any convincing clue to the reasons of the change in party leadership. True, Honecker was critical of East Germany's economic development; he even condemned the past practices of subjectivism and the abuse of the collective and proclaimed, as every new communist team does, faithfulness to the principle of collective leadership. However, in foreign affairs he followed in Ulbricht's path, confirming indestructible links with the Soviet Union and defining his attitude toward West Germany and West Berlin in similar, though somewhat softer, terms to what Ulbricht had used in the preceding year. If Moscow is truly interested in extending the policy of détente to intra-German relations—and without it no détente in Europe is thinkable—it could not have welcomed Honecker's attack against Bonn's "counter-revolutionary attempts" to restore capitalism in East Germany, against its revanchist policy, pursued by "the ruling circles of the FRG." [81] Even Ulbricht had recently abstained from such extreme accusations of the Bonn government. However, past experience suggests that oratorical outbursts do not bind

[81] Radio Free Europe, Research, *GDR, Party,* June 16, 1971.

any communist leader to any particular line and that Honecker too may soft-pedal his stand if "the interests of the socialist commonwealth" require such a change. The paramount question that remains is: what are the Soviet Union's intentions and its perceptions of détente in its European entirety?

At the moment, intra-German relations continue to be in suspense. Since the autumn of 1970, the State Secretary, Egon Bahr, for the FRG and for the GDR, Michael Kohl, met regularly but instead of discussing intra-German relations they focused on preparing an agreement on Berlin which was to complement the Quadripartite Agreement.

When serious negotiations start they will undoubtedly be arduous and long. If they succeed, the East German regime will have to reconcile itself to a relationship between the "two German states of one nation" as one of "special nature." It will have to pay this price for an intra-German détente. Then the magnetic attractiveness of "one nation" may weaken the artificial cohesiveness of the East German socialist nation, separated from the West German "bourgeois" nation. The GDR regime is aware of this danger and it will face it in the light of Moscow's interests.

The attitude of the Soviet government toward East Berlin's policy depends on the broader question of how its relations with the FRG will progress. If its policy of détente is genuine it will press Honecker to reach an agreement with Brandt. If it is a device to keep intra-German relations disgruntled and Western Europe's relations with the East in tensions, the East German government will be given a free hand not only in an agreement with West Germany but also in undermining all the other pacts. Once again, here is proof that the key to détente is in Moscow; it remains to be seen whether and for what purpose it will use it in the case of East Germany.

Taken all together, the picture is a veritable web of issues, national and international, at times complementary, at times contradictory, some apparently soluble, others apparently equally insoluble, all of them forming supposedly one whole. The intra-German cauldron persists; on its solution depends Brandt's daring *Ostpolitik* in its entirety and on this depends détente in Europe. These are the vagaries of the whole problem: that years of effort that now yield some hope for realization also inescapably entail, in equal measure, grave risks of failure of unpredictable consequences.

A Conclusion

Is DETENTE in Europe real? durable? Or is the term destined to join the host of threadbare political clichés?

The evidence of almost fifteen years of East-West European relations suggests that the détente is real, although limited in nature and scope, but that its durability is at best uncertain and at worst illusory. It may be that, given the character of international relations, one cannot expect more positive and permanent results. Perhaps nations and governments must be confined to modest goals of an immediate nature in the long process of the settlement of conflicting issues. However, the results of real statesmanship are ultimately measured not by the appearances of today but by the reality of years and decades. History has taught us well that events which give a semblance of success today may prove to be the very cause of failure tomorrow. Thus, the current achievements in détente are still on trial and will be for years to come.

Current achievements are not inconsiderable. The political configuration of Europe in the first part of the 1970's is undoubtedly materially different from the situation in the 1950's. The partition of Europe is not so rigid today as it was then. Trade between its two parts has grown steadily and cultural contacts have expanded. But experience has clearly demonstrated the limits of both economic and cultural détente: the first has failed to overcome the basic problems arising from two different economic and social systems; the latter has rarely affected, and has always been subservient to, vicissitudes and conflicting ideological and political considerations.

However, in politics (if not in ideology) fundamental changes have taken place. Negotiation has been substituted for confrontation and major conflicts resulting from the war and the postwar division of Europe are on the way toward a settlement. West Germany has normalized her relations with her erstwhile enemies in the east and will most probably reach an accommodation with East Germany. West Berlin will be quasi-legally assured of its ties with the FRG although, in fact, continuously exposed to the tenuousness of its unalterable geopolitical position.

There is no value in attempting to establish a balance sheet of gains and losses in the negotiations that have led toward European détente. The Soviet Union and its allies have achieved what they had been striving for for twenty years— recognition of the status quo in East Europe, short only of two demands: full recognition of the GDR and of West Berlin as an independent entity. The West, and in particular West Germany, has been able to minimize, though not exclude, tensions around Berlin and has preserved the hope against hope that a close relationship of "two German states of one German nation" can be developed.

The West paid a high price for questionable Soviet concessions. But since it is evident that there was no other alternative (given Soviet intransigence) if détente was to be achieved, the cardinal issue is not positing gains against losses but to look beyond present achievements. The spirit of détente does create a new situation in Europe, but the future remains a winding, rocky path that may lead to a higher plateau of consolidation and cooperation or to a precipice of aggravated conflicts. The danger of the latter will increase if the West fails to take most carefully calculated looks at each "next step."

The principal obstacle to a policy beyond current détente remains continuing suspicion on both sides. As evidenced by their attitude toward various aspects of détente, the Soviet Union and its allies perceive West Europe's motives for such a policy as a capitalist ruse to undermine the communist system in East Europe and to free that area from Soviet domination. This perception is justified only indirectly and that to an insignificant extent. West Europe believes that

East Europe, reaping benefits from détente, will shake off the most rigid aspects of a communist regime, but it hardly expects—particularly after the Soviet invasion of Czechoslovakia—that any country of the area could act against Soviet will. Moreover, modern history has demonstrated the inability of a democratic country successfully to infiltrate and subvert a totalitarian regime.

On the other hand, West Europe has no single perception of the Soviet policy of détente. It varies from country to country and within each nation. France, for instance, is more trusting of Soviet intentions than is West Germany, and Great Britain stands aloof from the possible political implications of détente. Within each nation, conservative parties tend to be more cautious than the progressive elements. On the whole, however, West Europe has accepted Soviet professions of détente in good faith and the "new Europe," fashioned according to the Soviet model of détente, is viewed with a sense of visible relief.

It is exactly this West European mood of relaxation, which approaches complacency, that is the grave danger accompanying any further progress beyond détente, a danger that could destroy détente itself. It will be only natural, from the Soviet point of view, for Moscow to probe into any avenue that could weaken the West. The evidence—as seen in Moscow's changing policy toward individual countries of the West, her sinuous approach to the question of European security, and her continuing attempts to weaken or eliminate the American presence in West Europe—indicates that Moscow will miss no opportunity to use détente to strengthen its own position toward the West and to exploit fully any indication of the West's own weakness. There is little consolation in the awareness that the consolidation of the West's strength lies in its own hand. Experience tells us that democracies rarely foresee or plan against crises until they face them directly and irrevocably. NATO grew out of just such a critical (and unpredicted) situation. But as détente in Europe progressed and the European members of the Atlantic alliance saw in détente an opportunity to foster their individual national interests, the thrust of NATO was quickly weakened. Now, British entry into the EEC may once again encourage not only the trend toward economic integration but also the political cohesion of Western Europe, a process that may create a strength approximate to the power of the United States or the Soviet Union. Moscow is clearly aware of this and will respond. Thus, the very development of such an integrated West Europe will tend only to deepen the artificial division of Europe and in terms of détente may well become counterproductive.

It is, indeed, a vicious circle: a weak West Europe offers Moscow an opportunity for exploiting détente; a strong West Europe would seem to immobilize détente and deepen Europe's partition. Détente cannot progress from its present level of mutual acceptance of currently achieved positions to a new relationship of an assured peace until the chief barrier between the East and West is removed: mistrust. As long as the East remains a secretive system, as long as it continues to see the West within the context of fixed and unyielding ideology, and as long as the West must base its every action on its knowledge of these realities, mistrust will remain as the principal ingredient of East-West relationships.

If this assumption is valid, then only a liberalization of the communist camp will turn an armed détente into a policy of peaceful, constructive cooperation. This will not be achieved overnight. It will be a long, seesaw struggle. But there is hope that with continuing and prolonged experimentation in reforms, with an increasing need of Western technology and under the impact of increased and more intimate association with the West, the East will come to realize that a modern, sophisticated society cannot finally prosper without a continuing response to man's longing for individual dignity.

250

Throughout history mankind has struggled toward this goal. Today, in the East, those desires have surfaced in a variety of forms: workers' protests, the insistence of intellectuals for greater freedom, and even moments of national upheaval. These activities have been suppressed, as they will be in the future, but, once they have occurred, the people concerned are never again the same. The hunger for freedom has deepened, and men will not be silenced forever. In what year or what decade this will happen, no one can say. But it will happen. For the perennial struggle of mankind for freedom is both man's uniqueness as man and the ultimate justification for his existence. Until the process of liberalization brings fundamental freedom, and with it trust and mutual goodwill, détente in Europe will be tentative in time and in reality.

TABLES

TABLE 1

Foreign Trade within the Communist Countries* (in percentages of total trade)

	1958 Imp	1958 Exp	1960 Imp	1960 Exp	1962 Imp	1962 Exp	1963 Imp	1963 Exp	1964 Imp	1964 Exp	1965 Imp	1965 Exp	1966 Imp	1966 Exp	1967 Imp	1967 Exp	1968 Imp	1968 Exp
USSR																		
"Socialist Bloc"	74.5	73.0	68.8	74.4	70.7	69.8	70.6	70.1	69.1	70.4	69.7	68.0	66.5	66.4	69.7	66.1	67.7	67.1
East European Bloc	50.7	54.0	50.1	56.1	55.6	56.5	58.7	57.2	57.5	58.6	58.0	55.7	56.4	53.1	59.7	52.2	60.0	53.0
Asian East Bloc	22.7	17.8	17.8	17.3	10.8	7.0	8.3	6.1	6.3	5.3	5.0	5.9	4.1	5.5	2.9	5.1	2.4	5.5
East Germany																		
"Socialist Bloc"	70.9	76.8	73.9	75.7	79.4	78.7	78.1	79.0	75.1	77.6	73.1	74.9	71.7	74.4	73.0	75.2	75.5	76.7
East European Bloc	62.8	65.0	66.7	68.7	75.0	74.8	73.3	75.3	71.0	73.3	68.0	70.7	67.3	68.7	68.5	69.9	71.5	71.4
Asian East Bloc	6.7	7.8	5.2	5.4	1.8	1.5	1.4	0.8	1.3	1.0	1.3	1.4	1.3	1.3	1.5	2.2	1.2	2.4
Poland																		
"Socialist Bloc"	58.2	58.6	62.7	62.3	66.1	62.8	67.0	63.5	63.0	64.4	66.1	63.2	64.3	61.6	65.7	63.7	64.4	65.5
East European Bloc	53.0	47.9	58.2	55.0	61.3	58.2	62.6	58.9	58.9	59.8	61.5	59.0	60.1	55.8	62.5	59.4	61.1	61.4
Asian East Bloc	3.4	7.4	3.5	4.6	1.7	1.4	1.7	1.2	1.7	1.3	1.7	1.5	1.4	2.1	1.1	2.2	1.7	2.2
Czechoslovakia																		
"Socialist Bloc"	70.5	70.4	71.2	71.7	74.0	74.3	73.5	75.5	72.6	73.8	73.4	73.1	70.3	70.2	72.0	71.6	72.1	71.5
East European Bloc	62.2	60.2	64.0	63.6	69.0	70.4	68.6	70.0	68.6	67.7	68.0	67.7	64.1	63.6	67.6	65.4	67.5	64.4
Asian East Bloc	7.3	8.6	5.9	6.9	2.2	1.2	2.1	1.8	1.7	1.0	1.2	1.6	1.7	1.8	1.1	1.7	1.2	1.8
Hungary																		
"Socialist Bloc"	71.4	71.9	70.4	71.3	71.4	73.7	68.9	70.4	66.6	71.2	67.0	70.0	64.9	68.3	66.6	68.6	68.5	71.9
East European Bloc	63.3	56.8	63.9	61.4	68.1	68.9	65.0	66.2	63.4	67.0	63.8	66.0	61.3	64.2	63.9	66.4	65.9	67.5
Asian East Bloc	5.7	9.5	4.4	5.6	1.5	1.8	2.0	0.9	1.6	0.9	1.3	1.6	1.5	1.9	0.7	1.8	0.8	2.2
Rumania																		
"Socialist Bloc"	79.2	76.2	73.1	73.0	67.4	68.4	67.9	69.9	68.0	68.8	61.2	68.6	57.2	62.0	48.2	56.6	51.4	59.5
East European Bloc	74.8	68.8	67.9	65.8	64.2	65.9	64.2	64.8	64.9	64.8	57.5	63.6	52.8	55.9	44.6	50.2	46.0	52.1
Asian East Bloc	3.7	6.4	4.4	6.0	1.6	1.3	2.5	2.8	2.3	2.4	2.6	3.3	3.0	4.0	2.6	4.7	3.2	4.6
Bulgaria																		
"Socialist Bloc"	85.3	86.4	83.9	83.9	82.9	82.4	82.4	82.1	75.6	80.0	74.2	79.4	69.5	76.4	74.0	77.9	76.7	78.6
East European Bloc	82.2	81.8	80.3	80.7	79.6	77.4	79.7	79.2	72.9	76.3	70.1	75.6	66.2	70.6	70.7	74.2	72.9	74.9
Asian East Bloc	2.5	3.1	2.3	1.8	0.6	0.9	0.7	0.7	0.6	0.7	0.4	0.5	0.4	0.8	0.3	0.9	0.4	0.7
Albania																		
"Socialist Bloc"	97.3	97.9	94.9	98.8	95.5	93.6	93.5	94.4	.	.	.	.	.	.	.	.	.	.
East European Bloc	94.5	92.1	85.9	93.0	26.9	60.9	.	.	.	.	.	.	.	.	.	.	.	.
Asian East Bloc	2.2	2.7	8.6	4.9	66.3	29.6	.	.	.	.	.	.	.	.	.	.	.	.

Note: . = data not available.   * Source: Compiled from Office statistique des Communautés Européenes. *Bloc Oriental 6,* 1969, no. 6, pp. 25-26.

TABLE II

Imports from Non-Communist Countries and the EEC to East Europe*
(in percentages of total imports)

	1958 Non-C	EEC	1960 Non-C	EEC	1962 Non-C	EEC	1963 Non-C	EEC	1964 Non-C	EEC	1965 Non-C	EEC	1966 Non-C	EEC	1967 Non-C	EEC	1968 Non-C	EEC
USSR	25.5	5.1	31.2	8.2	29.3	8.4	29.4	6.0	30.9	5.4	30.3	5.1	33.5	6.0	30.3	8.0	32.3	9.6
East Germany	29.1	14.9	26.1	12.7	20.6	10.4	21.9	10.9	24.9	12.5	26.9	13.1	28.3	15.0	27.0	13.6	24.5	11.7
Poland	41.8	11.2	37.3	10.1	33.9	7.1	33.0	8.3	37.0	9.0	33.9	9.0	35.7	9.6	34.3	10.4	35.6	12.7
Czechoslovakia	29.5	9.0	28.8	7.5	26.0	7.6	26.5	5.7	27.4	6.6	26.6	7.1	29.7	8.2	28.0	8.3	27.9	9.4
Hungary	28.6	11.6	29.6	13.5	28.6	11.6	31.1	13.1	33.4	12.7	33.0	12.5	35.1	13.2	33.4	12.6	31.5	12.2
Rumania	20.8	10.6	26.9	14.5	32.6	16.7	32.1	16.2	32.0	17.0	38.8	21.0	42.8	23.2	51.8	32.8	48.6	26.3
Bulgaria	14.7	8.1	16.1	9.1	17.1	7.3	17.6	7.9	24.4	10.4	25.7	11.9	30.5	16.3	26.0	12.8	23.3	11.0
Albania	2.7	2.3	5.1	3.6	4.5	2.9	6.5	5.2	.	.	.	.	.	.	.	.	.	.

Note: . = data not available.

* Source: Compiled from Office statistique des Communautés Européenes, *Bloc Oriental* 6, 1969, no. 6, p. 25.

TABLE III

Exports from East Europe to Non-Communist Countries and EEC*
(in percentages of total exports)

	1958 Non-C	EEC	1960 Non-C	EEC	1962 Non-C	EEC	1963 Non-C	EEC	1964 Non-C	EEC	1965 Non-C	EEC	1966 Non-C	EEC	1967 Non-C	EEC	1968 Non-C	EEC
USSR	27.0	6.3	25.6	6.7	30.2	6.3	29.9	6.4	29.6	6.2	32.0	6.3	33.6	7.0	33.9	7.5	32.9	7.1
East Germany	23.2	13.3	24.3	13.6	21.3	11.3	21.0	11.3	22.4	11.7	25.1	12.6	25.6	12.7	24.8	12.0	23.3	12.3
Poland	41.4	11.3	37.7	10.4	37.2	10.4	36.5	10.1	35.6	9.9	36.8	10.4	38.4	11.2	36.3	10.4	34.5	10.3
Czechoslovakia	29.6	7.3	28.3	7.0	25.7	6.9	24.5	6.9	26.2	7.5	26.9	7.4	29.8	7.9	28.4	8.3	28.5	9.6
Hungary	28.1	11.0	28.7	11.0	26.3	10.1	29.6	12.5	28.8	11.4	30.0	11.7	31.7	13.0	31.4	12.4	28.1	11.2
Rumania	23.8	11.9	27.0	13.1	31.6	15.4	30.1	15.7	31.2	14.3	31.4	14.7	38.0	18.4	43.4	19.2	40.5	17.4
Bulgaria	13.6	6.7	16.1	6.5	17.6	8.7	17.9	8.3	20.0	8.2	20.6	8.0	23.6	9.8	22.1	9.9	21.4	7.8
Albania	2.1	2.1	1.2	1.0	6.4	3.2	5.6	5.2	.	.	.	.	.	.	.	.	.	.

Note: . = data not available.

* Source: Compiled from Office statistique des Communautés Européenes, *Bloc Oriental* 6, 1969, no. 6, p. 26.

TABLE IV

Shares of the Trade of the Communist Countries in the EEC Trade
With the Third Countries*
(in percentages)

	1958	1960	1961	1962	1963	1964	1965	1966	1967	1968
Imports	7.0	8.1	6.7	7.7	8.9	7.7	8.4	8.9	9.6	9.3
Exports	8.6	10.1	8.8	8.5	8.0	8.5	8.6	9.8	11.4	11.2

* Source: Compiled from Office statistique des Communautés Européenes, *Bloc Oriental* 6, 1969, no. 6, pp. 31-35.

TABLE V

EEC Shares in East Europe's Foreign Trade with non-Communist Countries*
(in percentages)

		1958	1960	1962	1963	1964	1965	1966	1967	1968
USSR	Import	20.0	26.4	28.7	20.5	17.5	16.9	17.9	26.2	29.8
	Export	23.4	26.2	20.7	21.4	20.8	19.9	20.8	22.0	21.7
Poland	Import	26.9	27.2	21.0	25.1	24.4	26.7	26.9	30.3	34.4
	Export	27.3	27.5	28.0	27.7	27.8	28.3	29.0	28.5	29.7
Czecho-slovakia	Import	30.55	26.0	29.2	21.6	23.6	26.5	27.6	29.7	33.7
	Export	24.5	24.7	26.9	28.3	28.8	27.4	26.5	29.1	33.8
Hungary	Import	40.6	45.7	40.6	42.1	38.0	36.9	37.5	37.9	38.7
	Export	39.2	38.4	38.3	42.1	39.7	37.8	41.0	39.3	39.8
Rumania	Import	51.3	53.8	51.1	50.4	53.2	54.2	54.3	64.1	54.1
	Export	50.0	48.6	48.8	52.1	45.9	47.0	48.3	44.2	42.8
Bulgaria	Import	55.0	56.2	42.6	44.9	42.6	46.2	53.5	49.3	47.3
	Export	49.6	40.3	49.5	46.4	40.7	38.9	41.4	44.6	36.5
Albania	Import	85.7	70.7	75.0	68.8	80.5	.	.	.	.
	Export				92.6					

		1958		1960		1962		1963		1964		1965		1966		1967		1968	
		A	B	A	B	A	B	A	B	A	B	A	B	A	B	A	B	A	B
East Germany	Import	20.2	51.4	20.0	48.6	19.2	50.5	12.4	49.7	19.3	50.5	22.4	48.7	23.9	53.2	24.2	50.5	19.9	47.8
	Export	17.8	53.7	19.9	56.1	19.3	52.8	19.7	53.9	20.0	52.3	20.1	50.3	20.0	49.9	21.1	48.5	24.3	52.8

A = without interzonal trade   B = with interzonal trade   Note: . = data not available.

* Source: Compiled from Office statistique des Communautés Européenes, *Bloc Oriental 6*, 1969, no. 6, pp. 27-30.

TABLE VI

East Europe's Foreign Trade with Non-Communist Countries*
(participation of individual EEC countries in percentages)

	1958	1960	1962	1963	1964	1965	1966	1967	1968
USSR									
IMP.									
West Germany	6.5	11.4	11.0	7.3	8.5	5.6	5.3	6.8	8.0
France	7.3	7.4	8.2	3.4	2.9	4.7	6.1	7.3	9.7
Italy	3.2	5.1	5.2	6.6	4.1	4.2	3.6	6.0	6.8
Benelux	3.1	2.5	4.3	3.2	2.0	2.5	3.0	6.2	5.4
EXP.									
West Germany	5.7	8.3	6.4	6.1	5.5	5.6	6.2	6.0	6.1
France	7.5	5.2	4.0	4.8	4.7	4.2	4.4	4.4	3.9
Italy	3.3	7.2	6.2	6.3	5.9	5.7	5.2	7.1	6.6
Benelux	6.9	5.5	4.2	4.2	4.7	4.4	5.0	4.5	5.0
Poland									
IMP.									
West Germany	13.1	12.8	9.8	9.2	9.6	11.0	7.6	11.1	11.6
France	4.1	4.7	4.0	7.0	5.8	4.5	6.7	6.9	8.8
Italy	3.9	3.9	4.6	5.4	4.3	6.2	7.9	7.2	8.4
Benelux	5.8	5.8	2.6	3.5	4.7	5.0	4.8	5.1	5.7
EXP.									
West Germany	16.2	15.0	13.6	13.8	12.4	13.7	14.0	12.7	13.0
France	4.6	3.0	4.2	3.2	4.9	3.7	4.1	4.2	4.2
Italy	3.4	6.1	6.5	7.0	7.0	6.8	6.4	7.3	7.8
Benelux	3.1	3.4	3.7	3.7	.3.6	4.0	4.5	4.3	4.8

TABLE VI (*Continued*)

	1958	1960	1962	1963	1964	1965	1966	1967	1968
Czechoslovakia									
IMP.									
West Germany	15.45	11.4	11.4	8.1	10.6	12.4	10.0	11.0	11.8
France	4.55	3.3	5.0	4.4	2.8	3.1	4.4	6.2	5.1
Italy	3.15	3.5	5.2	4.0	5.0	5.7	7.1	6.4	5.9
Benelux	7.5	7.9	7.6	5.1	5.2	5.3	6.1	6.1	10.8
EXP.									
West Germany	12.0	12.5	11.9	12.6	12.2	12.7	11.5	12.6	14.7
France	3.9	2.3	3.4	3.6	5.2	3.7	3.5	4.0	4.8
Italy	3.2	4.2	5.8	6.2	4.7	4.6	5.1	6.8	8.0
Benelux	5.4	5.8	5.8	6.0	6.7	6.3	6.3	5.7	6.4
Hungary									
IMP.									
West Germany	19.6	19.1	15.1	15.6	16.1	15.1	16.7	17.4	14.1
France	7.9	8.8	9.7	11.2	6.1	5.3	6.0	5.9	6.1
Italy	5.8	9.3	8.1	7.6	7.0	9.6	8.7	9.1	12.3
Benelux	7.2	8.5	7.6	7.6	8.8	6.9	6.1	5.3	6.1
EXP.									
West Germany	17.8	17.8	18.5	16.1	17.4	17.1	16.9	13.8	15.6
France	5.7	5.4	4.5	4.5	3.2	3.8	5.4	4.5	4.0
Italy	9.6	8.3	9.5	16.3	13.1	11.6	13.4	15.4	12.3
Benelux	6.1	6.9	5.9	5.1	6.0	5.3	5.3	5.6	7.9

Rumania

IMP.

West Germany	22.4	26.4	26.1	23.3	23.5	26.5	28.5	32.3	22.0
France	15.7	14.2	6.7	7.3	12.1	11.8	10.9	10.1	10.3
Italy	8.1	9.4	15.2	14.9	12.9	12.4	9.4	11.0	13.1
Benelux	5.0	3.6	3.2	4.9	4.6	3.5	5.5	10.6	8.8

EXP.

West Germany	23.5	22.6	20.0	19.5	17.2	18.3	16.4	15.9	17.7
France	13.8	10.1	10.8	11.7	8.4	6.3	11.4	9.0	8.3
Italy	10.0	13.2	11.9	17.2	15.7	19.1	16.6	15.5	12.7
Benelux	2.7	2.7	6.1	3.7	4.7	3.2	4.0	3.7	4.0

Bulgaria

IMP.

West Germany	28.3	37.0	16.4	20.2	19.9	22.6	29.3	16.5	17.3
France	10.0	7.7	8.3	9.5	10.0	8.3	10.6	8.5	11.7
Italy	8.1	6.5	10.5	10.8	9.7	10.7	9.1	15.4	13.8
Benelux	8.5	5.5	7.3	4.4	3.1	4.5	4.6	8.9	4.4

EXP.

West Germany	24.4	20.7	21.3	23.7	16.2	17.1	13.3	17.1	15.5
France	9.6	5.3	9.7	6.1	4.9	2.8	4.5	6.7	5.2
Italy	10.4	10.2	13.9	13.3	16.2	16.2	18.7	17.1	12.6
Benelux	5.6	4.2	4.6	3.2	3.3	2.9	4.8	3.7	3.2

TABLE VI (*Continued*)

	1958 A	1958 B	1960 A	1960 B	1962 A	1962 B	1963 A	1963 B	1964 A	1964 B	1965 A	1965 B	1966 A	1966 B	1967 A	1967 B	1968 A	1968 B
Albania																		
IMP.																		
West Germany	.		.		26.9		17.4		.		.		.		.		.	
France	.				4.0		10.9		.		.		.		.		.	
Italy	85.7		70.7		37.9		52.2		.		.		.		.		.	
Benelux	.		.		.		.		.		.		.		.		.	
EXP.																		
West Germany	.		.		0.4		3.7		.		.		.		.		.	
France	.				.		22.2		.		.		.		.		.	
Italy	83.3		83.3		48.8		66.7		.		.		.		.		.	
Benelux	.		.		0.0		.		.		.		.		.		.	
East Germany																		
IMP.																		
West Germany		39		36.5		38.8		37.7		38.6		33.9		38.5		34.7		34.8
France	5.5	3.4	5.0	3.2	4.9	3.0	5.3	3.3	5.7	3.5	8.5	5.6	8.2	5.1	6.7	4.3	5.0	3.3
Italy	2.2	1.4	3.2	1.4	3.8	2.3	5.1	3.2	3.8	2.4	4.7	3.1	4.7	2.9	4.8	3.2	5.9	3.8
Benelux	12.6	7.6	11.8	7.5	10.5	6.5	8.9	5.5	9.8	6.0	9.2	6.1	11.0	6.8	12.8	8.3	9.0	5.8
EXP.																		
West Germany		48.1		45.2		41.5		42.6		40.3		37.8		37.4		34.7		37.6
France	3.7	1.9	2.9	1.6	3.3	2.0	3.3	1.9	3.2	1.9	3.4	2.1	4.4	2.7	4.6	3.0	6.2	3.9
Italy	2.6	1.4	4.6	2.5	4.2	0.5	4.4	2.5	3.4	2.0	3.3	2.1	4.0	2.5	5.3	3.5	5.6	3.5
Benelux	11.5	6.0	12.4	6.8	11.9	6.9	12.0	6.9	13.4	8.0	13.4	8.4	11.6	7.3	11.2	7.3	12.4	7.8

A = without interzonal trade　　B = with interzonal trade　　. = no data available

* Source: Compiled from Office statistique des Communautés Européenes, *Bloc Oriental 6*, 1969, n. 6. pp. 27-30.

TABLE VII

Distribution of EEC Exports to East Europe*
(in percentages of exporting countries' participation)

	1958	1966	1967	1968	1969
France	23.3	23.0	19.4	20.7	20.6
Benelux	18.2	14.1	15.3	14.5	13.4
West Germany	44.4	41.6	37.7	38.0	41.3
Italy	14.1	21.4	27.5	26.8	24.7

* Source: Compilation of data from Commission des Communautés Européenes, Direction générale du commerce extérieur, I/773/68-F, p. 3; XI/7.316/69-F, p. 2; XI/16.243/70-F, p. 20.

TABLE VIII

Distribution of EEC Exports to East Europe*
(in percentages of recipients' participation)

	1958	1966	1967	1968	1969
Albania	0.3	0.6	0.2	0.4	0.4
Bulgaria	4.1	12.9	8.0	6.9	5.5
Hungary	9.3	10.5	9.5	8.8	8.7
Poland	22.6	15.2	13.5	14.6	14.0
Rumania	7.4	14.9	16.8	14.2	14.4
Czechoslovakia	17.6	16.9	11.4	12.8	13.5
USSR	33.2	21.0	34.6	37.6	39.5
East Germany	5.5	7.9	6.0	5.0	4.0

* Source: Compilation of data from Commission des Communautés Européenes, Direction générale du commerce extérieur, I/773/68-F, p. 3; XI/7.316/69-F, p. 3; XI/16.243/70-F, p. 20.

TABLE IX

Trade of Four European Powers with the Communist Countries, 1961-1969*

(in percentages of total trade)

	1961		1962		1963		1964		1965		1966		1967		1968		1969	
	Exp	Imp	Exp	Imp	Exp	Imp	Exp	Imp	Exp	Imp	Exp	Imp	Exp	Imp	Exp	Imp	Exp	Imp
West Germany	5.8	6.2	5.6	6.0	4.6	5.7	5.3	5.4	5.4	5.5	6.0	5.9	6.7	6.0	5.9	5.9	6.4	5.6
United Kingdom	4.0	4.3	3.6	4.2	3.5	4.2	3.0	4.0	3.2	4.4	3.7	4.7	4.3	4.5	4.2	4.4	4.1	4.5
Italy	6.0	6.1	5.6	5.7	5.8	6.4	5.1	5.7	5.4	6.6	5.4	6.8	6.2	7.7	6.3	6.9	4.4	6.3
France	3.8	2.8	4.3	2.9	3.6	3.2	3.4	3.0	3.8	3.2	4.6	3.5	5.2	3.4	5.6	3.2	5.4	3.1

* Source: U.S. Department of State, Director of Intelligence and Research, *Research Memorandum*, "Trade of NATO Countries with Communist Countries," a compilation from Research Memoranda, covering the period from 1961 to 1969.

TABLE X

Trade of Four Powers with East Europe, 1960-1969*

IMPORTS
(Millions of dollars c.i.f.)

Country of Origin	1960 France	W.G.	Italy	U.K.	1961 France	W.G.	Italy	U.K.
Albania	insig	0.1	0.4	insig	0.1	insig	0.6	insig
Bulgaria	3.9	19.6	13.7	6.3	4.4	23.6	16.8	9.1
Czechoslovakia	11.3	61.7	23.2	31.5	15.4	62.0	28.8	38.1
East Germany	7.1	267.3	14.5	17.6	8.4	234.0	14.3	18.7
Hungary	8.2	44.5	19.3	12.1	7.1	47.2	17.5	11.9
Poland	15.0	76.3	36.9	101.0	16.7	84.4	39.2	103.4
Rumania	14.4	42.0	31.5	11.1	17.1	52.3	41.9	17.0
USSR	94.7	136.3	125.8	209.8	97.3	142.9	150.1	238.3

Country of Destination	EXPORTS (Millions of dollars f.o.b.)							
Albania	1.7	0.2	2.1	0.1	0.5	0.2	5.0	0.1
Bulgaria	7.1	29.2	8.0	7.7	12.0	18.0	9.5	5.2
Czechoslovakia	16.7	65.2	16.9	24.7	23.9	76.2	26.1	31.4
East Germany	14.1	228.4	6.8	23.2	21.6	216.7	10.8	27.5
Hungary	18.6	52.7	22.6	12.6	21.4	50.8	22.2	16.5
Poland	21.6	72.1	20.7	41.0	22.0	69.3	29.6	65.1
Rumania	25.2	35.7	16.3	11.9	23.6	57.9	23.2	41.4
USSR	115.6	185.3	78.6	148.9	109.9	204.0	89.5	194.4

TABLE X (*Continued*)

Trade of Four Powers with East Europe, 1960-1969*

IMPORTS
(Millions of dollars c.i.f.)

Country of Origin	1962				1963			
	France	*W.G.*	*Italy*	*U.K.*	*France*	*W.G.*	*Italy*	*U.K.*
Albania	insig	0.1	1.3	0.4	0.3	0.2	1.8	0.1
Bulgaria	9.0	26.8	15.9	9.3	12.8	29.3	25.2	10.2
Czechoslovakia	14.8	65.9	32.9	37.1	15.8	65.4	40.5	45.7
East Germany	8.5	228.6	11.4	18.5	12.6	255.6	12.3	21.1
Hungary	8.1	48.8	23.0	13.4	10.9	58.0	49.1	16.2
Poland	24.1	81.9	45.5	107.8	23.3	80.5	57.0	112.5
Rumania	22.1	61.8	35.2	19.8	34.3	56.2	62.1	20.8
USSR	110.7	186.8	165.8	235.5	141.1	163.7	175.8	254.7

Country of Destination	*EXPORTS* (Millions of dollars f.o.b.)							
Albania	4.0	0.6	1.0	0.1	0.8	0.7	2.2	0.5
Bulgaria	9.9	24.5	13.3	3.5	17.0	23.6	16.7	6.0
Czechoslovakia	25.6	75.0	27.1	39.7	21.0	58.8	21.4	33.5
East Germany	16.0	213.5	7.8	26.9	18.1	214.9	12.8	22.4
Hungary	28.0	49.5	23.2	19.6	40.2	63.2	26.6	21.0
Poland	25.0	65.7	28.0	92.3	44.0	65.4	33.8	78.6
Rumania	20.6	82.1	37.3	25.6	20.8	73.3	41.9	33.3
USSR	138.1	206.8	102.5	161.0	64.2	153.6	114.3	178.8

TABLE X (*Continued*)

Trade of Four Powers with East Europe, 1960-1969*

IMPORTS

(Millions of dollars c.i.f.)

Country of Origin	1964				1965			
	France	W.G.	Italy	U.K.	France	W.G.	Italy	U.K.
Albania	1.3	0.1	1.6	insig	0.4	0.1	1.4	insig
Bulgaria	8.1	30.3	20.0	12.0	7.3	41.3	31.0	15.1
Czechoslovakia	22.8	72.0	36.1	47.3	26.7	84.1	36.3	48.7
East Germany	14.2	256.8	14.8	29.0	15.9	315.1	14.1	33.6
Hungary	11.8	61.8	42.8	20.6	15.9	71.9	51.7	19.0
Poland	30.8	90.7	52.9	134.8	31.2	108.8	61.2	135.8
Rumania	29.0	61.3	54.9	25.0	28.8	72.4	61.2	31.4
USSR	141.1	170.4	147.0	252.9	146.0	210.5	181.3	333.0

Country of Destination	*EXPORTS*							
	(Millions of dollars f.o.b.)							
Albania	0.6	0.9	2.1	0.4	0.6	1.6	6.3	0.3
Bulgaria	21.0	38.9	27.7	7.8	23.7	55.2	32.6	10.8
Czechoslovakia	16.0	82.9	36.0	36.6	35.4	100.6	41.9	40.6
East Germany	26.3	287.7	13.3	17.0	69.1	301.5	16.1	23.2
Hungary	24.3	73.8	32.0	24.7	20.7	76.7	37.2	21.6
Poland	29.6	78.4	31.3	69.5	35.6	91.5	50.2	70.6
Rumania	42.9	82.7	42.4	23.5	43.8	115.6	47.1	27.1
USSR	64.1	193.6	90.7	111.2	72.0	146.5	98.1	128.6

TABLE X (*Continued*)

Trade of Four Powers with East Europe, 1960-1969*

IMPORTS
(Millions of dollars c.i.f.)

Country of Origin	1966 France	W.G.	Italy	U.K.	1967 France	W.G.	Italy	U.K.
Albania	0.4	0.5	1.8	insig	0.3	0.1	3.1	insig
Bulgaria	12.1	42.8	46.8	17.3	13.1	44.4	57.6	17.3
Czechoslovakia	28.2	86.6	42.0	54.7	26.3	90.3	54.7	56.4
East Germany	25.9	336.3	26.3	37.9	25.7	316.0	36.4	33.4
Hungary	26.3	80.3	60.6	20.5	24.2	69.0	83.2	26.4
Poland	41.5	120.4	64.5	150.3	44.9	109.9	76.1	154.6
Rumania	42.4	74.5	81.8	42.5	39.3	87.7	100.6	70.6
USSR	171.8	245.3	189.9	351.8	187.1	264.8	274.6	339.6

Country of Destination	EXPORTS (Millions of dollars f.o.b.)							
Albania	0.6	0.8	8.4	insig	0.8	1.0	4.1	1.1
Bulgaria	42.3	108.2	37.6	20.8	36.0	84.9	54.7	17.1
Czechoslovakia	63.3	125.7	53.8	52.2	41.8	131.3	44.0	41.4
East Germany	62.3	406.3	20.4	46.0	34.3	370.7	24.4	47.0
Hungary	25.2	92.5	37.2	29.3	26.5	105.0	43.3	34.3
Poland	67.1	93.7	63.8	101.6	61.7	122.8	67.5	134.3
Rumania	50.1	139.5	46.3	30.0	81.8	240.3	82.2	27.5
USSR	75.8	135.3	89.3	141.1	155.3	198.0	125.0	177.2

TABLE X (*Continued*)

Trade of Four Powers with East Europe, 1960-1969*

IMPORTS

(Millions of dollars c.i.f.)

Country of Origin	1968				1969			
	France	W.G.	Italy	U.K.	France	W.G.	Italy	U.K.
Albania	0.4	0.9	4.1	0.2	0.3	0.7	4.6	insig
Bulgaria	12.2	53.0	48.5	17.9	17.4	53.0	49.8	17.6
Czechoslovakia	29.6	115.2	64.1	55.5	34.4	177.4	70.4	51.6
East Germany	36.0	359.9	28.8	42.3	50.8	401.5	30.9	35.1
Hungary	24.4	77.7	63.7	24.0	30.6	104.1	99.7	22.6
Poland	43.7	119.6	81.9	145.2	58.9	137.1	104.0	136.8
Rumania	44.4	104.2	79.1	62.1	53.9	119.1	99.2	59.9
USSR	182.8	292.3	285.9	379.4	205.8	334.2	247.1	473.2

Country of Destination	EXPORTS							
	(Millions of dollars f.o.b.)							
Albania	0.9	1.7	9.1	0.2	1.0	1.9	9.0	0.3
Bulgaria	45.3	75.8	48.8	9.7	24.8	62.8	49.9	12.2
Czechoslovakia	38.3	176.8	56.0	44.8	45.0	210.7	62.0	43.6
East Germany	26.3	358.0	23.5	30.0	27.0	584.1	28.4	30.6
Hungary	30.7	84.2	60.5	30.5	40.5	90.5	64.9	32.0
Poland	83.1	148.1	88.3	106.8	81.8	157.2	90.1	132.2
Rumania	76.1	185.1	84.2	76.7	72.6	187.2	75.3	69.7
USSR	256.4	273.4	179.5	249.5	265.2	405.7	287.0	233.2

* Source: Department of State, Bureau of Intelligence and Research, "Trade of NATO Countries with Communist Countries," Compilation from Research Memoranda, 1960-1969.

TABLE XI *

Trade of NATO with Communist Countries, 1962-1969 **

(In percentages of world trade)

	1962	1963	1964	1965	1966	1967	1968	1969
Imports								
European NATO	4.3	4.4	4.1	4.4	4.6	4.7	4.4	4.2
Canada	0.4	0.6	0.5	0.7	0.8	1.0	0.9	0.8
U.S.	0.6	0.5	0.5	0.7	0.7	0.7	0.6	0.5
Total, NATO	3.2	3.3	3.1	3.3	3.4	3.4	3.2	3.1
Exports								
European NATO	4.3	3.9	3.9	4.1	4.6	5.2	4.9	4.8
Canada	3.2	4.5	8.1	5.3	6.2	2.8	2.5	1.3
U.S.	0.6	0.9	1.3	0.5	0.7	0.6	0.6	0.7
Total, NATO	3.2	3.1	3.5	3.3	3.7	3.8	3.6	3.5

* Source: U.S. Department of State, Director of Intelligence and Research, Research Memorandum, "Trade of NATO Countries with Communist Countries," a compilation of Research Memoranda, covering the period from 1962 to 1969.

** Albania, Bulgaria, Czechoslovakia, East Germany, Hungary, Poland, Rumania, USSR, Communist China, North Korea, North Vietnam, Outer Mongolia, and Cuba.

TABLE XII *

Trade in value of NATO Countries With Communist Countries, 1964-1969
(In percentages of change)

	Imports						Exports					
	1964	1965	1966	1967	1968	1969	1964	1965	1966	1967	1968	1969
European NATO	3.0	17.7	12.7	4.8	5.7	12.3	10.3	18.4	21.0	18.8	5.9	15.1
Canada	5.1	52.5	30.2	37.5	-4.5	5.7	114.8	-31.5	38.9	-51.1	11.1	-43.9
U.S.	11.7	38.1	28.7	-1.3	11.7	-1.5	67.3	-5.9	42.3	-1.5	9.8	15.0
Total NATO	3.3	18.9	13.7	5.1	5.7	11.5	26.4	1.0	24.3	7.8	6.4	11.2

* Source: U.S. Department of State, Director of Intelligence and Research, Research Memoranda, data compiled from six issues, 1964-1969, Table II.

TABLE XIII

West Germany's Trade with East Germany, 1960-1969*
(Millions of dollars)

	Imports	Exports
1960	267.3	228.4
1961	234.0	216.7
1962	228.6	213.5
1963	255.6	214.9
1964	256.8	287.7
1965	315.1	301.5
1966	336.3	406.3
1967	316.0	370.7
1968	359.9	358.0
1969	401.5	584.1

* Source: Department of State, Bureau of Intelligence and Research, "Trade of NATO Countries with Communist Countries," compilation from Research Memoranda, 1960-1969.

TABLE XIV *

East-West Contacts
July 1968 – January 1969

	Jul	Sep	Oct	Nov	Dec	Jan
Bulgaria	9	5	8	9	3	4
CSSR	25	19	35	51	25	18
Hungary	9	5	11	21	11	21
Poland	27	17	19	21	14	22
USSR	20	8	14	14	6	16
Rumania	16	30	43	30	31	33
Yugoslavia	3	12	15	10	10	10

* Source: Radio Free Europe, Research. *East-West Contacts*, A Monthly Survey, January 1969, Introduction.

TABLE XVa

East-West Europe Travel 1958-1968*

FROM

To	1958 France	1958 W.G.	1958 Italy	1958 U.K.	1959 France	1959 W.G.	1959 Italy	1959 U.K.	1960 France	1960 W.G.	1960 Italy	1960 U.K.
Bulgaria	...	...	...	...	...	...	...	...	...	...	...	...
Czech.	...	8,376	...	815	...	6,953	...	1,038	...	...	...	1,264
E. Germany	...	...	...	...	...	...	...	...	...	...	...	...
Hungary	...	...	...	...	...	...	...	...	...	...	...	1,129
Poland	...	15,451	...	...	...	9,398	...	6,175	...	...	...	6,199
Rumania	...	...	...	...	...	...	...	99	...	...	...	142

To	1961 France	1961 W.G.	1961 Italy	1961 U.K.	1962 France	1962 W.G.	1962 Italy	1962 U.K.	1963 France	1963 W.G.	1963 Italy	1963 U.K.
Bulgaria	...	...	...	...	...	...	...	...	...	...	...	...
Czech.	...	...	...	1,355	...	7,723	...	1,405	...	...	...	...
E. Germany	...	...	...	...	...	...	...	...	...	...	...	...
Hungary	...	...	...	1,349	...	...	...	2,150	...	...	...	...
Poland	...	...	...	6,483	...	9,378	...	8,111	...	...	...	...
Rumania	...	...	...	155	...	...	...	190	...	...	...	...

To	1964 France	1964 W.G.	1964 Italy	1964 U.K.	1965 France	1965 W.G.	1965 Italy	1965 U.K.	1966 France	1966 W.G.	1966 Italy	1966 U.K.
Bulgaria	...	...	...	...	...	...	...	...	...	...	...	...
Czech.	...	15,054	...	...	...	21,778	...	...	...	28,585	...	...
E. Germany	...	...	...	...	...	...	...	...	...	...	...	...
Hungary	...	...	...	...	...	...	...	...	...	14,363	...	...
Poland	...	12,487	...	...	...	13,206	...	...	...	...	...	...
Rumania	...	...	...	...	...	...	...	...	...	...	...	...

To	1967 France	1967 W.G.	1967 Italy	1967 U.K.	1968 France	1968 W.G.	1968 Italy	1968 U.K.
Bulgaria	...	...	...	...	...	...	...	...
Czech.	...	36,649	...	...	...	62,333	...	...
E. Germany	...	...	...	...	...	...	...	...
Hungary	...	...	...	...	...	...	...	...
Poland	...	15,770	...	...	...	13,130	...	...
Rumania	...	...	...	...	...	...	...	...

TABLE XVb

West-East Europe Travel 1958-1968*

From	1958 France	1958 W.G.	1958 Italy	1958 U.K.	1959 France	1959 W.G.	1959 Italy	1959 U.K.	1960 France	1960 W.G.	1960 Italy	1960 U.K.
TO												
Bulgaria	...	Not Listed		...	...	Not Listed	Not Listed	...	4,551	9,839	...	...
Czech.		Not Listed				Not Listed	Not Listed			Not Listed	Not Listed	
E. Germany		Not Listed				Not Listed	Not Listed			Not Listed	Not Listed	
Hungary	5,608	37,105	760	...	7,477	43,200	1,019	4,600	5,590	...	1,758	2,944
Poland					1,033	23	62	46	9,426	...	1,067	7,328
Rumania		Not Listed							1,460	...	...	...

From	1961 France	1961 W.G.	1961 Italy	1961 U.K.	1962 France	1962 W.G.	1962 Italy	1962 U.K.	1963 France	1963 W.G.	1963 Italy	1963 U.K.
Bulgaria	5,322	15,364	714	...	6,501	18,010	2,678	4,707	9,415	26,533	3,825	8,806
Czech.	8,184	1,046	1,526	4,007	8,848	2,867	2,393	4,238	10,228	5,314	3,554	5,999
E. Germany		Not Listed	Not Listed			Not Listed	Not Listed			Not Listed	Not Listed	
Hungary	9,363	...	1,390	...	6,176	14,472	4,808	4,171	8,407	31,772	1,561	5,733
Poland		...	211	8,343	9,271	63,168	1,822	8,406	11,802	54,042	2,215	10,016
Rumania	2,111	...	...	692	2,601	3,584	...	2,541	3,446	11,076	...	2,034

From	1964 France	1964 W.G.	1964 Italy	1964 U.K.	1965 France	1965 W.G.	1965 Italy	1965 U.K.	1966 France	1966 W.G.	1966 Italy	1966 U.K.
Bulgaria	12,803	58,569	5,717	13,306	20,538	84,160	11,140	18,645	33,915	100,194	14,632	21,919
Czech.	26,977	159,711	12,109	17,089	29,916	177,213	22,367	18,895	37,876	223,311	26,877	21,267
E. Germany		Not Listed	Not Listed			Not Listed	Not Listed			Not Listed	Not Listed	
Hungary	10,723	53,447	...	13,416	14,030	71,407	...	...	18,367	86,585	19,550	14,166
Poland	15,071	14,067	2,926	5,942	19,274	17,347	4,284	16,328	39,110	31,806	10,827	28,466
Rumania	4,243	15,835	...	...	14,368	93,826	...	8,394	16,738	65,394	10,192	8,124

From	1967 France	1967 W.G.	1967 Italy	1967 U.K.	1968 France	1968 W.G.	1968 Italy	1968 U.K.
Bulgaria	41,741	128,579	18,562	27,122	40,285	120,071	...	31,289
Czech.	40,255	248,415	30,765	24,921	35,840	232,809	34,121	24,526
E. Germany		Not Listed	Not Listed			Not Listed	Not Listed	
Hungary	16,914	87,977	...	...	25,792	151,773	...	...
Poland	37,341	31,588	11,568	29,406	33,597	22,880	10,722	27,212
Rumania	23,326	65,868	15,777	10,977	24,587	16,402	20,527	14,704

Notes: ... = data not available.

* Source: UN Statistical Yearbook, New York, United Nations, 1961, pp. 378-384; 1962, pp. 394-492; 1964, pp. 470-479; 1966, pp. 470-479; 1968, pp. 462-472; 1969, pp. 440-450.

TABLE XVI

University Stipends in France, 1963-1968*

	1963	1964	1965	1966	1967	1968
East Europe[1]	105	291	398	584	721	912
North America	109	116	105	153		172
Latin America	472	476	519	613	794	973
Total	2,341	3,180	3,344	4,456	5,137	5,505

* Source: Ministère des Affaires Étrangères, Direction Générale des Affaires Culturelles et Techniques, 1965, pp. 59, 61; 1968-1969, p. 15.
[1] Includes USSR, Yugoslavia, and Albania.

TABLE XVII*

Higher Education Foreign Students Enrolled, 1955-1967

Country	1955	1960	1965	1966	1967
Bulgaria	350	693	1,138	1,283	1,505
Czechoslovakia	975	1,849	3,303	3,314	3,464
Hungary	...	285	691	763	895
Poland	575	740	1,364	1,679	1,946
Rumania	...	736	439	729	971
USSR	12,300	...	16,200	15,800	15,000
Yugoslavia	343	559	1,816	2,019	2,502
Total	14,543	4,862	24,951	25,587	26,283
United States	36,494	53,107	82,709	100,262	110,315

Note: ... = data not available.
* Source: UNESCO, Statistical Yearbook, 1969, pp. 384-386. East Germany is not included in the UNESCO table.

TABLE XVIII*

Higher Education of Foreign Students by Country of Origin and Study, 1966

Country of origin	USA	France	West Germany	U.K.	Italy	Total
Bulgaria	19	48	34	5	7	113
Czechoslovakia	72	19	36	10	8	145
East Germany	– –	123	– –	. . .	1	124
Hungary	136	103	233	8	17	497
Poland	273	184	22	37	28	544
Rumania	48	82	9	2	8	149
USSR	56	43	5	14	3	121
Yugoslavia	255	186	248	57	44	790
Total	859	788	587	133	116	2,483

Notes: – – = magnitude nil or negligible.
    . . . = data not available.
* Source: UNESCO, *Statistical Yearbook, 1968*, pp. 280-288. The UNESCO table lists twenty selected countries of studies.

TABLE XIX*

Book Translations by Country of Publication, 1964-1967

Translated From	Year	English	French	German	Russian
COUNTRY					
Bulgaria	1964	29	23	34	292
	1965	37	25	31	250
	1966	30	30	32	210
	1967	41	34	39	194
Czechoslovakia	1964	164	133	143	285
	1965	182	133	146	289
	1966	200	150	156	198
	1967	199	140	149	220
Hungary	1964	72	84	107	154
	1965	92	76	98	146
	1966	85	77	106	126
	1967	71	49	75	112
Poland	1964	188	54	72	172
	1965	180	73	53	170
	1966	188	89	72	202
	1967	222	96	93	200
Rumania	1964	50	47	34	182
	1965	53	66	46	101
	1966	56	74	59	72
	1967	83	92	54	73

* Source: UNESCO, *Statistical Yearbook, 1969*, pp. 572-576.

BIBLIOGRAPHY

Bibliography

DOCUMENTS

Die Bemühungen der deutschen Regierung und ihrer Verbündeten um die Einheit Deutschlands, 1955-1966. Bonn: Auswärtiges Amt, 1966.

Brandt, Willy. *A Peace Policy for Europe.* New York: Holt, Rinehart and Winston, 1969.

The British Council. *Programme of Cultural, Educational, and Scientific Exchanges between Britain and Czechoslovakia* [etc.]. 1970-1972.

Bulletin des Presse- und Informationsamtes der Bundesregierung. (Bonn).

Das Bundesministerium für innerdeutsche Beziehungen. "Flucht von Bewohnern der DDR in das Bundesgebiet," 11/3-35-214. Bonn, January 15, 1970.

CEE. Direction générale des relations extérieures. "Structure et evolution des exportations de la CEE vers les pays de l'Est de 1958 a 1966." 1/773/68-F.

Die deutsche Ostpolitik 1961-1970. Kontinuität und Wandel. Documents. Edited by Boris Meissner. Köln: Verlag Wissenschaft und Politik, 1970.

Dokumente des geteilten Deutschland. Ed. Ingo von Münch. Stuttgart: Alfred Kröner, 1968.

Für Frieden und Entspannung. Eine Dokumentation über die deutsche Bemühungen um Frieden und Entspannung. 1949 bis August 1968. Bonn: Presse- und Informationsamt der Bundesregierung.

The Germans. Public Opinion Polls 1947-1966. Ed. Elisabeth Noelle and Erich Peter Neumann. Allensbach: Verlag für Demoskopie, 1967.

Die Internationale Politik 1966. Zeittafel. Register. Munich: R. Oldenbourg, 1967.

Kiesinger, Kurt Georg. *Entspannung in Deutschland. Friede*

in Europa. Reden und Interviews 1967. Bonn: Presse- und Informationsamt der Bundesregierung.

———. *Reden und Interviews 1968.* Bonn: Presse- und Informationsamt der Bundesregierung.

Major Addresses, Statements, and Press Conferences of General Charles de Gaulle. New York: Ambassade de France. Service de Presse et d'Information.

Ministère de l'Economie et des Finances. Service d'Information. *Les Échanges Commerciaux entre la France et les Pays de l'Est.* (n.d.)

Ministère des Affaires Étrangères. *Relations culturelles, scientifiques et techniques.*

The Policy of Renunciation of Force. Documents on German and Soviet Declarations on the Renunciation of Force. 1949 to July 1968. Bonn: Press and Information Office of the Federal Government.

La Politique Étrangère de la France. Textes et documents.

Sicherheit und friedliche Zusammenarbeit in Europa. Dokumente 1954-1967. East Berlin: Staatsverlag der DDR, 1968.

Statistiches Amt der Europäischen Gemeinschaften. Ostblock.

Texte zur Deutschlandpolitik, Five volumes, 1966-1970. Bonn: Federal Ministry for Intra-German Relations, 1970.

United Nations. Economic and Social Council. Economic Commission for Europe. "Analytical Report on the State of Intra European Trade." E/ECE/761. January 14, 1970.

———. Department of Economic and Social Affairs, Statistical Office of the United Nations. *Yearbook of International Statistics.* New York: United Nations.

———. *Fifteen Years of Activity of the Economic Commission for Europe, 1947-1962.* New York: United Nations, 1964.

———. *Yearbook of International Trade Statistics.* New York: United Nations.

U.S. Department of State. Director of Intelligence and Research. *Research Memoranda,* 1964-1969.

Voyage en Pologne du Général de Gaulle. Textes et Notes.

Wiedervereinigung und Sicherheit Deutschlands. Ed. Heinrich von Siegler. Two volumes, 1944-1967. Bonn: Verlag für Zeitarchive, 1968.

SELECTED GENERAL WORKS

Akademiia nauk SSSR. *Sovremennye burzhuaznye teorii o sliianii kapitalisma i sotsializma.* Moskva: Izdatel'stvo "Nauka," 1970.

The Atlantic Institute. *The Atlantic Community and Eastern Europe: Perspectives and Policy.* Report of a Conference held in Rome October 21-23, 1966. Boulogne-sur-Seine: The Atlantic Institute 1967.

Baring, Arnulf. *Aussenpolitik in Adenauers Kanzlerdemokratie.* Munich: R. Oldenbourg Verlag, 1969.

Barth, Herbert. *Bonner Ostpolitik gegen Frieden und Sicherheit.* East Berlin: Staatsverlag der DDR, 1969.

Barzel, Rainer. *Gesichtspunkte eines Deutschen.* Düsseldorf: Econ Verlag, 1968.

Bender, Peter. *Offensive Entspannung.* Köln-Berlin: Kiepenheur and Witsch, 1964.

Birnbaum, Karl E. *Frieden in Europa.* Voraussetzungen, Chancen, Versuche. Opladen: Leske Verlag, 1970.

Brentano, Heinrich von. *Germany and Europe.* New York: F. A. Praeger, 1964.

Brzezinski, Zbigniew. *Alternative to Partition.* New York: McGraw-Hill, 1965.

Communist States and the West. Ed. Adam Bromke, Philip E. Uren. New York: F. A. Praeger, 1967.

Denken an Deutschland. Ed. Theo Sommer. Hamburg: Nannen-Verlag, 1966.

Deutschland und die Östlichen Nachbarn. Ed. Reinhard Henkys. Stuttgart: Kreuz-Verlag, 1966.

Djilas, Milovan. *The Unperfect Society*. New York: Harcourt, Brace, 1969.

Economic Development for Eastern Europe. Ed. Michael Kaser. London: Macmillan, 1968.

Erler, Fritz. *Politik für Deutschland*. Stuttgart: Seewald Verlag, 1968.

Faust, Fritz. *Das Potsdamer Abkommen*. Frankfurt am Main: A. Metzner Verlag, 1959.

Freund, Gerald. *Unholy Alliance*. New York: Harcourt, Brace, 1957.

Geschichte der Aussenpolitik der Deutschen Demokratischen Republik. Ed. Peter Klein. East Berlin: Dietz Verlag, 1968.

Grewe, Wilhelm G. *Deutsche Aussenpolitik der Nachkriegszeit*. Stuttgart: Deutsche Verlags-Anstalt, 1960.

Grosser, Alfred. *Deutschlandbilanz*. Munich: Carl Hanser, 1970.

―――. *French Foreign Policy under De Gaulle*. Boston: Little, Brown, 1967.

Hallstein, Walter. *Europa 1980*. Bonn: Eichholz-Verlag, 1968.

―――. *Der unvollendete Bundesstaat*. Düsseldorf: Econ Verlag, 1969.

Hanrieder, Wolfram S. *West German Foreign Policy 1949-1963*. Stanford: Stanford University Press, 1967.

―――. *The Stable Crisis. Two Decades of German Foreign Policy*. New York: Harper & Row, 1970.

Hartmann, Frederick H. *Germany between East and West*. Englewood Cliffs, N.J.: Prentice-Hall, 1965.

Heidenheimer, Arnold J. *The Governments of Germany*. New York: Crowell Comp., 1966.

Hunter, Robert. *Security in Europe*. London: Elek Books, 1969.

The Institute for Strategic Studies, *The Military Balance, 1970-1971*. London, 1970.

Jaspers, Karl. *Freiheit und Wiedervereinigung.* Munich: R. Piper, 1960.

——. *Antwort.* Munich: R. Piper, 1967.

Kaiser, Karl. *German Foreign Policy in Transition.* London: Oxford University Press, 1968.

Keller, John W. "German Elites and Foreign Policy." Mimeographed. Pennsylvania State College, Penn. (n.d.)

Majonica, Ernest. *East-West Relations: A German View.* New York: F. A. Praeger, 1969.

——. *Möglichkeiten und Grenzen der deutschen Aussenpolitik.* Stuttgart: W. Kohlhammer Verlag, 1969.

Meissner, Boris. *Die Sowjetunion und das Selbstbestimmungsrecht des deutschen Volkes.* Köln: Wissenschaft und Politik, 1965.

Müller-Hermann, Ernst. *Bonn zwischen den Weltmächten.* Düsseldorf: Econ Verlag, 1969.

Nach 25 Jahren. Ed. Karl Dietrich Bracher. Munich: Kindler Verlag, 1970.

Osten, Walter. *Die Aussenpolitik der DDR.* Opladen: Leske Verlag, 1969.

Perspektiven deutscher Politik. Ed. Walter Scheel. Düsseldorf: E. Diederichs Verlag, 1969.

Pisar, Samuel. *Coexistence and Commerce.* New York: McGraw-Hill, 1970.

Planck, Charles R. *The Changing Status of German Reunification in Western Diplomacy, 1955-1966.* Baltimore: The Johns Hopkins Press, 1967.

Richardson, James L. *Germany and the Atlantic Alliance.* Cambridge, Mass: Harvard University Press, 1966.

Riklin, Alois. *Das Berlinproblem.* Köln: Verlag Wissenschaft und Politik, 1964.

Ritter, Gerhard. *The German Problem.* Columbus: Ohio State University Press, 1965.

Schmidt, Helmut. *Strategie des Gleichgewichts.* Stuttgart: Seewald Verlag, 1969.

Schulz, Eberhard and Schulz, Hans Dieter. *Braucht der Osten die DDR?* Opladen: Leske Verlag, 1968.

Schütz, Wilhelm Wolfgang. *Deutschland-Memorandum.* Frankfurt am Main: Fischer Bücherei, 1968.

―――. *Rethinking German Policy.* New York: F. A. Praeger, 1967.

Sethe, Paul. *Öffnung nach Osten.* Frankfurt am Main: Verlag H. Scheffler, 1966.

Siewert, Regina and Bilstein, Helmut. *Gesamtdeutsche Kontakte.* Opladen: Leske Verlag, 1969.

Smith, Jean Edward. *Germany Beyond the Wall.* Boston: Little, Brown, 1967.

Stanley, Timothy W. and Whitt, Darnell M. *Detente Diplomacy: United States and European Security in the 1970's.* Cambridge: University Press of Cambridge, 1970.

Strauss, Franz Josef. *Challenge & Response.* London: Weidenfeld and Nicolson, 1969.

―――. *Entwurf für Europa.* Stuttgart: Seewald Verlag, 1966.

Tauber, Arnošt, "The European Economic Community and Czechoslovakia." *Series of Studies, 1968,* Vol. 30, Prague: Institute of International Politics and Economics.

Ulbrichts Grundgesetz. Die sozialistische Verfassung der DDR. Köln: Verlag Wissenschaft und Politik, 1968.

Váli, Ferenc A. *The Quest for a United Germany.* Baltimore: The Johns Hopkins Press, 1967.

Wehner, Herbert. *Beiträge zur Deutschlandpolitik.* Bonn: Bundesministerium für gesamtdeutsche Fragen, 1967.

―――. *Wandel und Bewährung.* Frankfurt am Main: Ullstein, 1968.

Wilczynski, Jozef. *The Economics and Politics of East-West Trade.* New York: F. A. Praeger, 1969.

Willis, F. Roy. *France, Germany, and the New Europe 1945-1967.* Stanford: Stanford University Press, 1968.

Windsor, Philip. *German Reunification.* London: Elek Books, 1969.

PERIODICALS

Andras, Charles. " 'European Security' and the Security of Europe," Radio Free Europe. Research. *East-West Relations/1,* March 1970.

——. "Through Berlin—to Europe," Radio Free Europe. Research. *East-West Relations/1,* February 11, 1971.

——. "Die Warschauer-Pakt-Staaten und ihr Konzept der europäischen Sicherheit," *Ost-europäische Rundschau,* Vol. XVI, No. 6, 1970.

Baade, Fritz. "Neugestaltung unserer Politik in Nah- und Mittelost," *Aussenpolitik,* Vol. 16, No. 4/65; pp. 243-251.

Bender, Peter. "The Special Case of East Germany," *Studies in Comparative Communism,* Vol. 2, No. 2, April 1969; pp. 14-33.

Benoit, Emil. "East-West Business Cooperation: A New Approach to Communist Europe," *New Republic,* Vol. 156, No. 7 (a reprint).

Bertram, Christoph. "West German Perspectives on European Security: Continuity and Change," *World Today,* March 1971; pp. 115-124.

Besson, Waldemar. "European Unification and the Present State of the East-West Conflict." A lecture presented at the session of the Atlantic Studies Committee at Villa Serbelloni, September 12-16, 1967 (mimeographed).

Bognar, J. "The Role of East-West Economic Relations in Promoting European Cooperation," Radio Free Europe. Research. *Hungarian Press Survey,* February 24, 1971.

Brzezinski, Zbigniew. "The Framework of East-West Reconciliation," *Foreign Affairs,* Vol. 46, No. 2; pp. 256-275.

Coulman, Peter. "Eine Rueckkehr zum Nationalismus," *Aussenpolitik,* Vol. 16, No. 11/65; pp. 733-739.

The Current Digest of the Soviet Press.

East-West. Brussels: Agenor

Gasteyger, Curt. "Europe's Future Challenges," *International Journal,* Vol. 24, No. 2, Spring 1969; pp. 277-288.

Goldman, Marshall I. "The East Reaches for Markets," *Foreign Affairs,* Vol. 47, No. 4; pp. 721-734.

Hanrieder, Wolfram F. "West German Foreign Policy: Background to Current Issues," *Orbis,* Vol. xiv, Winter 1970; pp. 1,029-1,049.

Imhoff, Christoph von. "Ein Dialog zwischen Deutschen und Polen," *Aussenpolitik,* Vol. 17, No. 2/66; pp. 100-109.

Inter Nationes. *Cultural News from Germany.*

Journal of International Affairs, Vol. xxii, No. 1, 1968 (entire issue on East-West détente).

Kaiser, Karl. "Deutsche Aussenpolitik nach der tschekoslowakischen Krise von 1968," *Europa-Archiv,* Vol. 23, No. 10, 1969; pp. 353-364.

Klingmüller, Erich. "Zur Strategie des Ost-West-Handels," *Osteuropa Wirtschaft,* Vol. 9, No. 3; pp. 1-20.

Korbel, Josef. "West Germany's Ostpolitik: i. Intra-German Relations," *Orbis,* Vol. xiii, No. 4, Winter 1970; pp. 1,050-1,072.

————. "West Germany's Ostpolitik: II. A Policy Toward the Soviet Allies," *Orbis,* Vol. xiv, No. 2, Summer 1970; pp. 326-348.

————. "German-Soviet Relations: The Past and Prospects," *Orbis,* Vol. x, No. 4, Winter 1967; pp. 1,046-1,060.

Kruger, Herbert. "The German Peace Note," *Modern World,* Vol. 5, 1967; pp. 19-36.

Löwenthal, Richard. "Der Einfluss Chinas auf die Entwicklung des Ost-West-Konflikts in Europa," *Europa-Archiv,* Vol. 22, No. 10; pp. 339-350.

Lukaszewski, Jerzy. "Western Integration and the People's Democracies," *Foreign Affairs,* Vol. 46, No. 2; pp. 377-387.

Marcoult, J. "Bonn et les difficultés de la politique de détente," *Revue de défense nationale,* Vol. 24, January 1968; pp. 50-58.

Le Marec, P. "La République Démocratique Allemande et la reunification," *Revue de défense nationale,* Vol. 22, October 1966; pp. 1,599-1,611.

Meier, Christian. "Neue Phase in den deutsch-sowjetischen Beziehungen," *Osteuropa,* Vol. 20, No. 3, 1970; pp. 152-163.

Meissner, Boris. "Die UdSSR zwischen Koexistenz- und Blockpolitik," *Aussenpolitik,* Vol. 20, No. 9, 1969; pp. 521-529.

Mosely, Philip E. "The United States and East-West Détente: The Range of Choice," *Journal of International Affairs,* Vol. XXII, No. 1, 1968; pp. 5-15.

Müller, Adolf. "Die Haltung der ČSSR gegenüber der Bundesrepublik während des Prager Demokratisierungsprozesses," *Osteuropa,* Vol. 19, No. 4, 1969; pp. 256-266.

NATO Letter.

Petrenkow, J. "Ueber einige völkerrechtliche Aspekte des Status von Westberlin," *Deutsche Aussenpolitik* (GDR), Vol. 15, No. 2, 1969; pp. 152-159.

Pierre, Andrew J. "The Bonn-Moscow Treaty of 1970: Milestone or Mirage?" *Russian Review,* Vol. 30, No. 1, January 1971; pp. 17-29.

Pritzel, Konstantin. "Der Interzonenhandel," *Aus Politik and Zeitgeschichte,* November 29, 1967.

Radio Free Europe. Research. (research papers and press translations)

Ransom, C. F. G. "Obstacles to the Liberalization of Relations between E.E.C. and Comecon," *Comparative Communism,* Vol. 2, Nos. 3 and 4; pp. 61-78.

Ray, G. F., "Export Competitiveness: British Experience in Eastern Europe," *National Institute Economic Review,* No. 36, May 1966; pp. 43-60.

Saeter, Martin. "Change of Course in German Foreign Policy," *Cooperation and Conflict* (Oslo), No. 11, 1967; pp. 82-101.

Sannwald, R. "Die Handelsbeziehungen zwischen der EWG und dem Ostblock," *Osteuropa Wirtschaft,* Vol. 12, No. 2; pp. 97-114.

Schaeffer, Henry. "Communist 'Westpolitik' and the EEC," Radio Free Europe. Research. *East-West Relations/2,* December 21, 1970.

Schulz, Eberhard. "Gedanken zu einer europäischen Friedensordnung," *Europa-Archiv,* Vol. 24, No. 17, 1969; pp. 589-599.

————. "Prag and Bonn. Politische Belastungen in deutschtschekoslovakischen Verhältnis," *Europa-Archiv,* Vol. 22, No. 4; pp. 105-125.

Sommer, Theo. "Bonn Changes Course," *Foreign Affairs,* Vol. 45, No. 3, April 1967; pp. 477-491.

Sontag, John. "International Communism and Soviet Foreign Policy," *The Review of Politics,* Vol. 32, No. 1, January 1970.

Uschakow, Alexander. "Deutschland in der Aussenpolitik Polens," *Aussenpolitik,* Vol. 21, No. 8, 1970; pp. 470-481.

Weber, Bernd. "Ulbricht zwischen BRD und UdSSR," *Aussenpolitik,* Vol. 21, No. 2, 1970; pp. 104-109.

Wettig, Gerhard. "Die Berlin-Politik der UdSSR und der DDR," *Aussenpolitik,* Vol. 21, No. 5, 1970; pp. 284-296.

————. "Bundesrepublik und DDR—Partner oder Gegner," *Deutschland-Archiv,* Vol. 3, April 1970; pp. 361-367.

————. "Die politische Leitsätze von Potsdam und die Feindstaatenartikel der UNO-Charta in der gegenwärtigen sowjetischen Deutschland-Politik," *Osteuropa,* Vol. 19, March 1969; pp. 173-186.

————. "Moskau und die grosse Koalition in Bonn," *Aus Politik und Zeitgeschichte,* March 6, 1968. B 10/68.

————. "Haupttendenzen der gegenwärtigen sowjetischen Deutschland-Politik," *Aus Politik und Zeitgeschichte,* October 18, 1967; B. 42/67.

————. "Der Sowjetische Kurs der europäischen Sicherheit— eine Entspannungspolitik neuen Typs," *Aus Politik und Zeitgeschichte,* August 1, 1970. B 31/70.

————. "Die Interessen der Sowjetunion und der DDR in der Anerkennungsfrage," *Deutschland-Archiv,* Vol. 3, No. 7, 1970; pp. 703-709.

Windsor, Philip. "The Boundaries of Détente," *The World Today,* June 1969; pp. 255-263.

Wolfe, James H. "West Germany and Czechoslovakia: The Struggle for Reconciliation," *Orbis,* Vol. xiv, Spring 1970; pp. 154-179.

Wyle, Frederick S. "Is European Security Negotiable?" *Survival,* Vol. xii, No. 6, June 1970; pp. 189-193.

NEWSPAPERS

Financial Times; Frankfurter Allgemeine Zeitung; Guardian; International Herald Tribune; Le Monde; Neue Zürcher Zeitung; Neues Deutschland; The New York Times; Times (London); Die Welt; Die Zeit;

(East European press reviewed from the translations by Radio Free Europe—Press.)

Index

Acheson, Dean, 200
Adenauer, Konrad, foreign policy of, 143-44; and Munich, 144, 159; reunification policy, 171-73; and trade, 163; with GDR, 174
Albania, 125, 129
Alten, Jürgen von, 235
Aron, Raymond, 20
Austria, and invasion of Czechoslovakia, 97

Bahr, Egon, 192, 230, 245; "Bahr Paper," 192-93, 195, 198
Ball, George, 200
Barzel, Rainer, 146, 199; on Brandt's visit in Soviet Union, 211
Bashev, Ivan, 131
Belgium, and invasion of Czechoslovakia, 97
Benelux, 28, 125
Bell, Daniel W., 20
Berlin Wall, 32, 216; and Quadripartite Agreement on Berlin, 223
Berlin (East), integration with GDR, 214
Berlin (West), 39, 61, 79, 193; background development, 213-14; Big Four Agreement on, 207, 218-21; responsibility for, 200; blockade, 175, 213; contacts with GDR, 180; in FRG Constitution, 124, 222; in FRG trade, 164; as independent entity, 174; and Khrushchev's ultimatum, 214; life in, 217; in polls, 214-16, 217, 226
    Quadripartite Agreement, 221-24, 245; German translation of, 224-25; as

related to FRG-Soviet treaty, 198; relations with FRG, 222-23; solution related to FRG-Soviet treaty (1970), 206-207; travel from and to, 223; visits to GDR, 178; West's position on, 194, 195; West Powers' rights in, 222-23, 224
Bild Zeitung, 192
Bismarck, Otto, 148, 170
Böll, Heinrich, 162
Boothby, Lord, 62, 130
Brandt, Willy, 20, 36, 143, 147, 153, 159; background to his *Ostpolitik,* 187; and FRG-Polish relations, 229; and FRG-Soviet treaty (1970), 201; foreign policy of, 148ff, 152; governmental declaration, 190-91; and intra-German relations, 188ff, 236; on invasion of Czechoslovakia, 90-91; meeting with Brezhnev, 207-208, 209; with Stoph, 98; motivations for signing FRG-Soviet treaty (1970), 201-204; negotiations with GDR, 98
    Nobel Peace Prize award, 212; on policy toward Poland, 154; and polls on FRG-Polish negotiations, 230; reaction to Gomulka's changed attitude, 156-57; and reunification, 169, 190; and treaty with Poland, 98; with Soviet Union, 98; trips in: Bucarest, 152; Czechoslovakia, 89, 161; Erfurt, 171, 239-40; Moscow, 196, 197-98; Warsaw, 232-33; on two Germanys, 188-89, 190-91

European Free Trade Association (EFTA), 111, 118; trade with COMECON, 113, 114

European Security Conference, 70-89; abolition of blocs, 74; agenda, 85-89; Canada's participation, 81; and cultural contacts, 86; and economic cooperation, 86-87; position of: France, Great Britain, Italy, U.S., 76-77; Belgium, Denmark, Iceland, Luxemburg, Netherlands, Norway, 78; NATO, 72-73 *reduction of forces,* 70-71, 72, 73, 79-80, 81, 82, 84-85, 208, 209; renunciation of force, 87-88; reunification, 71; and technological cooperation, 86; U.S. participation, 74, 75, 81; and Warsaw Pact Declarations: Bucarest (1966), 70-71; Bucarest (1971), 82; Budapest, 74, 80-81; East Berlin, 81; Karlovy Vary, 71-72; Prague and Moscow, 74-75; and principle of sovereignty, 88; and United States, 70, 71

FDR. *See* Free Democratic Party

Federal Republic of Germany, 25, 28, 33; cultural contacts, 167-68, 180, 181; entry in UN, 208; exports to COMECON, 125; and external representation of Berlin, 224; and goals of détente, 36; intra-German relations in election campaign, 189, 190; industrial cooperation with Hungary, 126; and invasion of Czechoslovakia, 90-92, 97, 102; on Munich, 235; polls on foreign relations of, 148; position on negotiations on Berlin, 219; on recognition of GDR, 241; West's attitude toward, 194
relations with: Bulgaria, 144; Czechoslovakia, 147, 151; during "Czechoslovak Spring," 161; trade missions, 160-61; Hungary, 144, 151; Poland, 88, 147, 149, 154-57, 191, and Catholic and Protestant Churches' position, 146; Rumania, 144, 150, 152; Soviet Union, 144, 149, 191; and treaty (1970), 34, 196-97, 205-206, 212. *See also* France, GDR, Great Britain
renunciation of force, 152-53, 191; and reunification, 68, 91, 169ff, 197; Security Conference, 76. *See also* European Security Conference *and tourist travel,* 166-67; in Czechoslovakia, 99; in East, 165-67; Table xv; trade with: Bulgaria, 129, 163, 164-65; COMECON, 127ff; communist countries, 112-13; Czechoslovakia, 129, 163, 164-65; GDR, 124, 129, 134-35, 174-76, 180-81; Poland, 128, 129, 163, 164-65; Rumania, 129; Soviet Union, 128, 203-204. *See also* Tables ix, x, xiii; trade missions in East Europe, 145; visits in GDR, 181-82

Finland, 9

Florek, Henry, 20

Fock, Jenö, 53, 97, 110n

France, 11; and Berlin, 223-24; and book translations, 45;